ECONOMIC IMPLICATIONS OF THE SIZE OF NATIONS

WITH SPECIAL REFERENCE TO LEBANON

BY

NADIM G. KHALAF

American University of Beirut

LEIDEN
E. J. BRILL
1971

TO MY FATHER

TABLE OF CONTENTS

PART TWO

LIST OF TABLES

LIST OF FIGURES

PREFACE

This is a modest attempt to evaluate the economic implications of the size of nations, for a sample of eighty countries, on (1) economic stability, (2) concentration in trade, (3) dependence on trade, and (4) economic growth and economic development. Only simple and multiple correlations, and a cross-classificatory scheme interpreted as crude partial correlations, are used to analyze the nature of the relationships between 'size' and the mentioned four aspects. The uneven quality of the data does not, perhaps, justify the use of more rigorous statistical techniques. Lebanon is also singled out as an example of a small country in an attempt to assess the impact of the size of the Lebanese economy on each of these aspects.

There are several acknowledgements that I owe and must make to those who have helped in the preparation of this study. I am indebted to the Economics Department and the Economic Research Institute of the American University of Beirut for making available to me their research facilities. My very sincere thanks are due to the Publication Committee of the American University of Beirut, without whose support this study would not have been published. A grant from the Rockefeller Foundation, through the Arts and Sciences Research Committee of the American University of Beirut, was of assistance in facilitating the work on the statistical part. I am deeply indebted to Professor Joseph D. Coppock who gave me freely of his time during his two years as Visiting Professor of Economics at the American University of Beirut. Since an earlier version of this was my Ph. D. thesis at Princeton University, my very sincere thanks are due to the members of my thesis committee, Professor Oskar Morgenstern, Chairman, and Professor Benjamin J. Cohen who suggested numerous improvements. My thanks are also due to Professors F. H. Harbison, R. E. Quandt, and H. G. Georgiadis who had read earlier drafts of the manuscript. I must admit that not all their good advice was heeded and, therefore, all remaining faults and shortcomings are solely mine.

Finally my sincere thanks are due to Miss Lamia Awad, Mr. Ilyas Barudi, Miss Mariana Khouri Makdisi and Mr. Walid Sulayman who helped prepare the statistical tables and scatter diagrams, and to Miss Suzie Baghachejian and Mrs. Soumaya Jebara who typed the manuscript.

Beirut, Lebanon   NADIM G. KHALAF
December, 1970

CHAPTER ONE

INTRODUCTION

Very little attention has so far been given to the question of size of a nation as a factor in economic growth and economic diversity, to the economic stability and vulnerability of small nations, and to the question of assessing the economic implications of some of the general features that characterize the economies of small nations. In the summer of 1957 a Symposium was held in Jerusalem, and one of the two major themes of the Symposium was to find out the extent to which the validity and applicability of concrete experience in the field of economic and social development was dependent on the size and the specific conditions of the country, and also to find out whether the development experience of large countries was meaningful for, or of any relevance to, small countries.[1] During September of the same year, the International Economic Association held a conference in Portugal which was mainly concerned with the relation of the size of nations to their economic prosperity and levels of per capita incomes.[2] Little else has been written on the subject since.[3] At a time when the increase in the number of small nations has been unprecedented, some questions pertaining to size have become relevant and often urgent.[4] It is not entirely irrelevant, for example, to investigate whether the small size of a nation is necessarily an impediment to its economic development; or to find out whether small nations, by virtue of their smallness, are more economically unstable than large nations; or to examine the extent to which small countries can rely on international trade,

---

[1] Hebrew University, *The Challenge of Development*, Jerusalem, 1958.

[2] The proceedings and papers of this conference are presented in E. A. G. Robinson (ed.), *Economic Consequences of the Size of Nations*, London: Macmillan & Co., Ltd., 1960.

[3] Mention should be made of William G. Demas, *The Economics of Development in Small Countries with Special Reference to the Caribbean*, Montreal: McGill University Press, 1965. D. B. Keesing, "Population and Industrial Development: Some Evidence from Trade Patterns," *American Economic Review*, June 1968; and Bela Belassa, "Country Size and Trade Patterns: Comment," *American Economic Review*, March 1969.

[4] Out of the 112 countries classified by the United Nations as underdeveloped, not less than 91 have a population of less than 15 million and 65 have less than 5 million. See Sidney Dell, *Trade Blocs and Common Markets*, New York, 1963.

without impairing their economic stability, in order to escape from (or compensate for) their smallness. It is the main purpose of this investigation to throw some light on these and other related questions.

The study will be mainly concerned with assessing the impact of size on four different aspects of the economy - (1) economic stability, (2) diversity of economic structure, (3) degree of dependence on international trade, and (4) rate of economic growth and level of economic development. Specifically, the study is an attempt to find out whether there is any relation between each of these aspects and the size of a country. Some of the generalizations made about small economies, and the special features that are often attributed to 'smallness' center around these four aspects. It is generally presumed, for example, that the economic structure of small countries is less diversified than that of large countries, and that small countries are, therefore, expected to have a high degree of specialization in their production, and also a strong degree of commodity and geographic concentration in their exports. It is suggested too that this limited diversity can obstruct the country's flexibility and reduce its capacity to accommodate sudden changes in demand for its products. This may prove to be a possible source of instability, and small countries may thus be more vulnerable than large countries to fluctuations in their economic activity. Small countries are also expected to depend more heavily on international trade than large countries. This dependence, it can be claimed, is also likely to be a source of instability since it exposes the economy to more outside influences, some of which may be destabilizing in nature. It is also worth investigating whether there is any relationship between the size of a country and its level of economic performance. Since it is claimed that 'smallness' may imply an irregular economic activity and an irregular rate of growth, it may likewise be claimed that 'smallness' may also imply a slow rate of economic growth.

The investigation is in two parts, and both parts deal with the four aspects mentioned above, namely, with economic stability, concentration of economic activity, dependence on foreign trade, and economic growth and development. Each part will thus be in four Chapters. The *second* (and shorter) part is mainly an inquiry into the impact of 'size' on the Lebanese economy. Lebanon is chosen as an example of a small country, and the implications of 'size' on its economic growth, diversity, foreign trade involvement, and economic stability are separately analyzed in four Chapters. The *first* part is designed to examine and interpret the nature and magnitude of the association between size of nations and each of the four aspects mentioned. This part will try to find out the extent to which economic stability, concentration, dependence on trade, and economic growth are related to size. The size of countries (in the economic sense, GNP, and the demographic sense, population) will be treated as the *independent* variables, and the indices measuring instability, concentration, dependence on trade, and economic growth, will be treated as the *dependent* variables. Twenty-five such dependent variables have been chosen. Eight are instability indices, measuring the instability of national income, of exports and imports, of capital movements, and of foreign exchange reserves and of the terms of trade; seven are concentration indices, measuring the commodity and geographic concentration of exports and imports; five are dependence-on-trade indices, measuring the extent of trade involvement in terms of foreign trade as a ratio of GNP, of foreign trade per capita, of exports of goods and services, and foreign capital and donations as a ratio of GNP; and finally five are economic growth and development indices, measuring the per cent increase in GNP, the increase in per capita GNP, the level of per capita GNP, and the growth of exports.

Two methods of analysis will be used throughout this part: two-variable analysis, and multi-variant analysis with two independent variables. In the two-variable analysis, simple regressions and correlations between the independent variables (size of nations in terms of both population and GNP) and each of the twenty-five dependent variables, will indicate the extent to which these variables are related to size. The dependent variables will also be ranked with reference to population and GNP, i.e., countries will be grouped in quartiles, and the medians for the quartiles of the countries ranked in increasing order of size, will reveal whether any directional pattern exists or not. This kind of analysis, along with the simple regressions and correlations, should demonstrate whether any systematic relationship exists and how significant the relationship is, between size of country (in terms of population and GNP) and the twenty-five variables (measuring instability, concentration, dependence on trade, and growth) considered in this investigation.

Since in a number of cases, the two-variable analysis failed to indicate a clear association between size and the dependent variables, it seemed appropriate to use multi-variant analysis to include other variables which plausible reasoning or allegations suggest as possibly affecting the association between size and the dependent variables under consideration. For this purpose, a crossclassificatory scheme, described on page 35, and formal multiple-correlation analysis with two independent variables are both used. This three-variable analysis will again interpret the strength of the association between size and the dependent variables, and will also indicate whether such an association will be affected by some other related variables. A brief illustration at this point will help clarify the purpose of this analysis. It is argued, for example, that commodity export concentration is not only related to the size of country (i.e., an inverse association is expected to exist between size and export concentration), but also and more importantly perhaps, to the degree of economic development (i.e., an inverse association is expected to exist between export concentration and economic development). Such an association between export concentration and economic development may affect and even alter the nature of the association between size and export concentration. Multivariant analysis, with export concentration as the dependent variable and with size and economic development as the two independent variables will indicate whether this is possible or not, i.e., whether the impact of size on export concentration will change with a change in the degree of economic development, or whether the same association between size and export concentration will prevail regardless of the degree of development.

It should be stated at the outset that no one specific definition of size of nations is adopted in this investigation. Any demarcation line between small and large countries is at best arbitrary. Kuznets defines country size in terms of population and draws the line at a population of 10 million.[1] Demas defines a small country as one with a population of 5 million or less and with usable land area of 10 to 20 thousand square miles or less.[2] There are others[3] who also use population as a measure of country size. In this study both population and Gross National Product will be used without, however, drawing any line between small and large countries. The choice of these two measures assumes that size can be defined in terms of inputs and/or in terms of output. Population is selected to represent inputs and GNP to represent output. Other inputs (like area or usable land) could and have

---

[1] S. Kuznets, "Economic Growth of Small Nations," E. A. G. Robinson (ed.), *op. cit.*, p. 14.

[2] W. G. Demas, *op. cit.*, p. 40.

[3] See for example D. B. Keesing, *op. cit.*, and B. Belassa, *op. cit.*

been selected. Population figures are, however, more readily available. Choice among variables representing output is rather limited. GNP figures have their defects but no other indicators are also as conveniently available and perhaps as comparable.

PART ONE

CHAPTER TWO

ECONOMIC STABILITY AND SIZE

Are small countries, by virtue of their 'smallness', more vulnerable than large countries to fluctuations in their economic activity? Is there any relation between the size of a country and economic stability? In a chapter to follow, on the relation between size and economic growth and development, it is inquired whether small size implies a slow rate of economic growth; i.e., whether size constitutes an impediment to economic growth. It is equally important, also, to find out whether small size necessarily implies an irregular economic activity and an irregular rate of economic growth. This is the main purpose of this chapter.

A priori reasons suggesting that size and economic stability may be related are several. Elsewhere in this investigation it is observed that a rather significant association exists between size and degree of dependence on foreign trade. In order to compensate for their 'smallness', small countries tend to depend more heavily on international trade. For more than one reason, this dependence on trade may impair a country's economic stability. It can be argued, for example, that destabilizing forces originating outside a country can be more easily transmitted into a small country heavily dependent on foreign trade than the case would be in a larger country not as heavily dependent on trade. The generally high foreign trade (or export) proportions that often characterize small countries render small countries unusually sensitive to fluctuations in their foreign trade. Any shift in demand for their exports will mean, because of the high proportion of exports to national income, a relatively large proportionate change in the demand for the country's total product. Likewise, any balance of payments disequilibria, which may result from the shift in demand for exports, will mean a relatively large disequilibria in relation to the small country's national product. It is possible also that a small country is not in as strong a position as a large country to effectively retaliate, or guard itself, against outside policy measures or developments threatening to impair its stability. In so far as this is true, a small country's exports may be subject to more manipulation by other countries, and hence provide another potential source of instability in exports and national product.

It should perhaps also be noted that just as the 'smallness' of a country and the resulting strong dependence on foreign trade are capable of impairing a country's economic stability, it is also possible that they may help to stabilize economic activity instead. 'Smallness' more often than not, particularly when the level of economic development permits it, means a high propensity to import, and a high propensity to import may enable a small country to export some of the consequences of destabilizing forces initiated inside the country. Under such conditions 'smallness' becomes a stabilizing force.

It is also observed elsewhere in this investigation that there is an observable association between size and diversity of production and exports; small countries are generally more specialized in their production and, consequently, in their exports. The smaller the country, that is, the stronger is the concentration in production and exports. Hence it is possible to argue that in so far as a small country's economic structure is characterized by a more limited diversity, its degree of economic instability is likely to be higher than that of a larger country where economic structure is more diversified. The more specialized a country is, the less capable it is of generating forces to offset developments that lead to fluctuations in economic activity. The unavailability of abundant and diversified resources and a limited domestic market, obstruct a small country's capacity to accommodate sudden changes in demand for its products. The degree of responsiveness of a country's exports to changes in demand, depends in the final analysis on the price and income elasticity conditions, and elasticities of demand for a small country's exports need not necessarily be different from those for a large country. But the diversity of exports is expected to influence the elasticity of demand for exports. The less diversified exports are, the higher are the elasticities of demand for exports likely to be, and the more vulnerable would exports become to changes in demand conditions. If this line of reasoning is correct, one may expect exports of small countries and hence their national income (due to the high export proportions) to show higher degree of instability than the exports and total products of large countries.

A survey of the literature on this subject does not indicate that any empirical investigation has as yet been undertaken to study the association between size and economic stability. This chapter attempts to provide some evidence on the nature of this association. Its purpose is to evaluate the impact of 'size' on economic stability, and to investigate the extent to which 'smallness' is necessarily a cause of instability in economic activity. The chapter is in two parts. The statistical methods used in these two parts have been briefly noted in the previous chapter. In the two-variable analysis, six different aspects of instability are considered—instability of national income, instability of exports, instability of imports, instability of capital movements, fluctuations of foreign exchange reserves, and fluctuations of the terms of trade. The multi-variant analysis examines the extent to which the association between size and some of these aspects of instability (e.g., income, export and import instabilities) is influenced by the degree of dependence on trade, by the degree of concentration in trade, and by economic growth and development. Income, export and import instability indices will be the dependent variables, and 'size' and each of dependence on trade, concentration in trade, economic growth and economic development, as the two independent variables. In other words, instability is separately analyzed as a function of size and dependence on trade, of size and concentration in trade, of size and economic growth, and of size and economic development. The cross-classifications will indicate whether any pattern in the instability variables can be observed as both size and each of the other independent variables change; and the multiple-correlation coefficients will be compared with the simple-correlation coefficients, and the influence of each of these independent variables on the relationship between instability and size will be analyzed.

1. Two-Variable Analysis: Patterns and Correlations

The dependent variables used here as measures of economic instability are eight: One index measures the instability of national income, two indices measure the instability of exports, one index measures the instability of imports, two indices measure the instability of capital movements, one index measures the fluctuations of foreign exchange reserves, and one index measures the fluctuations of the terms of trade.[1] Each one of these instability variables will be separately analyzed. Simple correlations between the instability variables and size of country in terms of population and GNP, and comparisons of the median instability for the quartiles of the countries ranked with reference to size, are both employed here for the purpose of interpre-

---

[1] These indices and all other indices used in this investigation are explained and their sources given in Appendix B. The values of these indices are also given in Appendix Table 1.

ting the nature and significance of the association between size and each of the aspects of instability mentioned above. Instability of national income is considered first.

A. *Instability of National Income and Size*

It can be claimed that small countries, on account of their limited domestic market and limited diversity in factor endowments, are generally expected to have a narrowly diversified economic structure. This narrow diversity is said to render small countries more vulnerable to fluctuations in their economic activity, and these fluctuations, among other things, may mean an unstable national product. Is this claim true? Are the national incomes of small countries more unstable than the national incomes of large countries? Are instability of national income and 'size' in any way associated? What do the facts show?

The index used here as a measure of the degree of instability of national income is a close approximation of the average year-to-year percentage variation in income, adjusted for trend (i.e., logarithmic variance method), for a sample of sixty countries (prepared by Coppock). This Instability Index of National Income (Y_1) is correlated to size of country in terms of both population and gross national product. The coefficients of correlation (r) between population (X_2) and income instability (Y_1) and between GNP (X_1) and income instability (Y_1) are $+.01$ and $+.03$ respectively. The scatter diagrams of Figure 1 show these relations. These very low correlation coefficients indicate that the relationship between instability of national income and size of a country (in terms of both population and GNP) is very weak or non-existent. Tests of significance indicate that these coefficients are well below the .05 level of significance and cannot, therefore, be taken with any confidence.

When the sixty countries are ranked in increasing order of size, and the median income instability of each quartile computed, a somewhat more significant association between size (particularly population) and income instability is revealed. When population is used as a measure of size and countries are ranked in increasing order of population, the median income instability (Y_1) is 6.0 for the first quartile, 6.6 for the second, 8.7 for the third, and 11.0 for the fourth quartile. This shows a consistent rising pattern. Thus a positive association is revealed between income instability and population, unlike the very weak positive association of formal correlation analysis. There is a tendency here

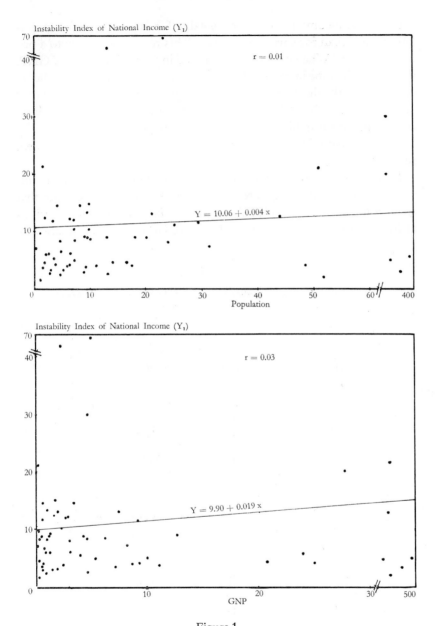

Figure 1
Scatter diagrams: Instability of national income and size.

for national income to be more unstable for larger countries (population wise) than for smaller countries. This result is contrary to a priori reasoning.[1] When countries are ranked in increasing order of GNP, the median income instability is 6.6 for the first quartile, 10.3 for the second, 8.3 for the third, and 4.7 for the fourth. No pattern between GNP and income instability is revealed. The fourth quartile has the lowest median income instability, but the first quartile has a median instability lower than that of the second and third quartiles. Table I gives these relations.

Results of formal correlation analysis and rankings of income instability medians do not, therefore, provide support for the claim that small countries are generally subject to more fluctuation in their national income than large countries. The correlation coefficients are low

Table 1

Relation between Size of Country (Population, GNP) and Instability of National Income (Y_1)

GROUPS OF COUNTRIES Countries Ranked in Increasing Order of Population Size (Quartiles)	Number of Countries	Average Population (millions)	Median Instability of National Income
	(1)	(2)	(3)
I	15	2.29	6.0
II	15	6.63	6.6
III	15	13.67	8.7
IV	15	86.13	11.0

Countries Ranked in Increasing Order of GNP Size (Quartiles)	Number of Countries	Average GNP ($ billions)	Median Instability of National Income
I	15	0.53	6.6
II	15	1.77	10.3
III	15	5.29	8.3
IV	15	66.40	4.7

[1] This result need not necessarily be contrary to *a priori* reasoning since large instability in larger (by population) countries can be admitted by *a priori* reasoning, owing to such factors as, e.g., agricultural fluctuations in India, or cyclical fluctuations in the U.S.A.

and statistically non-significant, but both of them are positive. And in one case, the rankings of the income instability medians reveal a positive pattern between population size and income instability, which suggests, contrary to expectations, that income instability tends to increase as size (in terms of population) increases.

B. *Instability of Export Proceeds and Size*

It can also be claimed that small countries, on account of their generally narrow diversity of economic structure, tend to have a higher degree of commodity and geographic concentration of exports[1], and that this high degree of concentration often generates instability in export proceeds. If this claim is true, small countries are expected to have a higher degree of export instability than large countries. What does our analysis show? Are instability of export proceeds and size of country in any way related?

Two different indices of export instability are utilized here and both of them are correlated to size of country in terms of population and GNP. The first (Y_2) is the same logarithmic variance method used in measuring instability of national income computed (by Coppock) for a sample of eighty-three countries. The second index (Y_3) is a "normalized standard error", i.e., the standard error of estimate (square root of the unexplained variance) divided by the mean of the observations, computed (by Massell) for a sample of thirty-six countries. Values of both indices are in columns Y_2 and Y_3, respectively, of Appendix Table 1. The coefficient of correlation (r) between export instability index (Y_2) and population (X_2) is $+.45$, and the correlation coefficient between export instability (Y_2) and GNP (X_1) is $+.20$. Figure 2 shows these relations. Both coefficients are positive which suggests that there is a tendency for instability of export proceeds (Y_2) to increase as size, particularly in terms of population, increases. Both correlation coefficients are relatively high, and the former is significant at both the .05 and .01 levels, and can be taken with reasonable amount of confidence.

When the Massell index of export instability (Y_3) is used, the direction of the association between export instability and size is altered. The correlation coefficient between export instability (Y_3) and population (X_2) is $-.10$, and between export instability (Y_3) and GNP (X_1) is $-.12$. Figure 3 shows these relations. These low coefficients indicate

---

[1] The relationship between size of country and export concentration is considered in Chapter III of this investigation.

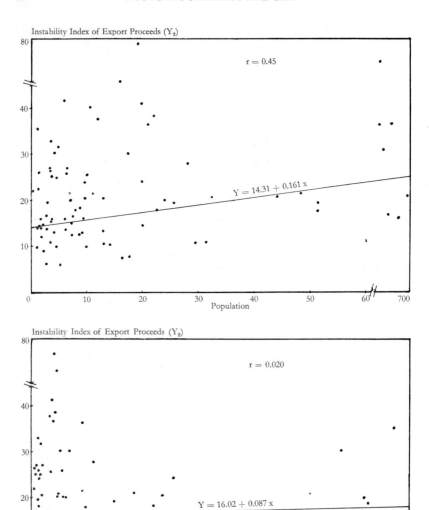

Figure 2
Scatter diagrams: Instability of export proceeds and size.

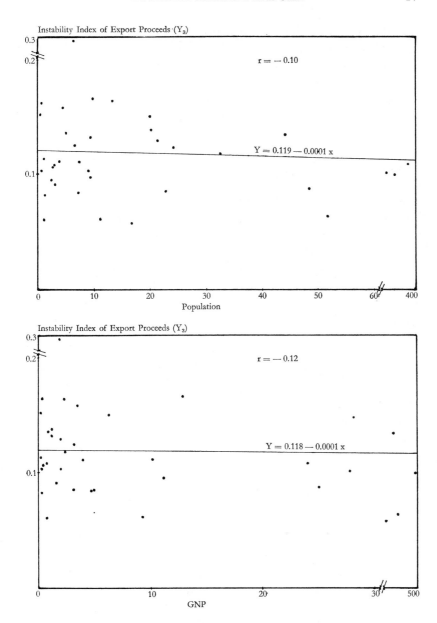

Figure 3
Scatter diagrams: Instability of export proceeds and size.

that the association between instability of export proceeds (Y_3) and size of a country is almost nonexistent. The coefficients are however negative, but they are below the .05 level of significance and cannot be taken with any confidence.

The rankings of the median export instability reveal the same association, as in the correlation analysis, between export instability and size of country. When the eighty-three countries of the Coppock sample are ranked in increasing order of population size, the median export instability (Y_2) is 16.0 for the first quartile, 18.2 for the second, 20.5 for the third, and 20.8 for the fourth. Thus the same positive association is revealed. There is here a pattern indicating a tendency for export instability to increase as population size increases. This result plus the fact that the correlation coefficient between Y_2 and population is $+.45$ and is significant at two levels of confidence, suggest that small countries tend to have more stable exports than large countries. This is contrary to commonly held opinion.[1] When the countries (80 of the 83) are ranked in increasing order of GNP, the median export instability (Y_2) is 18.9 for the first quartile, 14.9 for the second, 21.1 for the third, and 18.1 for the fourth. No trend is revealed. This is not unexpected since the correlation coefficient between export instability and GNP ($+.20$) was not statistically significant. The rankings of the thirty-six countries of the Massell sample fail also to reveal any association between export instability (Y_3) and size of country. When the countries are ranked in increasing order of population size, the median export instability (Y_3) is 10.6 for the first quartile, 11.1 for the second, 13.2 for the third, and 10.0 for the fourth. No directional pattern emerges. The last quartile has the lowest median, the third quartile has the highest, and the first and last quartiles have almost the same medians. Export instability and population size are not related. A similar pattern is also revealed when the countries are ranked in increasing order of GNP size. The median export instability (Y_3) is 10.8 for the first quartile, 12.9 for the second, 11.1 for the third, and 10.1 for the fourth. Thus any directional pattern also fails to emerge. The last quartile has the lowest median, the second quartile has the highest, and the first and last quartiles have similar

---

[1] It is worthwhile to note that J. D. Coppock who correlated export instability with three measures of size of an economy—national income, population, and area—found out also "that there is a tendency, though a weak one, for exports to be more unstable for larger economies than for smaller ones." See his *International Economic Instability*, New York, McGraw-Hill Book Co., Inc., 1962, p. 105.

medians. Export instability and GNP size are not significantly related to each other. These relations are given in Table 2.

The claim that small countries are more vulnerable than large countries to fluctuations in their export proceeds does not find support here. Both correlation analysis and rankings of median export insta-

Table 2

Relation between Size of Country (Population, GNP) and Instability of Export Proceeds (Y₂, Y₃)

Relation between Size of Country (Population, GNP) and Instability of Export Proceeds (Y_2, Y_3)

GROUPS OF COUNTRIES *Countries Ranked in Increasing Order of Population Size (Quartiles)*	*Number of Countries*	*Y₂ (Coppock)*		*Number of Countries*	*Y₃ (Massell)*	
		Average Population (millions)	*Median Instability of Export Proceeds*		*Average Population (millions)*	*Median Instability of Export Proceeds*
I	21	2.05	16.0	9	1.20	10.6
II	21	6.17	18.2	9	5.70	11.1
III	21	14.06	20.5	9	14.44	13.2
IV	20	105.01	20.8	9	97.44	10.0

Countries Ranked in Increasing Order of GNP Size (Quartiles)	*Number of Countries*	*Average GNP ($ billions)*	*Median Instability of Export Proceeds*	*Number of Countries*	*Average GNP ($ billions)*	*Median Instability of Export Proceeds*
I	20	0.43	18.95	9	0.32	10.8
II	20	1.37	14.95	9	1.87	12.9
III	20	3.62	21.15	9	6.28	11.1
IV	20	51.96	18.10	9	77.13	10.1

bility do not reveal a significant inverse pattern between instability of export proceeds and size of country. Two of the correlation coefficients are negative, but they are very low and cannot be taken with confidence, and the relevant median instability rankings fail to indicate any trend. In fact, the only significant result which our analysis reveals is a positive association between export instability (Y_2) and population size. This was apparent, to repeat, in the statistically significant correlation coefficient of $+.45$, and in the increasing trend of the median export instability when countries were ranked in increasing order of population size.

C. *Instability of Imports and Size*

A priori thinking does not suggest that a relationship exists between import instability and size of country. There are no reasons to assume that the degree of import instability will change with a change in the size of countries. Results of the correlation analysis and of the median import instability rankings support this view.

The index used as a measure of the instability of imports (Y_4) is the same logarithmic variance method used in measuring the instability of national income and of export proceeds. The values of this index, computed by Coppock for a sample of eighty-three countries, are given in column Y_4 of Appendix Table 1. The corrrelation coefficient (r) between the import instability index (Y_4) and population (X_2) is —.13, and the correlation coefficient between import instability index (Y_4) and GNP (X_1) is +.01. Figure 4 shows these relations. These low correlation coefficients indicate that the degree of association between instability of imports and size of country, in terms of both population and GNP, is very weak or nonexistent. The coefficient for the association between import instability and population size is negative, while the coefficient for the association between import instability and GNP size is positive, and both are not significant at any level and cannot be taken with any confidence.

The import instability medians of the countries ranked in increasing order of size reveal the same lack of association between import instability and size of country. When the eighty-three countries are ranked in increasing order of population size, the median import instability (Y_4) is 20.0 for the first quartile, 19.4 for the second, 24.3 for the third, and 19.9 for the fourth. Thus no apparent trend between import instability and population size is indicated. The second quartile has the lowest median, the third quartile has the highest median, and the first and last quartiles have the same medians. Import instability and population size are not related. When the countries (80 of the 83) are ranked in increasing order of GNP, the median import instability (Y_4) is 19.9 for the first quartile, 21.0 for the second, 22.8 for the third, and 19.0 for the fourth. Here again, no trend between import instability and GNP size is indicated. The fourth quartile has the lowest instability median, but the third quartile has a higher median than the first two

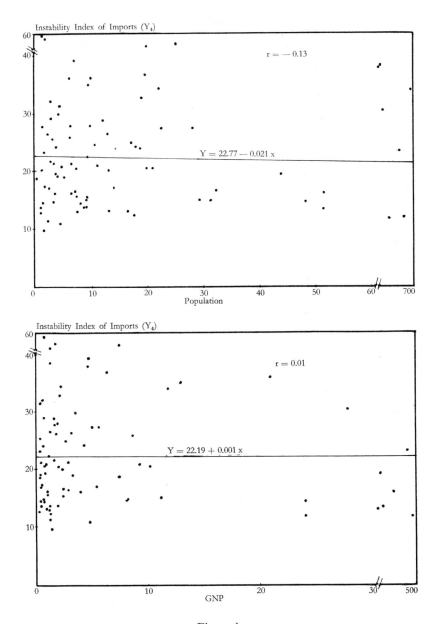

Figure 4
Scatter diagrams: Instability of imports and size.

Table 3

Relation between Size of Country (Population, GNP) and Instability of Imports (Y_4)

GROUPS OF COUNTRIES Countries Ranked in Increasing Order of Population Size (Quartiles)	Number of Countries	Average Population (million)	Median Instability of Imports
I	21	2.05	20.0
II	21	6.17	19.4
III	21	14.06	24.3
IV	20	105.01	19.9

Countries Ranked in Increasing Order of GNP Size (Quartiles)	Number of Countries	Average GNP ($ billions)	Median Instability of Imports
I	20	0.425	19.9
II	20	1.365	21.0
III	20	3.615	22.8
IV	20	51.96	19.0

quartiles, and the second quartile has a higher instability median than the first. These relations are given in Table 3.

It is apparent, therefore, from the correlation analysis and from the rankings of the median import instability that no association exists between instability and size of country in terms of both population size and GNP size.

D. *Instability of Capital Movements and Size*

Does instability of capital movements have anything to do with the size of country? Are small countries expected, again by virtue of their smallness, to be more vulnerable to fluctuating in their capital movements? A priori reasoning seems to suggest an inverse association between size of country and instability of capital movements. So long as small countries are assumed to have a less diversified economic structure and therefore a more limited scope of investment opportunities, they cannot be expected to command a strong control over their capital movements, and these movements as a result will be sub-

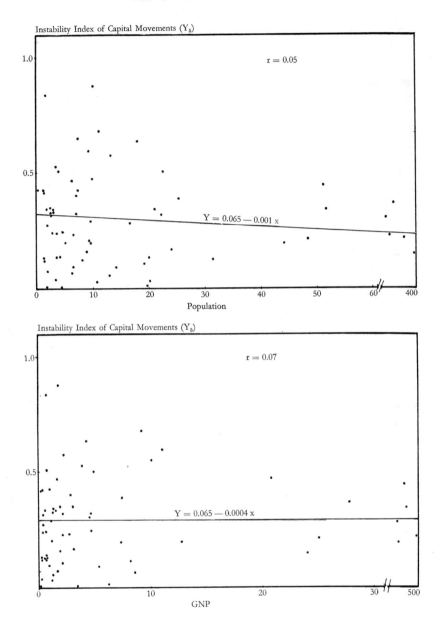

Figure 5
Scatter diagrams: Instability of capital movements and size

ject to sudden interruption and more fluctuation. It can also be argued that the retaliatory powers of small countries against policy restrictions imposed by large countries on capital movements are rather limited and ineffective, and that this provides another reason for the greater instability of their capital movements.

Can this line of argument be supported? What do the facts show? Two different instability indices of capital movements are used for this purpose, and both are correlated to size of country in terms of population size and GNP size. Values of these indices, both computed by Coppock for a sample of sixty-seven countries, are given in columns Y_5 and Y_6 of Appendix Table 1. The first index (Y_5) consists of applying linear correlation technique, with time (1947 to 1958) on the x-axis and the net capital movements on the y-axis, and where low r-values represent high instability. The second index (Y_6), the so called U.N. method, consists of obtaining the absolute difference in values from year to year, expressing this difference as a percentage of the larger of the two annual values, and then averaging these percentages.

The coefficient of correlation (r) between instability index of capital movements (Y_5) and population (X_2) is $+.05$, and between instability index of capital movements (Y_5) and GNP (X_1) is $+.07$. Figure 5 shows this relation. Both of these coefficients are very low and therefore indicate that no relationship exists between size of country and instability of capital movements.

A similar weak association between instability of capital movements and size is also revealed when the second index of instability is used. The coefficient of correlation (r) between instability index of capital movements (Y_6) and population (X_2) is $—.13$, and between instability index (Y_6) and GNP (X_1) is $—.05$. Figure 6 shows these relations. Both these coefficients are negative but both of them are statistically insignificant and cannot be taken with any confidence.

Correlation analysis, therefore, does not indicate that a significant association exists between instability of capital movements and size of country. Two of the correlation coefficients are negative, two are positive, and all four coefficients are too low to be taken with any confidence.

The rankings of the median instability of capital movements do not reveal also any consistent pattern between instability of capital movements and size of country. When instability index (Y_5) is used and the sixty-seven countries are ranked in increasing order of population size, the median instability of capital movements (Y_5) is 0.326 for the first

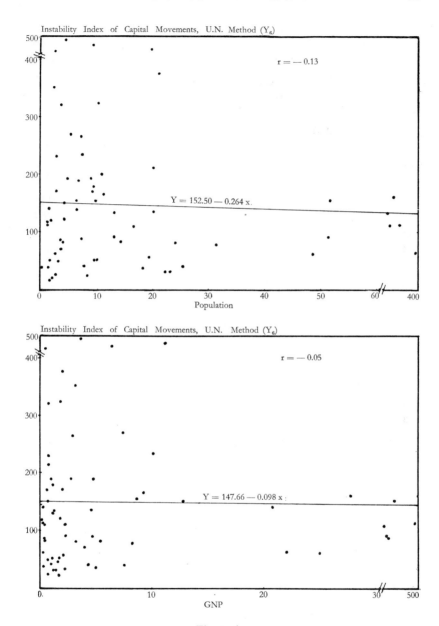

Figure 6
Scatter diagrams: Instability of capital movement sand size.

quartile, 0.237 for the second, 0.203 for the third, and 0.266 for the fourth. Thus no directional pattern is indicated. The first quartile has the highest median, and the third quartile has a lower median than the second quartile, but the fourth quartile has a higher median than the middle two quartiles. No systematic relationship is observed between population size and instability of capital movements. When the countries (65 of the 67) are ranked in increasing order of GNP size, also no trend is observed. The median instability of capital movements (Y_5) is 0.187 for the first quartile, 0.308 for the second, 0.311 for the third, and 0.282 for the fourth quartile. The middle two quartiles have higher medians than the first and last quartiles, and no directional pattern between GNP size and instability of capital movements is thus revealed.

When the second instability index (Y_6) is used and the sixty-seven countries are ranked in increasing order of population, the median instability of capital movements (Y_6) is 83 for the first quartile, 154 for the second, 155 for the third, and 90 for the fourth. Again no directional pattern is observed. The first quartile has the lowest median, but the fourth quartile has a lower median than the middle two quartiles. No relationship is indicated between population size and instability of capital movements. When the countries (65 of the 67) are ranked in increasing order of GNP, also no trend is indicated. The median instability of capital movements (Y_6) is 117 for the first quartile, 89 for the second, 99 for the third, and 138 for the fourth. The second and third quartiles have a lower instability median than the first quartile, but the fourth quartile has the highest instability median. These relations are given in Table 4.

The argument that small countries cannot command a strong control over their capital movements and that as a result they are more prone, than large countries, to experience fluctuations in their capital movements, does not find strong support in this analysis. Both the formal correlation analysis and the rankings of the instability medians do not reveal any significant association between instability of capital movements and size of country in terms of population and GNP. There is no reason to assume therefore that the instability of capital movements has a tendency to increase with a decrease in the size of country.

E. *Fluctuations of Foreign Exchange Reserves and Size*

The same reasoning which suggested an inverse association between size of country and instability of both export proceeds and capital

Table 4

Relation between Size of Country (Population, GNP) and Instability of
Capital Movements (Y$_5$, Y$_6$)

GROUPS OF COUNTRIES

Countries Ranked in Increasing Order of Population Size (Quartiles)	Number of Countries	Average Popula- tion (millions)	Median Insta- bility of Capital Movements	Number of Countries	Average Popula- tion (millions)	Median Insta- bility of Capital Movements
		(Y$_5$) (r)			(Y$_6$) (U.N.)	
I	17	1.85	0.326	17	1.85	83
II	17	5.58	0.237	17	5.88	154
III	17	13.09	0.203	17	13.09	155
IV	16	74.19	0.266	16	74.19	90

Countries Ranked in Increasing Order of GNP Size (Quartiles)	Number of Countries	Averages GNP ($ billions)	Median Insta- bility of Capital Movements	Number of Countries	Average GNP ($ billions)	Median Insta- bility of Capital Movements
I	16	0.388	0.187	16	0.388	117
II	16	1.35	0.308	16	1.35	89
III	16	3.75	0.311	16	3.75	99
IV	17	47.41	0.282	17	47.41	138

movements, can also suggest a similar inverse association between size of country and fluctuations of foreign exchange reserves. If it can be argued that small countries are more susceptible to fluctuations in their export proceeds and capital movements, it can likewise be argued that they are more susceptible to experience disequilibria in their balance of payments and consequently more fluctuations in their foreign exchange reserves.

The index used as a measure of fluctuations of foreign exchange reserves (Y$_7$) is essentially the same as the U.N. method used in measuring the instability of capital movements (Y$_6$). The values of this index, computed by Michaely for a sample of thirty-two countries (for the period 1948-58), are given in column Y$_7$ of Appendix Table 1. This index is correlated to size of country in terms of both population size

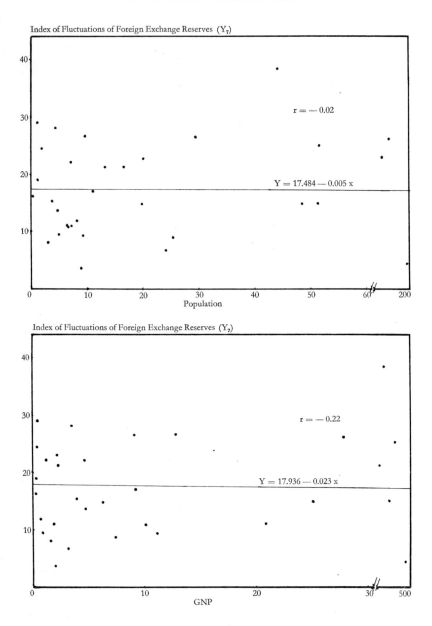

Figure 7
Scatter diagrams: Fluctuations of foreign reserves and size.

and GNP size. The coefficient of correlation (r) between the index of fluctuations of foreign exchange reserves (Y_7) and population (X_2) is —.02, and between the same index (Y_7) and GNP (X_1) is —.22. The scatter diagrams of Figure 7 show these relations. Both of these coefficients are negative which can imply that there is a tendency for fluctuations of foreign exchange reserves to decrease as size of country (particularly GNP size) increases. But one cannot place any confidence even in the latter coefficient of —.22, since both of them are below the .05 level of significance.

The rankings of the median fluctuations of foreign exchange reserves do not also show any strong association between fluctuation of foreign reserves and size of country. When the thirty-two countries are ranked in increasing order of population size, the median fluctuation of foreign exchange reserves (Y_7) is 17.6 for the first quartile, 11.0 for the second, 19.2 for the third, and 24.0 for the fourth. Unlike the negative (and almost nonexistent) coefficient of the correlation analysis, these medians show a tendency to increase with an increase in population size. The fourth quartile has the highest fluctuation median, and the third quartile has a higher median than the first two quartiles, but the second quartile has the lowest median. When the thirty-two countries are ranked in increasing order of GNP size, the median fluctuations of foreign reserves (Y_7) is 17.6 for the first quartile, 18.3 for the second, 14.2 for the third, and 18.1 for the fourth. Despite the negative coefficient of —.22 between fluctuations of foreign reserves and GNP size, the rankings of the median fluctuations do not show a declining trend. The third quartile has the lowest fluctuation median, but the fourth quartile has a higher median than the third and first quartiles. Both rankings fail to show a clear pattern between fluctuations of foreign reserves and size of country. They do show at least that the median fluctuation does not tend to decrease with an increase in size of country. Table 5 shows these relations.

The view that small countries are more susceptible than large countries to fluctuations in their exchange reserves, does not find adequate support in our analysis. Results of the correlation analysis and the rankings of the median fluctuations fail to indicate a significant association between fluctuations in foreign reserves and size of country in terms of population and GNP. The two correlation coefficients are negative, one is approximately zero and can be ignored, the other is comparatively high but still cannot be taken with any confidence, and the median rankings do not reveal a declining pattern.

Table 5

Relationship between Size of Country (Population, GNP) and Fluctuations of Foreign Exchange Reserves (Y_7)

GROUPS OF COUNTRIES *Countries Ranked in Increasing Order of Population Size (Quartiles)*	*Number of Countries*	*Average Population (millions)*	*Median Fluctuations of Foreign Reserves*
I	8	2.4	17.6
II	8	7.25	11.0
III	8	17.49	19.2
IV	8	63.45	24.0
Countries Ranked in Increasing Order of GNP Size (Quartiles)	*Number of Countries*	*Average GNP ($ billions)*	*Median Fluctuations of Foreign Reserves*
I	8	0.63	17.6
II	8	2.88	18.3
III	8	8.83	14.2
IV	8	88.41	18.1

F. *Fluctuations of the Terms of Trade and Size*

The last of the instability indices concerns the association between the degree of fluctuations of the terms of trade and size of country. Can one claim that small countries are likely to have more fluctuations than large countries in their terms of trade? Do the facts support this claim? Again, a priori reasoning seems to suggest an inverse association between fluctuations of the terms of trade and size of country. The smaller the country, that is, the less is the control it has over the prices of exports and imports and the more are the fluctuations of its terms of trade.

The index used here as a measure of fluctuations of the terms of trade (Y_8) consists of the range between the highest and lowest positions of the country's terms of trade (for the period 1948-1958), expressed as a ratio of the average level of the terms of trade during that period. The values of this index, computed by Michaely for a sample of thirty-six countries, are given in column Y_8 of Appendix Table 1. This index is correlated to size of country in terms of both population size and GNP size. The coefficient of correlation (r) be-

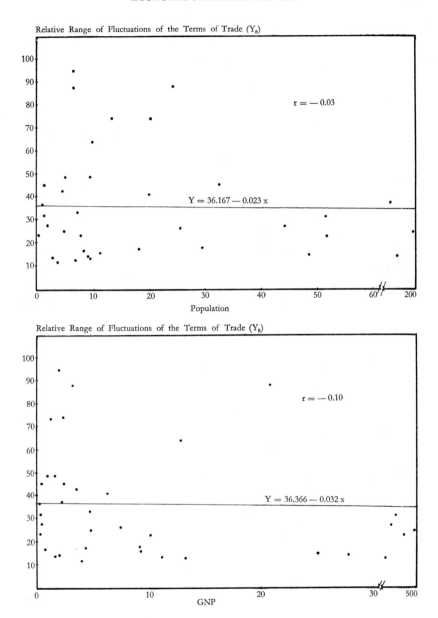

Figure 8
Scatter diagrams: Fluctuations of the terms and trade and size.

tween the index of fluctuations of terms of trade (Y_8) and population (X_2) is —.03, and the coefficient between the same index (Y_8) and GNP is —.10. The scatter diagrams of Figure 8 show these relations. As in the previous index of instability, both of these coefficients are negative which again implies that there is a tendency perhaps for fluctuations of the terms of trade to decrease as size of country (in terms of population and GNP) increases. But these coefficients are low and one cannot place any confidence in them since they are not significant at the .05 level. The association between fluctuations of the terms of trade and size of country is therefore very weak.

The rankings of the median fluctuations of the terms of trade, as in formal correlation analysis, fail to reveal a consistent pattern between fluctuations of the terms of trade and size of country. When the thirty-six countries of the sample are ranked in increasing order of population size, the median fluctuations of the terms of trade (Y_8) is 27.4 for the first quartile, 33.0 for the second, 40.8 for the third, and 24.6 for the fourth. No trend is thus revealed. The fourth quartile has the lowest median fluctuation, but the second quartile has a higher median than the first, and the third quartile has a higher median than the first two quartiles. When the same countries are ranked in increasing order of GNP size, the median fluctuations of the terms of trade (Y_8) is 36.5 for the first quartile, 42.8 for the second, 22.9 for the third, and 24.6 for the fourth. Also no clear trend is indicated. But the last two quartiles have lower median fluctuations than the first two quartiles. These relations are given in Table 6.

The results of both correlation analysis and the rankings of the median fluctuations fail to indicate a strong association between the fluctuations in the terms of trade and size of country in terms of population and GNP. Therefore, the view that small countries are expected to have more fluctuations in their terms of trade than large countries, is not supported by our analysis.

To *conclude*, the two-variable analysis, rankings and simple correlations, of the relationship between size and the different aspects of economic instability considered here, suggests the following results— there is no significant association between size and instability of national income, although in one case the rankings revealed a positive pattern between income instability and population size; there is a significant positive association between population size and export instability; there is no association between size and import instability; there is likewise no association between size and instability of capital

Table 6

Relation between Size of Country (Population, GNP) and Fluctuations of the Terms of Trade (Y₈)

GROUPS OF COUNTRIES Countries Ranked in Increasing Order of Population Size (Quartiles)	Number of Countries	Average Population (millions)	Median Fluctuations of Terms of Trade
I	9	2.21	27.4
II	9	7.48	33.0
III	9	17.54	40.8
IV	9	67.20	24.6

Countries Ranked in Increasing Order of GNP Size (Quartiles)	Number of Countries	Average GNP ($ billions)	Median Fluctuations of Terms of Trade
I	9	0.57	36.5
II	9	2.47	42.8
III	9	7.40	22.9
IV	9	80.01	24.6

movements; and finally there is no association also between size and either of the fluctuations of foreign exchange reserves or of the terms of trade. Such results, therefore, do not provide any support for the claim that small countries, by virtue of their 'smallness', are generally expected to be more vulnerable than large countries to fluctuations in their economic activity.

2. THREE-VARIABLE ANALYSIS: CROSS-CLASSIFICATIONS AND CORRELATIONS

The three-variable analysis is designed to investigate the degree to which the association between size and economic instability, interpreted in the first part of this chapter, is affected by dependence on trade, by concentration in trade, and by economic growth and development. Three aspects of economic instability are chosen for this analysis—instability of national income, instability of export proceeds, and instability of imports. It is often assumed in the literature that a high dependence on foreign trade could be a source of instability in national income. Multi-variant analysis, with income instability as the dependent variable, and with size and dependence on trade as the independent variables, will indicate the nature of the relationship between income instability and dependence on trade, and will also indicate the impact of dependence on trade on the association between size and income instability.

It can also be claimed that a strong concentration in production and, hence, exports is capable, too, of impairing the stability of national income. Multi-variant analysis, with income instability as the dependent variable, and with size and export concentration as the independent variables, will indicate whether such a contention can be supported or not. It will reveal the nature of the relationship between income instability and export concentration, and will also reveal the impact of export concentration on the association between size and income instability.

Levels of economic development and rates of economic growth may also influence the stability of national income and, therefore, change the association between size and income instability. Three-variable analysis, with instability as the dependent variable, and with size and economic development or economic growth as the two independent variables, will interpret such a possibility. This analysis, in other words, will indicate the nature and strength of the association between income instability and economic growth or economic development, and will also indicate the impact of economic growth or development, on the association between size and income instability.

The treatment of export instability will be similar to that of income instability, since some of the factors that are capable of impairing a country's export stability are generally the same as those that can impair income stability. Three-variable analysis, with instability in export proceeds as the dependent variable, and with each of size and dependence on trade, size and export concentration, and size and economic development or growth as the two independent variables, will indicate the extent to which the association between size and export instability may change as a result of a change in the degree of dependence on trade, or export concentration, or the levels of economic development and growth. A priori reasoning, for example, suggests a tendency for export instability to increase with an increase in the dependence on trade, and perhaps also to increase with an increase in export concentration. The three-variable analysis of export instability variables will investigate whether such reasoning can be supported.

The last aspect of instability treated here is instability of imports. With instability of imports as the dependent variable, and with size and dependence on trade, and size and economic growth or development as the two independent variables, the multi-variant analysis will try to show whether the association between size and import instability is likely to change with a change in the degree of dependence on trade, and in the level of economic development and growth. The limited data on import concentration does not permit the inclusion of import concentration as another independent variable, and hence its impact on the association between size and import instability will not be considered.

Two methods of analysis will be used throughout—the cross-classification method of analysis, and formal multiple-correlation analysis with two independent variables, since the latter includes only those variables used by the cross-classification technique. The cross-classification method of analysis needs some explanation. Countries are first ranked in increasing order of each of the two independent variables (population and GNP) and divided into thirds, low (L), middle (M), and high (H). Second, countries in each of the thirds are ranked, also in increasing order, with respect to another variable, say dependence on trade or export concentration, so that there will be nine cells in all. Then, finally, the median value of the variable under consideration is calculated for the countries in each of the nine cells. Such a table can be interpreted as a crude partial correlation table. Comparing the median values across any row, down any column, or diagonally will indicate whether any directional pattern can be observed. An example may clarify this. Simple correlation analysis has shown the nature of the relationship between, say, export instability and size. Now, it has been alleged that this relationship may change if, say, commodity export concentration is taken into account. Cross-classifying export instability indices by size and by export concentration will demonstrate whether this allegation is true or not. Countries are, therefore, ranked in increasing order of size (both population and GNP) and divided into thirds, low (L), middle (M), and high (H). Then countries in each of the thirds are ranked, also in increasing order, with respect to export concentration and also divided into thirds, low (L), middle (M) and high (H), so that there were nine cells in all. Then the median value of the export instability indices is calculated for the countries in each of the nine cells. Comparison of these median values across any row, down any column, or diagonally will reveal whether any directional pattern prevails. This will reveal, in other words, the manner in which instability of export proceeds changes as both size and export concentration change, and will, thus, answer the allegation concerning the impact of export concentration on the association between size and export instability.

A. *Income Instability and Size*

There are five factors that are considered here for their impact on the association between size and income instability. They are—level of economic development, economic growth, dependence on trade, commodity concentration of exports, and geographic concentration of exports. The relationship between income instability and size and each of the above factors will be separately analyzed.

1. *Income Instability, Development, and Size*

This is mainly an analysis of the effect of the level of economic development on the association between income instability and size. Income instability medians (Y_1) classified by size (GNP and population) and by economic development (Y_{23}) reveal an inverse association between economic development and income instability, and reveal no association between size and income instability. Table 7 shows these results. The median values of income instability observe a directional pattern down all columns, and also (with one exception) diagonally. No directional pattern is, however, observed across all rows. The inverse association between income instability and economic development is observed regardless of the size of country; whereas no consistent pattern is observed between income instability and size. A positive directional pattern is observed between income instability and size in the population breakdown, across any row and also diagonally, but such a pattern disappears in the GNP breakdown. These results are in line with the two-variable analysis where a positive pattern was indicated between income instability and population size. It is now further indicated that such a positive pattern is not offset by a change in the level of economic development.

Formal multiple-correlation analysis, with income instability (Y_1) as the dependent variable, and with size (X_1 or X_2) and economic development (Y_3) as the two independent variables, provides more or less similar results. Multiple regression equations, given below, show a positive coefficient between income instability (Y_1) and size (X_1 and

Table 7

*Income Instability Medians (Y_1) by Size (GNP) and by Degree
of Development (Y_{23})*

	Small Countries	Large Countries	TOTAL
Underdeveloped *Countries*	9.0 *Range* (1.6-14.8) n = 11	20.0 *Range* (4.3-66.8) n = 3	9.0 *Range* (1.6-66.8) n = 14
Developed *Countries*	6.0 *Range* (3.1-6.1) n = 3	4.5 *Range* (2.0-21.5) n = 12	5.4 *Range* (2.0-21.5) n = 15
TOTAL	7.4 *Range* (1.6-14.8) n = 14	4.7 *Range* (2.0-66.8) n = 15	6.0 *Range* (1.6-66.8) n = 29

*Income Instability Medians (Y_1) by Size (Population) and by Degree of
Development (Y_{23})*

	Small Countries	Large Countries	TOTAL
Underdeveloped *Countries*	4.4 *Range* (1.6-14.6) n = 8	13.4 *Range* (4.2-66.8) n = 7	9.0 *Range* (1.6-66.8) n = 15
Developed *Countries*	4.1 *Range* (2.5-10.4) n = 7	8.7 *Range* (2.0-21.5) n = 7	5.4 *Range* (2.0-21.5) n = 14
TOTAL	4.3 *Range* (1.6-14.6) n = 15	8.9 *Range* (2.0-66.8) n = 14	6.0 *Range* (1.6-66.8) n = 29

X_2), and a negative coefficient between income instability and economic development (Y_{23})

$$Y_1 = 0.1265X_1 - 0.0088Y_{23} + 13.0910$$
$$\quad\;\; (.157) \qquad (.006) \qquad\;\; (2.86) \qquad R = .269$$
$$Y_1 = 0.1643X_2 - 0.0069Y_{23} + 10.7946$$
$$\quad\;\; (.107) \qquad (.005) \qquad\;\; (3.20) \qquad R = .359$$

The standard deviations of these coefficients, however, are all quite high, and these coefficients are not statistically acceptable. Hence, the positive association between income instability and size, and the negative association between income instability and economic development are both not significant. The level of economic development, therefore, is not likely to have an impact on the association between income instability and size.

2. Income Instability, Economic Growth, and Size

This is similarly an analysis of the effect of economic growth on the relationship between income instability and size. Income instability medians (Y_1) classified by size (GNP and population) and by economic growth (Y_{21}), indicate a positive pattern between income instability and economic growth, and also indicate the same inconsistent pattern between income instability and size. See Table 8. The median values

Table 8

Income Instability Medians (Y_1) by Size (GNP) and by Economic Growth (Y_{21})

	Small Countries	Large Countries	TOTAL
Low Economic Growth	6.1 Range (3.1-14.8) n = 7	4.2 Range (2.0-8.9) n = 7	5.2 Range (2.0-14.8) n = 14
High Economic Growth	9.1 Range (1.6-14.6) n = 7	11.5 Range (4.1-66.8) n = 8	9.6 Range (1.6-66.8) n = 15
TOTAL	7.4 Range (1.6-14.8) n = 14	4.7 Range (2.0-66.8) n = 15	6.0 Range (1.6-66.8) n = 29

Income Instability Medians (Y_1) by Size (Population) and by Economic Growth (Y_{21})

	Small Countries	Large Countries	TOTAL
Low Economic Growth	4.1 Range (2.5-9.0) n = 8	8.7 Range (2.0-14.8) n = 6	5.2 Range (2.0-14.8) n = 14
High Economic Growth	4.4 Range (1.6-14.6) n = 7	13.0 Range (4.1-66.8) n = 8	9.6 Range (1.6-66.8) n = 15
TOTAL	4.3 Range (1.6-14.6) n = 15	8.9 Range (2.0-66.8) n = 14	6.0 Range (1.6-66.8) n = 29

of income instability observe a rising directional pattern down any column, and also (with one exception) diagonally. There is, in other words, a positive relationship between income instability and economic growth, and this positive relationship seems to hold regardless of size of country. The income instability medians, however, do not observe a consistent directional pattern across all rows, which means that there is no clear association between income instability and size. A positive directional pattern is, nevertheless, observed between income instability and population size, across any row and also diagonally, but such a pattern disappears in the GNP breakdown. These results, again, are in line with the two-variable analysis where, to repeat, a positive pattern was observed between income instability and population size. It is now further observed that such a positive pattern need not change with a change in the level of economic growth.

Multiple-correlation analysis, with size (X_1 and X_2) and economic growth (Y_{21}) as the two independent variables, provides a similar picture. Multiple regression equations, given below show a positive coefficient between income instability (Y_1) and economic growth (Y_{21}), and two coefficients with different signs between income instability and size. This latter result is evidence of the inconsistent pattern between income instability and size already observed in the cross-classi-

$$Y_1 = +0.0129X_1 + 1.0547Y_{21} + 4.4177$$
$$(.143) \qquad (.868) \qquad (4.82) \qquad R = .242$$
$$Y_1 = -0.0213X_2 + 1.0852Y_{21} + 4.7784$$
$$(.117) \qquad (.880) \qquad (4.73) \qquad R = .244$$

fication method of analysis. Moreover, the standard deviations of these coefficients are higher than the coefficients themselves and, therefore, the relationship between income instability and size is not acceptable. The standard deviations of the economic growth coefficients are relatively smaller but not small enough to accept the coefficients, and the positive relationship between income instability and economic growth remains statistically non-significant. In the light of this result, economic growth is not, perhaps, expected to have an influence on the relationship between income instability and size.

3. Income Instability, Dependence on Trade, and Size

The three-variable analysis here will try to interpret the impact of dependence on trade on the association between income instability and size. The three-by-three classifications of income instability medians

Table 9

Income Instability Medians (Y₁) by Size (GNP) and by Dependence on Trade (Y₁₆)

DEPENDENCE ON TRADE	G N P INCOME INSTABILITY MEDIANS			
	LOWEST THIRD	MIDDLE THIRD	HIGHEST THIRD	TOTAL
LOWEST THIRD	10.9 Range (2.4-14.6) n = 4	11.6 Range (3.9-66.8) n = 6	7.2 Range (3.5-20.0) n = 10	9.6 Range (2.4-66.8) n = 20
MIDDLE THIRD	4.4 Range (1.6-21.1) n = 7	11.3 Range (3.2-14.8) n = 8	7.3 Range (2.0-21.5) n = 5	8.5 Range (1.6-21.5) n = 20
HIGHEST THIRD	7.2 Range (3.6-9.6) n = 9	5.8 Range (2.5-53.4) n = 6	4.1 Range (3.5-4.7) n = 5	6.0 Range (2.5-53.4) n = 20
TOTAL	7.8 Range (3.7-9.6) n = 20	10.4 Range (2.5-66.8) n = 20	4.9 Range (2.0-21.5) n = 20	7.8 Range (1.6-66.8) n = 60

Income Instability Medians (Y₁) by Size (Population) and by Dependence on Trade (Y₁₆)

DEPENDENCE ON TRADE	POPULATION INCOME INSTABILITY MEDIANS			
	LOWEST THIRD	MIDDLE THIRD	HIGHEST THIRD	TOTAL
LOWEST THIRD	8.5 Range n = 1	10.3 Range (2.4-14.6) n = 5	10.0 Range (3.5-66.8) n = 14	9.6 Range (2.4-66.8) n = 20
MIDDLE THIRD	8.1 Range (1.6-21.1) n = 8	9.6 Range (3.2-14.8) n = 6	7.8 Range (2.0-21.5) n = 6	8.5 Range (1.6-21.5) n = 20
HIGHEST THIRD	5.5 Range (2.5-9.6) n = 11	8.3 Range (3.9-53.4) n = 9	 n = 0	6.0 Range (2.5-53.4) n = 20
TOTAL	5.8 Range (1.6-21.1) n = 20	9.0 Range (2.4-53.4) n = 20	8.7 Range (2.0-66.8) n = 20	7.8 Range (1.6-66.8) n = 60

(Y_1) by size (GNP and population) and by dependence on trade (Y_{16}), fail to indicate any one directional pattern between size and income instability, and also fail to indicate any steady pattern between income instability and dependence on trade. See Table 9. The median values of income instability do not observe a steady directional pattern across any row, down any column, and also diagonally. There is, however, a tendency, unsteady but nevertheless a tendency, for the income instability medians to decline down most of the columns. Countries at 'high' levels of dependence on trade show lower income instability medians than countries at 'low' levels of dependence on trade. This suggests a weak inverse association between dependence on trade and income instability. Since the medians do not, on the other hand, follow any directional pattern across any row, this suggests that no association exists between income instability and size.

Multiple-correlation analysis, with size (X_1 and X_2) and dependence on trade (Y_{16}) as the two independent variables, provides similar conclusions. The multiple regression equations show a negative coefficient between income instability (Y_1) and size, and a negative coefficient also between income instability and dependence on trade. The R-values of these equations are, however, fairly low, and the standard deviations of the size and dependence-on-trade coefficients are as high as the coefficients themselves. The inverse relationships, therefore, between income instability and size, and between income instability and dependence on trade are both not acceptable. The equations are given below:

$$Y_1 = -0.0284X_1 - 0.0514Y_{16} + 13.1388$$
$$\quad\quad (.023) \quad\quad (.049) \quad\quad (2.48) \quad\quad R = .198$$
$$Y_1 = -0.0110X_2 - 0.0506Y_{16} + 12.8719$$
$$\quad\quad (.026) \quad\quad (.053) \quad\quad (2.90) \quad\quad R = .126$$

Since the association between dependence on trade and income instability is weak, if not nonexistent, dependence on trade is not likely to have an impact on the association between income instability and size. Hence, regardless of the level of dependence on trade, the same relationship will prevail between income instability and size. It is, nevertheless, significant to remember that the cross-classifications and the multiple-correlations both suggest that a weak, yet, inverse association exists between income instability and dependence on trade. This result is contrary to a priori reasoning and implies that dependence on trade is not necessarily a source of extra income instability. Small countries, therefore, who generally depend more heavily on trade as an escape from their 'smallness', need not, by virtue of their heavy dependence on trade, experience greater income instability.

4. Income Instability, Commodity Export Concentration, and Size

It is also pertinent to inquire whether commodity export concentration has any influence on the association between income instability and size. The a priori case again suggests a positive relationship between commodity export concentration and income instability. The

Table 10

Income Instability Medians (Y_1) by Size (GNP) and by commodity-Export Concentration (Y_9)

COMMODITY-EXPORT CONCENTRATION	G N P INCOME INSTABILITY MEDIANS			
	LOWEST THIRD	MIDDLE THIRD	HIGHEST THIRD	TOTAL
LOWEST THIRD	*3.1* Range (2.4-3.7) n = 2	7.2 Range (3.2-14.8) n = 6	4.7 Range (2.0-12.7) n = 11	4.8 Range (2.0-14.8) n = 19
MIDDLE THIRD	11.8 Range (6.6-21.1) n = 6	10.4 Range (2.5-66.8) n = 7	8.8 Range (3.9-21.5) n = 6	9.1 Range (2.5-66.8) n = 19
HIGHEST THIRD	7.8 Range (1.6-13.4) n = 11	*13.0* Range (8.3-53.4) n = 5	4.2 Range (4.1-4.3) n = 2	8.5 Range (1.6-53.4) n = 19
TOTAL	8.4 Range (1.6-21.1) n = 20	11.3 Range (2.5-66.8) n = 18	4.7 Range (2.0-21.5) n = 19	8.3 Range (1.6-66.8) n = 57

Income Instability Medians (Y_1) by Size (Population) and by Commodity-Export Concentration (Y_9)

COMMODITY-EXPORT CONCENTRATION	POPULATION INCOME INSTABILITY MEDIANS			
	LOWEST THIRD	MIDDLE THIRD	HIGHEST THIRD	TOTAL
LOWEST THIRD	5.5 Range (3.7-12.4) n = 3	*4.4* Range (2.4-14.8) n = 6	5.4 Range (2.0-12.7) n = 10	4.8 Range (2.0-14.8) n = 19
MIDDLE THIRD	6.1 Range (2.5-21.1) n = 7	9.1 Range (3.9-14.6) n = 7	*20.0* Range (8.7-66.8) n = 5	9.1 Range (2.5-66.8) n = 19
HIGHEST THIRD	*4.4* Range (1.6-11.8) n = 9	10.5 Range (4.3-53.4) n = 6	10.8 Range (8.3-30.0) n = 4	8.5 Range (1.6-53.4) n = 19
TOTAL	5.5 Range (1.6-21.1) n = 19	8.9 Range (2.4-53.4) n = 19	8.7 Range (2.9-66.8) n = 19	8.3 Range (1.6-66.8) n = 57

lack of diversity in production and, hence, in exports can jeopardize the stability of national income. The three-by-three classifications of income instability medians (Y_1) by size (GNP and population) and by commodity export concentration (Y_9), fail to reveal any association between income instability and size, and also fail to reveal any association between income instability and commodity export concentration. The median values of income instability do not observe any directional pattern across any row, down any column and also diagonally. See Table 10 for these results. There is, therefore, hardly any indication here that income instability and size, or that income instability and commodity export concentration are in any apparent manner associated.

Multiple-correlation analysis provides a similar picture. With size $(X_1$ and $X_2)$ and commodity export concentration (Y_9) as the two independent variables, the two multiple regression equations yield R-values that are very low (.136 and .128). The regression equations also yield a negative coefficient between income instability (Y_1) and size, and also a negative coefficient between income instability and commodity export concentration (Y_9). The standard deviations of all these coefficients, however, are high and these relationships, therefore, are not statistically acceptable. The two equations are given below:

$$Y_1 = -0.0242X_1 - 0.0238Y_9 + 12.3138$$
$$(.024) \qquad (.104) \qquad (7.24) \qquad R = .136$$
$$Y_1 = -0.0243X_2 - 0.0297Y_9 + 12.9261$$
$$(.026) \qquad (.106) \qquad (7.50) \qquad R = .128$$

It is of interest to note that while the association between income instability and commodity export concentration is weak it is, nevertheless, negative, which suggests that commodity export concentration is not a likely cause of extra income instability. This is contrary to a priori reasoning since commodity concentration is a commonly accepted explanation of export instability, and is, as a result, a possible source of extra income instability. If these results are true, small countries who are likely to have relatively high commodity export concentration, need not experience extra income instability on account of their commodity export concentration.

5. *Income Instability, Geographic Export Concentration, and Size*

Geographic export concentration is also a commonly accepted explanation of export instability, and may, consequently, be a possible cause of extra income instability. It is, therefore, relevant to find out whether geographic export concentration has any impact on the association between income instability and size. The cross-classfications of income instability medians (Y_1) by size (GNP and population) and

Table 11

Income Instability Medians (Y_1) by Size (GNP) and by Country-Export Concentration (Y_{10})

COUNTRY-EXPORT CONCENTRATION	G N P INCOME INSTABILITY MEDIANS			
	LOWEST THIRD	MIDDLE THIRD	HIGHEST THIRD	TOTAL
LOWEST THIRD	5.4 *Range* (3.7-7.2) n = 2	8.9 *Range* (3.2-30.0) n = 7	4.2 *Range* (2.0-21.5) n = 11	6.4 *Range* (2.0-30.0) n = 20
MIDDLE THIRD	8.7 *Range* (2.4-21.1) n = 9	12.2 *Range* (2.5-14.8) n = 7	8.8 *Range* (5.7-11.0) n = 4	9.0 *Range* (2.4-21.1) n = 20
HIGHEST THIRD	7.8 *Range* (1.6-11.8) n = 8	9.1 *Range* (3.2-66.8) n = 6	4.7 *Range* (4.1-7.3) n = 5	5.0 *Range* (1.6-66.8) n = 19
TOTAL	8.3 *Range* (1.6-21.1) n = 19	10.4 *Range* (2.5-66.8) n = 20	4.9 *Range* (2.0-21.5) n = 20	8.3 *Range* (1.6-66.8) n = 59

Income Instability Medians (Y_1) by Size (Population) and by Country-Export Concentration (Y_{10})

COUNTRY-EXPORT CONCENTRATION	POPULATION INCOME INSTABILITY MEDIANS			
	LOWEST THIRD	MIDDLE THIRD	HIGHEST TIRD	TOTAL
LOWEST THIRD	5.5 *Range* (3.5-12.4) n = 5	4.1 *Range* (3.2-10.3) n = 5	10.2 *Range* (2.0-30.0) n = 10	6.4 *Range* (2.0-30.0) n = 20
MIDDLE THIRD	8.5 *Range* (2.5-21.1) n = 5	9.7 *Range* (2.4-14.8) n = 10	8.7 *Range* (5.7-13.0) n = 5	9.0 *Range* (2.4-21.1) n = 20
HIGHEST THIRD	4.1 *Range* (1.6-11.8) n = 9	9.1 *Range* (4.3-53.4) n = 20	5.0 *Range* (3.9-66.8) n = 5	5.0 *Range* (1.6-66.8) n = 19
TOTAL	5.5 *Range* (1.6-21.1) n = 19	9.0 *Range* (2.4-53.4) n = 20	8.7 *Range* (2.0-66.8) n = 20	8.3 *Range* (1.6-66.8) n = 59

by geographic export concentration (Y_{10}), again fail to indicate any association between income instability and size, and also fail to indicate any association between income instability and geographic export concentration. The median values of income instability still fail to follow any directional pattern across any row, down any column, and also diagonally. The same irregular pattern in the income instability medians is observed, regardless of geographic export concentration and regardless of size. See Table 11 for these results. The cross-classification method of analysis, therefore, does not indicate that it is likely for geographic export concentration to affect the association between income instability and size.

Multiple-correlation analysis provides further support for this conclusion. The multiple regression equations, with size (X_1 and X_2) and geographic export concentration (Y_{10}) as the two independent variables, yield very low R-values. The size coefficients are negative, but the standard deviations of these coefficients are as large as the coefficients themselves and, hence, the association between income instability and size is not acceptable. The geographic export concentration coefficients are positive, unlike those of commodity export concentration. Again, however, the standard deviations of these coefficients are very high, and the association, therefore, between income instability and geographic export concentration is not significant. The equations are given below. This latter result suggests that geographic export concentration is not likely to influence the association between income

$$Y_1 = -0.0208X_1 + 0.0732Y_{10} + 7.3235$$
$$(.023) \qquad (.088) \qquad (3.84) \qquad R = .169$$
$$Y_1 = -0.0187X_2 + 0.0693Y_{10} + 7.6208$$
$$(.024) \qquad (.089) \qquad (3.98) \qquad R = .157$$

instability and size. This proposition is borne out by both the cross-classification method of analysis and by multiple-correlation analysis. The contention, therefore, that geographic export concentration is a likely source of extra income instability does not find support in this analysis. And small countries who generally have a comparatively strong geographic export concentration (see a forthcoming chapter), are not expected to experience extra income instability due to their geographic export concentration.

6. *Conclusions.*

The foregoing multi-variant analysis (the cross-classifications and multiple-correlations) of the association between size and income instability suggests the following results: (a) There is no significant association between size and income instability. The cross-classifications do not reveal any steady pattern, and formal correlation analysis does not yield significant correlation coefficients between size and income instability. (b) There is no evidence that the level of economic development is likely to influence the association between size and income instability. The cross-classifications do not reveal a steady pattern (although a declining directional pattern was observed) between income instability and economic development, and correlation analysis does not yield statistically acceptable coefficients between income instability and economic development. (c) There is no evidence, also, that the rate of economic growth is likely to influence the association between size and income instability. The cross-classifications indicate a positive directional pattern between income instability and economic growth, but multiple-correlation analysis does not yield acceptable coefficients between income instability and economic development. The coefficients are, however, positive and so is the pattern in the cross-classifications. Economic growth, therefore, implies more income instability than does, perhaps, economic development. (d) There is no support for the contention that dependence-on-trade is a likely source of extra income instability. The cross-classifications reveal a negative directional pattern between income instability and dependence on trade, and correlation analysis does not yield acceptable (they are nevertheless negative) coefficients between income instability and dependence on trade. (e) There is, also, no support for the view that commodity export concentration is a likely source of extra income instability. The cross-classifications fail to indicate any pattern between income instability and commodity export concentration, and the multiple correlations do not yield acceptable (they are nevertheless negative) coefficients between income instability and commodity export concentration. (f) Finally, there is no support for the view that geographic export concentration is a likely source of extra income instability. Again cross-classifications fail to reveal a steady dirctional pattern between income instability and gepgraphic export concentration, and correlation analysis does not yield acceptable coefficients between income instability and geographic export concentration.

The last three of the above propositions are of some relevance to the economies of small nations. Dependence-on-trade, commodity-export concentration, and geographic export concentration are generally more prevalent in the case of small countries than they are in the large countries. Our results now indicate that small countries, as a consequence of these features, need not necessarily experience extra income instability. But perhaps they are more likely to experience extra export instability. Let us see what do the facts show.

B. *Export Instability and Size*

The treatment of export instability and size will be similar to that of income instability, since the factors considered in this investigation as capable of influencing export instability are more or less the same as those that are likely to influence income instability. The purpose of this analysis, therefore, is not only to describe the nature of the association between size and export instability, but, more importantly, to investigate the extent to which this association is influenced by such factors as economic development and growth, and commodity and geographic concentration of exports. The relationship between export instability and size and each of these factors will be separately analyzed.

1. *Export Instability, Development, and Size*

It was previously inquired whether economic development has an effect on the association between income instability and size. We do likewise now with the effect of economic development on the association between export instability and size. Export instability is interpreted as a function of size and economic development. The cross-classifications of export instability medians (Y_2) by size (GNP and population) and by economic development (Y_{23}), reveal a steady positive directional pattern between export instability and economic development. The median values of export instability observe a positive pattern across any row and also diagonally (in northeasterly and southeasterly directions). Irrespective of the level of development, 'small' countries repeatedly show lower export instability medians than 'large' countries. The median values of export instability, however, do not observe any steady pattern down all columns. There is no apparent relationship, in other words, between export instability and economic development. See Table 12. These results can be interpreted to mean that there is a positive relationship between export instability and size, and that economic development does not seem to have an observable influence on this relationship.

Multiple-correlation analysis provides additional support for these

Table 12

Export Instability Medians (Y_2) by Size (GNP) and by Degree of Development (Y_{23})

	Small Countries	Large Countries	TOTAL
Underdeveloped Countries	15.0 Range (9.9-27.5) n = 12	18.3 Range (13.8-31.0) n = 3	15.2 Range (9.9-31.0) n = 14
Developed Countries	9.2 Range (6.3-14.7) n = 3	20.2 Range (7.5-41.3) n = 12	18.5 Range (6.3-41.3) n = 15
TOTAL	14.7 Range (6.3-25.7) n = 15	19.4 Range (7.5-41.3) n = 15	16.2 Range (6.3-41.3) n = 30

Export Instability Medians (Y_2) by Size (Population) and by Degree of Development (Y_{23})

	Small Countries	Large Countries	TOTAL
Underdeveloped Countries	14.8 Range (9.9-25.2) n = 8	17.3 Range (10.0-31.0) n = 8	15.7 Range (9.9-31.0) n = 16
Developed Countries	14.7 Range (6.3-21.4) n = 7	20.9 Range (7.5-41.3) n = 7	18.1 Range (6.3-41.3) n = 13
TOTAL	14.7 Range (6.3-25.2) n = 15	18.8 Range (7.5-41.3) n = 15	16.2 Range (6.3-41.3) n = 30

conclusions. Multiple regression equations, with export instability (Y_2) as the dependent variable, and with size (X_1 and X_2) and economic development (Y_{23}) as the two independent variables, yield positive coefficients between export instability and size, and negative coefficients between export instability and economic development. The standard deviations of the latter coefficients are very high, and hence, this relationship between export instability and economic development is not acceptable. The standard deviations of the size coefficients, however, are relatively lower and the positive relationship between export instability and size, therefore, is relatively more acceptable. See the two equations below. It should be noted that the two R-values yielded here, are not any higher than the simple-correlation coefficients be-

$$Y_2 = 0.1145X_1 - 0.0022Y_{23} + 16.8558$$
$$\quad\quad (.097) \quad\quad (.004) \quad\quad\quad (1.77) \quad\quad R = .226$$
$$Y_2 = 0.1618X_2 - 0.0005Y_{23} + 14.5809$$
$$\quad\quad (.062) \quad\quad (.003) \quad\quad\quad (1.86) \quad\quad R = .455$$

tween export instability and size. Pairing size with economic development did not yield higher correlation coefficients. Apparently, economic development does not have any influence on the association between export instability and size.

2. Export Instability, Economic Growth, and Size

One would similarly want to inquire whether a country's rate of economic growth has any effect on the association between export instability and size. What kind of a relationship exists between export instability and economic growth? Is it strong enough to influence the relationship between export instability and size? Export instability medians (Y_2) classified by size (GNP and population) and by economic growth (Y_{21}), reveal the same positive directional pattern between export instability and size, and also reveal an unsteady positive pattern between export instability and economic growth. The median values of export instability observe a steady positive trend across any row, and also diagonally. The 'small' countries consistently show lower export instability medians than 'large' countries, regardless of the level of economic growth. The export instability medians also observe a positive pattern across any row, but not diagonally. The positive association between export instability and economic growth is not therefore as steady as the positive association between export instability and size. See Table 13. The cross-classification analysis suggests that economic growth is not likely to influence the positive association between export instability and size.

What does multiple-correlation analysis show? Multiple regression equations, with export instability (Y_2) as the dependent variable, and with size (X_1 and X_2) and economic growth (Y_{21}) as the two independent variables, yield positive coefficients between export instability and size, and also positive coefficients between export instability and economic growth. The two R-values of these equations are very low, and the standard deviations of the size and of the economic growth coefficients are all higher than the coefficients themselves. Hence, the positive relationship between export instability and size, and the same

Table 13

Export Instability Medians (Y_2) by Size (GNP) and by Economic Growth (Y_{21})

	Small Countries	Large Countries	TOTAL
Low Economic Growth	13.8 Range (6.3-25.7) n = 8	18.5 Range (10.0-41.3) n = 7	14.7 Range (6.3-41.3) n = 15
High Economic Growth	16.1 Range (9.9-25.2) n = 7	20.6 Range (7.5-31.0) n = 8	18.2 Range (7.5-31.0) n = 15
TOTAL	14.7 Range (6.3-25.7) n = 15	19.4 Range (7.5-41.3) n = 15	16.2 Range (6.3-41.3) n = 30

Export Instability Medians (Y_2) by Size (Population) and by Economic Growth (Y_{21})

	Small Countries	Large Countries	TOTAL
Low Economic Growth	13.4 Range (6.3-18.5) n = 8	21.5 Range (10.0-41.3) n = 7	14.7 Range (6.3-41.3) n = 14
High Economic Growth	16.1 Range (9.9-15.2) n = 7	18.8 Range (7.5-31.0) n = 8	18.2 Range (7.5-31.0) n = 15
TOTAL	14.7 Range (6.3-25.2) n = 15	18.8 Range (7.5-41.3) n = 15	16.2 Range (6.3-41.3) n = 30

relationship between export instability and economic growth are both not statistically acceptable. See the two equations below.

$$Y_2 = 0.0857X_1 + 0.0246Y_{21} + 16.2092$$
$$\quad\ (.087) \qquad (.528) \qquad (2.94) \qquad R = .197$$
$$Y_2 = 0.0269X_2 + 0.0083Y_{21} + 16.8492$$
$$\quad\ (.072) \qquad (.545) \qquad (2.93) \qquad R = .077$$

Neither size nor economic growth, therefore, are significant sources of export instability. Cross-classification analysis and multiple-correlation analysis both yield a positive association between export instability and size, and also a positive association between export instability and economic growth. These associations are not statistically strong, but they are, perhaps, sufficient to indicate that 'small' countries need not experience extra export instability, and that economic growth is not likely to change this relationship.

3. *Export Instability, Commodity Export Concentration, and Size*

Commodity export concentration is a generally accepted explanation of export instability, and the a priori case for a positive association between export instability and commodity export concentration is quite convincing. It is, therefore, pertinent to find out whether commodity export concentration has any influence on the association between export instability and size, and to determine the extent to which commodity export concentration is a source of extra export instability. It is for this purpose that export instability is interpreted as a function of size and commodity export concentration. Export instability medians (Y_2) classified by size (GNP and population) and by commodity export concentration (Y_9), fail to indicate a steady pattern between instability and size, and also fail to indicate a steady pattern between export instability and commidity export concentration. The median values of export instability do not observe any directional tendency across any row, down any column, and also diagonally. *Table 14* shows these results. The cross-classification analysis, therefore, does not provide any support for the view that 'small' countries are more likely to experience greater export instability; nor for the view that commodity export concentration is an important source of extra export instability.

Multiple-correlation analysis provides the same evidence. Multiple regression equations, with export instability (Y_2) as the dependent variable, and with size $(X_1$ and $X_2)$ and commodity export concentration (Y_9) as the two independent variables, yield very low R-values. They also yield positive coefficients between export instability and size, and positive coefficients between export instability and commodity export concentration. The standard deviations of the size coefficients are very high; hence, the relationship between export instability and size is not acceptable. The coefficient is, nevertheless, positive and one can at least suggest that export instability does not show a tendency to increase with a decrease in size. The standard deviation of one of the commodity export concentration coefficients is small enough to accept the positive association between export instability and commodity export concentration. But the R-value of the whole equation is very low (.154), and this positive association cannot be very significant. See the two equations below.

Table 14

Export Instability Medians (Y_2) by Size (GNP) and by Commodity-Export Concentration (Y_9)

COMMODITY-EXPORT CONCENTRATION	GNP EXPORT INSTABILITY MEDIANS			
	LOWEST THIRD	MIDDLE THIRD	HIGHEST THIRD	TOTAL
LOWEST THIRD	18.6 *Range* (15.7-25.9) n = 4	21.1 *Range* (10.0-57.2) n = 8	16.8 *Range* (7.5-36.2) n = 13	16.8 *Range* (7.5-57.2) n = 25
MIDDLE THIRD	18.2 *Range* (12.5-33.0) n = 7	22.6 *Range* (6.3-73.8) n = 8	19.4 *Range* (6.2-41.3) n = 10	19.4 *Range* (6.2-73.8) n = 25
HIGHEST THIRD	19.5 *Range* (9.9-27.2) n = 14	20.2 *Range* (13.0-36.6) n = 9	*15.0* *Range* (13.8-16.1) n = 2	20.1 *Range* (9.9-36.6) n = 25
TOTAL	18.2 *Range* (9.9-33.0) n = 25	20.2 *Range* (6.3-73.8) n = 25	18.3 *Range* (6.2-41.3) n = 25	18.5 *Range* (6.2-73.8) n = 75

Export Instability Medians (Y_2) by Size (Population) and by Commodity-Export Concentration (Y_9)

COMMODITY-EXPORT CONCENTRATION	POPULATION EXPORT INSTABILITY MEDIANS			
	LOWEST THIRD	MIDDLE THIRD	HIGHEST THIRD	TOTAL
LOWEST THIRD	21.3 *Range* (12.0-30.4) n = 4	18.6 *Range* (6.2-41.9) n = 10	17.2 *Range* (7.5-46.1) n = 12	17.2 *Range* (6.2-46.1) n = 26
MIDDLE THIRD	*14.7* *Range* (6.3-33.0) n = 9	18.5 *Range* (10.7-37.8) n = 9	*34.8* *Range* (18.3-73.8) n = 8	19.0 *Range* (6.3-73.8) n = 26
HIGHEST THIRD	22.1 *Range* (9.9-35.7) n = 13	16.3 *Range* (13.4-40.4) n = 7	22.4 *Range* (14.7-36.6) n = 6	20.4 *Range* (9.9-40.4) n = 26
TOTAL	16.2 *Range* (6.3-35.7) n = 26	18.3 *Range* (6.2-41.9) n = 26	20.6 *Range* (7.5-73.8) n = 26	19.4 *Range* (6.2-73.8) n = 78

$$Y_2 = 0.0019X_1 + 0.0021Y_9 + 19.0402$$
$$(.019) \quad\quad (.082) \quad\quad (5.72) \quad\quad R = .014$$
$$Y_2 = 0.0228X_2 + 0.2749Y_9 + 16.6932$$
$$(.020) \quad\quad (.082) \quad\quad (5.85) \quad\quad R = .154$$

Neither size nor commodity export concentration are, therefore, important sources of export instability. Cross-classification analysis did not indicate any steady pattern between export instability and size, nor between export instability and commodity export concentration; and the multiple-correlation analysis did not also yield strong associations, but they were sufficient to suggest that 'smallness' is not a source of extra export instability, and neither is commodity export concentration. This latter result is contrary to a priori thinking, since it is generally contended that the more diversified a country's exports are, the more stable are its export proceeds likely to be. The practical implications of this result are quite significant. This means that attempts designed to increase the diversity of exports are not likely to have any appreciable effect on reducing export instability.[1]

The implications of such a conclusion on 'small' nations is also worth noting. Since commodity export concentration is not an important source of extra export instability, 'small' countries, whose exports by virtue of their smallness are genrally more concentrated than those of 'large' countries, need not necessarily experience greater export instability.

4. *Export Instability, Geographic Export Concentration, and Size*

Geographic export concentration is also commonly referred to as an explanation of export instability, and the a priori case for a positive association between export instability and geographic export concentration is similarly convincing. Hence, it is appropriate to find out whether geographic export concentration has any impact on the association between export instability and size, and to determine the extent to which geographic export concentration is a source of extra export instability. The relevance of such questions to the economies of 'small' nations is apparent. Since geographic export concentration is relatively more conspicuous in the case of small countries, it becomes important to know whether this feature is necessarily a cause of extra

---

[1] It is interesting to mention in this regard that Massell has also found out that "The relationship between instability of export earnings and concentration of exports is a tenuous one indeed." See B. F. Massell, "Export Concentration and Fluctuations in Export Earnings: A Cross-Section Analysis", *American Economic Review*, March 1964, p. 61. J. D. Coppock reports, too, a very low correlation coefficient*(+.04) between commodity export concentration and export instability. See J. D. Coppock, *op. cit.*, p. 104. More recently also, Macbean has found out that export concentration misses the mark as an explanation of extra instability of exports. See A. I. Macbean, *Export Instability and Economic Development*, London, George Allen & Unwin, 1966.

export instability. For this reason, export instability is here analyzed as a function of size and of geographic export concentration.

Export instability medians (Y_2) classified by size (GNP and population) and by geographic export concentration (Y_{10}), do not indicate any steady association between export instability and size, nor between export instability and geographic export concentration. The median values of export instability fail to observe any directional pattern across any row, down any column, and also diagonally. There is a tendency for export instability to decrease with an increase in geographic export concentration, but this is not a steady pattern. Table 15 shows these results. The cross-classifications again indicate that the relationship between export instability and size is very tenuous, and that geographic export concentration, like commodity concentration, is not a likely source of export instability. In fact, there is a tendency, unsteady but nevertheless a tendency, for export instability to decrease with an increase in geographic export concentration.

Formal correlation analysis provides the same conclusions. Multiple regression equations, with export instability (Y_2) as the dependent variable, and with size (X_1 and X_2) and geographic export concentration (Y_{10}) as the two independent variables, yield very low R-values. They also yield negative coefficients between export instability and geographic export concentration, which supports the inverse unsteady pattern observed in the cross-classification between export instability and geographic concentration. They yield, as well, two different coefficients between export instability and size, which is further proof of the fact that the relationship between export instability and size is nonexistent. It should also be noted that the standard deviations of all coefficients are very high. The relationships, therefore, between export instability and size, and between export instability and geographic export concentration cannot be significant. The two equations are given below.

$$Y_2 = -0.0010X_1 - 0.0907Y_{19} + 23.3374$$
$$ (.018) \qquad (.070) \qquad (3.03) \qquad R = .171$$
$$Y_2 = 0.0165X_2 - 0.0812Y_{19} + 22.4606$$
$$ (.019) \qquad (.070) \qquad (3.12) \qquad R = .205$$

Cross-classification analysis and multiple-correlation analysis both demonstrate that neither 'smallness' nor geographic export concentration are likely causes of extra export instability. This latter result is contrary to a priori reasoning and is of significance to small nations.

Table 15

Export Instability Medians (Y_2) by Size (GNP) and by Country-Export Concentration (Y_{10})

COUNTRY-EXPORT CONCENTRATION	GNP EXPORT INSTABILITY MEDIANS			
	LOWEST THIRD	MIDDLE THIRD	HIGHEST THIRD	TOTAL
LOWEST THIRD	22.1 *Range* (15.7-25.9) n = 3	25.4 *Range* (12.0-73.8) n = 10	20.9 *Range* (6.2-41.3) n = 13	21.2 *Range* (6.2-73.8) n = 26
MIDDLE THIRD	20.1 *Range* (13.0-31.9) n = 12	20.2 *Range* (10.0-57.2) n = 7	16.2 *Range* (10.0-28.1) n = 7	19.6 *Range* (10.0-57.2) n = 26
HIGHEST THIRD	15.2 *Range* (9.9-33.0) n = 12	23.2 *Range* (6.3-28.4) n = 8	13.8 *Range* (7.5-18.3) n = 5	16.1 *Range* (6.3-38.4) n = 25
TOTAL	16.9 *Range* (9.9-33.0) n = 27	20.6 *Range* (6.3-73.8) n = 25	18.3 *Range* (6.2-41.3) n = 25	19.4 *Range* (6.2-73.8) n = 77

Export Instability Medians (Y_2) by Size (Population) and by Country-Export Concentration (Y_{10})

COUNTRY-EXPORT CONCENTRATION	POPULATION EXPORT INSTABILITY MEDIANS			
	LOWEST THIRD	MIDDLE THIRD	HIGHEST THIRD	TOTAL
LOWEST THIRD	19.2 *Range* (12.0-30.4) n = 6	10.3 *Range* (6.2-41.9) n = 9	26.2 *Range* (10.9-73.8) n = 12	21.4 *Range* (6.2-73.8) n = 27
MIDDLE THIRD	19.7 *Range* (10.0-31.9) n = 7	16.2 *Range* (10.0-27.2) n = 12	26.2 *Range* (14.7-57.2) n = 8	19.4 *Range* (10.0-57.2) n = 27
HIGHEST THIRD	15.4 *Range* (6.3-35.7) n = 14	21.2 *Range* (12.5-37.8) n = 6	17.6 *Range* (7.5-38.4) n = 6	16.7 *Range* (6.3-38.4) n = 26
TOTAL	16.4 *Range* (6.3-33.0) n = 27	18.2 *Range* (6.2-41.9) n = 27	21.2 *Range* (7.5-73.8) n = 26	19.0 *Range* (6.2-73.8) n = 80

If, as is often assumed, geographic export concentration is relatively more conspicuous in small countries, this need not mean that they are, as a result, expected to experience extra export instability.

5. *Conclusions.*

The multi-variant analysis of the association between export instability and size suggests the following conclusions: (a) There is no significant association between export instability and size. The cross-classifications did not indicate a steady pattern, and multiple correlations did not yield significant correlation coefficients between export instability and size. It should be noted, however, that the correlation coefficients were mostly positive, and that, in those cases where a steady pattern was observed in the cross-classifications, it was a positive pattern. While there is no evidence of a strong association between export instability and size, there is a suggestion, therefore, that export instability is not likely to increase with a decrease in size. (b) There is no association between export instability and economic development. The cross-classifications failed to reveal any pattern, and multiple-correlations did not yield significant coefficients between export instability and economic development. There is, therefore, no evidence that the level of economic development is expected to influence the association between export instability and size. (c) There is, also, no evidence that the rate of economic growth is likely to influence the association between export instability and size. The cross-classifications indicated an unsteady pattern between export instability and economic growth, and multiple-correlations did not yield significant coefficients. The coefficients are, however, positive and so is the unsteady pattern in the crosss-classifications. This again suggests, as the case was with income instability, that economic growth implies, perhaps, more export instability than does the level of economic development. (d) There is no strong support for the a priori case that commodity export concentration is an important source of export instability. The cross-classifications fail to indicate any steady pattern between export instability and commodity export concentration, and multiple-correlations yield a positive but non-significant coefficient between export instability and commodity export concentration. (e) Finally, there is also no support for the a priori case that geographic export concentration is an important source of extra export instability. The cross-classifications do not reveal any steady pattern between instability medians and geographic export concentration medians, and the multiple-correlations yield a non-significant, yet negative, correlation coefficient between export instability and geographic export concentration.

The result that commodity and geographic export concentration are not important sources of extra export instability, has significant implications on the economies of small nations. If export concentration is relatively more predominant among small nations, then these nations need not be very apologetic about this fact since it is not a cause of export instability. Nor should they expect policies aimed at increasing the diversity of their exports, in the commodity and geographic sense, to be very effective in reducing the instability of their export proceeds.

C. *Import Instability and Size*

The last instability treated here is import instability, and the purpose of this treatment is again twofold: to describe the nature of the association between import instability and size, and to investigate whether this association is influenced by such factors as the level of economic development, economic growth, and dependence on trade. Since data on import concentration is not available, the impact of import concentration on the association between import instability and size will not be analyzed. The relationship between import instability and size and each of these factors (economic development, economic growth, and dependence on trade) will be separately treated.

1. *Import Instability, Economic Development, and Size*

The previous section on export instability inquired whether economic development has an influence on the association between export instability and size. It is pertinent to find out whether economic development has any influence on the association between import instability and size. For this purpose, import instability is now treated as a function of size and economic development. The cross-classifications of import instability medians (Y_4) by size (GNP and population) and by economic development (Y_{23}), do not indicate any steady pattern between import instability and size, nor between import instability and economic development. The median values of import instability fail to reveal any pattern across any row, down any column, and also diagonally. Apparently, there is no association between import instability and size, and also no association between import instability and economic devlopment. See Table 16 for these results. Two interesting patterns are, however, revealed by these classifications. There is a tendency for import instability of 'small' countries to increase with an increase in development, whereas the tendency of import instability of 'large' countries is to decrease with an increase in development. Also observed is the tendency of import instability of the underdeveloped countries to increase with size, whereas the tendency of import instability of the developed countries is to decrease with an

Table 16

Import Instability Medians (Y$_4$) by Size (GNP) and by Degree of Development (Y$_{23}$)

	Small Countries	Large Countries	TOTAL
Underdeveloped Countries	18.3 Range (12.6-41.4) n = 12	*30.5* Range (27.5-36.1) n = 3	22.4 Range (12.5-41.4) n = 15
Developed Countries	21.6 Range (11.2-26.3) n = 3	*17.7* Range (10.7-39.3) n = 12	19.3 Range (10.7-39.3) n = 15
TOTAL	19.4 Range (11.2-41.4) n = 15	20.8 Range (10.7-39.3) n = 15	20.1 Range (10.7-41.4) n = 30

Import Instability Medians (Y$_4$) by Size (Population) and by Degree of Development (Y$_{23}$)

	Small Countries	Large Countries	TOTAL
Underdeveloped Countries	14.0 Range (12.6-36.1) n = 8	27.6 Range (14.4-41.4) n = 8	20.9 Range (12.6-41.4) n = 16
Developed Countries	21.6 Range (10.7-39.3) n = 7	19.3 Range (12.9-36.8) n = 7	20.0 Range (10.7-39.3) n = 14
TOTAL	15.0 Range (10.7-39.3) n = 15	26.5 Range (12.9-41.4) n = 15	20.1 Range (10.7-41.4) n = 30

increase in size. Perhaps as a result of these two tendencies, the large-underdeveloped countries show the highest import instability medians.

Multiple-correlation analysis also shows that there is no strong association between import instability and size, nor between import instability and economic development. Multiple regression equations, with import instability (Y$_4$) as the dependent variable, and with size (X$_1$ and X$_2$) and economic development (Y$_{23}$) as the two independent variables, yield low R-values. They also yield negative coefficients between import instability and economic development, and two different coefficients between import instability and size. The standard deviations of all these coefficients are higher than the coefficients themselves, hence, the association between import instability and size, and between import instability and economic development are both not acceptable. See the two equations below.

$$Y_4 = -0.0358X_1 - 0.0030Y_{23} + 23.9370$$
$$ (.122) \qquad (.005) \qquad (2.23) \qquad R = .182$$
$$Y_4 = 0.0326X_2 - 0.0039Y_{23} + 23.4077$$
$$ (.086) \qquad (.004) \qquad (2.57) \qquad R = .188$$

Therefore, neither size nor economic development are, apparently, important sources of import instability. Cross-classification analysis did not reveal any steady pattern between import instability and size, nor between import instability and economic development. Multiple-correlation analysis also failed to yield any significant results. There is no indication that size is a cause of extra import instability, and it does not seem likely for economic development to change this situation.

2. *Import Instability, Economic Growth, and Size*

It is perhaps equally relevant to inquire whether economic growth has any impact on the relationship between import instability and size. It has been just suggested that economic development is not expected to influence the relationship between import instability and size. Can the same be said about economic growth? For this reason, import instability is now interpreted as a function of size and economic growth. Import instability medians (Y_4) classified by size (GNP and population) and by economic growth (Y_{21}), fail to indicate a steady directional pattern between import instability and size, and also between import instability and economic growth. The median values of import instability do not observe any steady trend across all rows, down all columns, and also diagonally. Table 17 summarizes these results. Apparently, there is no association between import instability and size, and also no association between import instability and economic growth. The cross-classification analysis, therefore, does not indicate that economic growth is likely to influence the association between import instability and size.

Multiple-correlation analysis provides similar conclusions. It is also indicated here that there is no strong association between import instability and size, nor between import instability and economic growth. Multiple regression equations, with import instability (Y_4) as the dependent variable, and with size (X_1 and X_2) and economic growth (Y_{21}) as the two independent variables, yield very low multiple-corre-

Table 17

*Import Instability Medians (Y$_4$) by Size (GNP) and by Economic
Growth (Y$_{21}$)*

	Small Countries	Large Countries	TOTAL
Low Economic Growth	23.9 Range (11.2-41.2) n = 8	16.1 Range (10.7-36.8) n = 7	21.6 Range (10.7-41.4) n = 15
High Economic Growth	17.2 Range (12.6-26.4) n = 7	23.3 Range (12.9-39.3) n = 8	19.4 Range (12.6-39.3) n = 15
TOTAL	19.4 Range (11.2-41.4) n = 15	20.8 Range (10.7-39.3) n = 15	20.1 Range (10.7-41.4) n = 30

*Import Instability Medians (Y$_4$) by Size (Population) and by Economic
Growth (Y$_{21}$)*

	Small Countries	Large Countries	TOTAL
Low Economic Growth	14.4 Range (10.7-36.1) n = 8	35.0 Range (14.4-41.4) n = 7	21.6 Range (10.7-41.4) n = 15
High Economic Growth	17.2 Range (12.6-39.3) n = 7	21.6 Range (12.9-30.5) n = 8	19.4 Range (12.6-39.3) n = 15
TOTAL	15.0 Range (10.7-39.3) n = 15	26.4 Range (12.9-41.4) n = 15	20.1 Range (10.7-41.4) n = 30

lation coefficients. The R-values here are even lower than the R-values yielded by the previous section. This implies that the association between import instability and economic growth is weaker than the association between import instability and economic development. The correlation analysis also yields negative coefficients between import instability and size, and between import instability and economic growth. But the standard deviations of all these coefficients are higher than the coefficients themselves. Therefore, the associations between import instability and size, and between import instability and economic growth cannot be significant. The two regression equations are given below.

$$Y_4 = -0.0643X_1 - 0.1831Y_{21} + 22.3789$$
$$\quad\;\;(.096) \qquad (.583) \qquad\;\; (3.24) \qquad R = .151$$
$$Y_4 = -0.0558X_2 - 0.1245Y_{21} + 22.2701$$
$$\quad\;\;(.079) \qquad (.590) \qquad\;\; (3.17) \qquad R = .159$$

Again, multi-variant analysis seems to suggest that neither size nor economic growth are important sources of import instability. Cross-classifications did not reveal any steady directional pattern between import instability and size, nor between import instability and economic growth. Similarly, multiple correlations failed to yield acceptable relationships between import instability and size, and between import instability and economic growth. There is, therefore, no indication that 'smallness' is a likely cause of extra import instability, and no evidence that it is likely for economic growth to change this result.

3. *Import Instability, Dependence on Trade, and Size*

Lastly, it is investigated whether a country's dependence on foreign trade has any influence on the relationship between import instability and size. 'Smallness' generally implies, as suggested by a forthcoming chapter, a relatively high dependence on trade. It is, therefore, relevant to find out whether this dependence on trade is itself a cause of extra import instability. For this purpose, import instability will be interpreted here as a function of size and degree of dependence on foreign trade. Import instability medians (Y_4) classified by size (GNP and population) and by dependence on trade (Y_{16}), fail to indicate any directional pattern between import instability and size, and also between import instability and dependence on trade. The median values of import instability do not follow any steady pattern across any row, down any column, and also diagonally. Table 18 shows these results. It is obvious that there is no association between import instability and size, nor between import instability and degree of dependence on trade. The cross-classifications, therefore, do not indicate that dependence on trade is necessarily a source of extra import instability, or that it is likely for the association between import instability and size to change due to dependence on trade.

Multiple-correlation analysis provides similar results. It is also apparent that there is no strong association between import instability and size, nor between import instability and dependence on trade. Multiple regression equations, with import instability (Y_4) as the dependent variable, and with size (X_1 and X_2) and dependence on trade

Table 18

Import Instability Medians (Y₄) by Size (GNP) and by Dependence on Trade (Y₁₆)

DEPENDENCE ON TRADE	GNP IMPORT INSTABILITY MEDIANS			
	LOWEST THIRD	MIDDLE THIRD	HIGHEST THIRD	TOTAL
LOWEST THIRD	19.8 Range (12.9-31.4) n = 8	26.7 Range (15.5-38.4) n = 8	27.5 Range (11.9-42.3) n = 11	24.3 Range (11.9-42.3) n = 27
MIDDLE THIRD	19.4 Range (14.3-41.4) n = 9	17.7 Range (9.6-44.2) n = 10	15.4 Range (12.9-35.0) n = 8	17.0 Range (9.6-44.2) n = 27
HIGHEST THIRD	17.4 Range (12.6-50.7) n = 10	21.6 Range (11.2-36.1) n = 9	20.4 Range (10.7-39.3) n = 7	20.5 Range (10.7-50.7) n = 26
TOTAL	19.1 Range (12.6-50.7) n = 27	24.3 Range (9.6-44.2) n = 27	19.8 Range (10.7-42.3) n = 26	20.4 Range (9.6-50.7) n = 80

Import Instability Medians (Y₄) by Size (Population) and by Dependence on Trade (Y₁₆)

DEPENDENCE ON TRADE	POPULATION IMPORT INSTABILITY MEDIANS			
	LOWEST THIRD	MIDDLE THIRD	HIGHEST THIRD	TOTAL
LOWEST THIRD	20.2 Range (16.9-31.4) n = 4	22.4 Range (12.9-36.1) n = 7	27.5 Range (11.9-42.3) n = 16	24.3 Range (11.9-42.3) n = 27
MIDDLE THIRD	23.7 Range (9.6-44.2) n = 10	16.4 Range (12.9-35.0) n = 7	16.3 Range (12.3-41.4) n = 10	17.0 Range (9.6-44.2) n = 27
HIGHEST THIRD	18.7 Range (10.7-50.7) n = 13	20.8 Range (13.7-39.3) n = 13	Range n = 0	20.5 Range (10.7-50.7) n = 26
TOTAL	19.4 Range (9.6-50.7) n = 27	20.4 Range (12.9-39.3) n = 27	22.0 Range (11.9-42.3) n = 26	20.7 Range (9.6-50.7) n = 80

(Y_{16}) as the two independent variables, still yield low multiple-correlation coefficients. They yield also negative coefficients between import instability and size, and negative coefficients between import instability and dependence on trade. The standard deviations of all these coefficients are, again, higher than the coefficients themselves. Hence, the relationship between import instability and size, and that between import instability and dependence on trade are both not acceptable. See the two equations below.

$$Y_4 = -0.0023X_1 - 0.0492Y_{16} + 24.6462$$
$$\quad\quad (.020) \quad\quad (.043) \quad\quad (2.17) \quad\quad R = .151$$
$$Y_4 = -0.0343X_2 - 0.0749Y_{16} + 26.7860$$
$$\quad\quad (.022) \quad\quad (.045) \quad\quad (2.46) \quad\quad R = .252$$

The cross-classifications and multiple-correlations suggest that neither 'smallness' nor dependence on trade are important sources of extra import instability. Cross-classifications did not indicate any steady pattern between import instability and size, nor between import instability and dependence on trade. Multiple correlations also failed to yield any significant relationships between import instability and size, and between import instability and dependence on trade. It should be noted, however, that the coefficient between import instability and dependence on trade is negative. While the coefficient is not acceptable, it can perhaps suggest that dependence on trade is not a cause of extra instability. And the relationship between import instability and size is not expected to change due to dependence on trade.

4. Conclusions.

The multi-variant analysis of the relationship between import instability and size suggests the following conclusions: (a) There is no significant association between import instability and size. The cross-classifications did not reveal any steady directional pattern, and multiple-correlations did not yield acceptable coefficients between import instability and size. It should be said, however, that unlike export instability, the coefficients between import instability and size were mostly negative. While there is no evidence of a strong association between import instability and size, there is a weak tendency, perhaps, for import instability to decrease with size. (b) There is no association between import instability and economic development. The cross-classifications failed to reveal any steady pattern, and multiple-correlations did not yield acceptable coefficients between import instability and economic development. There is, therefore, no evidence that economic development is likely to change the association between import instability and size. (c) There is, similarly, no evidence that the association between import instability and size is likely to change due to economic growth. The cross-classifications did not indicate any steady directional pattern, and the multiple-correlations did not yield acceptable coefficients between import instability and economic growth. The association between import instability and economic growth was even weaker than that between import instability and economic development. (d) Finally, there is also no strong evidence of an association between import instability and degree of dependence on trade. The cross-classifications did not indicate any steady pattern, and the multiple-correlations yielded a non-significant, yet negative, coefficient between import instability and dependence on trade. 'Small' countries who usually depend more heavily on trade as an escape from 'smallness', need not experience extra import instability on account of their dependence on trade.

CHAPTER THREE

CONCENTRATION IN TRADE AND SIZE

The economic structure of small countries is generally less diversified than that of large countries, and this limited diversity has implied that small countries usually specialize in a relatively few export commodities and may, consequently, depend on a few export markets to sell their products. It is, in other words, presumed that an inverse association exists between size of country and commodity export concentration, i.e., the smaller the country the stronger is the commodity concentration of exports. It is also presumed, since countries specializing in a few export commodities may find it more convenient to rely on a few export markets, that a positive association exists between commodity concentration of exports and geographic concentration of exports, i.e., the stronger the commodity concentration of exports, the stronger the geographic concentration.

Several observations have been made in the literature with respect to the association between size of country and commodity and geographic concentration in international trade. Not all these observations are, however, clear as to the nature of this association, and as to the impact of 'size' on the degree of concentration in exports and imports. Hirschman, who is responsible for the construction of the coefficient now commonly used to measure degree of concentration, was in his pioneering work[1] mainly concerned with geographic concentration in Trade. One of his conclusions is that there is a positive correlation between commodity and geographic concentration of exports. Later on, Kuznets took Hirschman's indices for three areas—Europe, the British Empire, and Latin America, calculated simple averages of the indices within each of these areas separately for the larger and smaller countries distinguished by size of population, and demonstrated that there is a "tendency for small countries to concentrate their foreign trade, particularly exports, in one or a few markets."[2] Michaely applied

---

[1] Albert O. Hirschman, *National Power and the Structure of Foreign Trade*, Berkeley, University of California Press, 1945. He develops his coefficient in Chapter VI, and measures only geographic concentration.

[2] Simon Kuznets, "Economic Growth of Small Nations," *op. cit.*, Table II, p. 22. The inverse relationship between size and geographic concentration of exports has also been more recently confirmed by Kuznets. See his "Quantitative Aspects

the Hirschman coefficient of concentration to a sample of forty-four countries, and also demonstrated, by calculating average coefficients for 'large' and 'small' countries, that there is an inverse association between size and geographic concentration, i.e., that exports of 'small' countries are more geographically concentrated than exports of 'large' countries.[1]

The effect of size on commodity concentration, however, has not been clearly demonstrated. The Michaely investigation seems to suggest, for example, that it is not so much the size of a country but rather its degree of development that has more of an influence on the degree of diversity of exports, and that the effect of size on commodity concentration of exports is not as conspicuous as its effects on geographic concentration of exports. Classifying his sample of forty-four countries into categories of 'large-small' and 'developed-underdeveloped', Michaely reports that among the underdeveloped countries the 'small' had on the average lower (not higher) coefficients of commodity concentration of exports than the 'large' countries.[2] This suggests that among underdeveloped countries the association between size and commodity concentration of exports could be positive instead of negative, and also that the impact of 'size' on commodity concentration differs among countries at different levels of economic development.

This chapter attempts to provide more evidence on the nature of the association between size and commodity and geographic concentration in trade. Its purpose is to assess the impact of 'size' on the concentration of exports and imports, and to investigate the extent to which 'smallness' in and of itself is necessarily a cause of a strong concentration in exports and imports. The chapter is in two parts. The *first* interprets the direction and magnitude of the association between size of country and degree of concentration in exports and imports. Formal simple-correlation analysis will be utilized, with the size of country (in terms of both size of population and size of GNP) as the independent variable, and the indices measuring concentration of exports and imports (seven such indices have been chosen) as the de-

---

of the Economic Growth of Nations: Level and Structure of Foreign Trade: Comparison for Recent Years," *Economic Development and Cultural Change*, Vol. XIII, No. 1, Part. II, Table 10, p. 37.

[1] Michael Michaely, "Concentration of Exports and Imports: An International Comparison," *op. cit.*, Table V, p. 735. Same results have also been reproduced in M. Michaely, *Concentration in International Trade*, Amsterdam, North-Holland Publishing Co., 1962, Table 6, p. 25.

[2] *Ibid.*, Table II, p. 729.

pendent variable. The dependent variables will also be ranked with reference to size of country, i.e., countries will be grouped in quartiles, and the medians for the quartiles of the countries ranked in increasing order of size, will indicate whether any pattern or directional tendency exists. Both of these techniques, should reveal the significance of the association between size of country and concentration in exports and imports. The *second* part, which is based on a multi-variant analysis, with two independent variables, tries to investigate the extent to which the association between 'size' and concentration in exports and imports is affected by the degree of dependence on foreign trade and by the level of economic development. It is relevant to pose these questions since an observable pattern has been established (Chapter IV of this investigation) between 'size' and dependence on trade; and since it has also been suggested in the literature that a more meaningful association exists between level of development and concentration, rather than between 'size' and concentration. Two methods of analysis will be utilized for this purpose: A cross-classification method of analysis, already described, and formal multiple-correlation anlysis, with two independent variables. Indices measuring degree of concentration will be the dependent variables, size and economic development, or size and dependence-on-trade, the two independent variables. In other words, concentration is taken as a function of 'size' and development, and as a function of 'size' and dependence-on-trade. Multiple correlation coefficients will be compared with simple correlation coefficients, and the impact of economic development and of dependence-on-trade on the association between 'size' and concentration in trade will be examined.

1. Two-Variable Analysis: Patterns and Correlations

Three different aspects of concentration will be considered—commodity concentration of exports, commodity concentration of imports, and geographic (both regional and country) concentration of exports.[1] The dependent variables used here to measure these aspects of concentration are seven: Two indices measure the commodity concentration of exports, one index measures the commmodity concen-

---

[1] Unavailability of comparable coefficients measuring geographic concentration of imports did not permit the consideration of this aspect of concentration. Furthermore, a priori reasons suggesting an association between geographic concentration of imports and size are not very strong.

tration of imports, one index is a ratio of export to import concentration, and three indices measure the regional and country concentration of exports. Each one of these three aspects will be separately analyzed. Simple correlations between concentration indices and size of country in terms of population and GNP, and comparisons of the median concentration for the quartiles of the countries ranked with reference to size of country, will be both utilized for the purpose of interpreting the significance of the association between size of country and commodity and geographic concentration of exports and imports. Commodity concentration of exports will be considered first.

A. *Commodity Concentration of Exports and Size*

Is the export sector of a country limited by the overall diversity of the economy? Should, in other words, the commodity exports of small countries be less diversified than the exports of large countries, because small countries have a generally less diversified economic structure than large countries? It is often argued that there is an inverse association between commodity export concentration and size of country, that is, the larger the country the less concentrated (the more diversified) are its commodity exports.

To find out whether this claim is true or not, two different indices measuring the commodity concentration of exports are utilized, and both indices are correlated to size of country in terms of population and GNP. The first index (Y_9) is the "Hirschman coefficient" of concentration applied (by Coppock) to the exports of seventy-eight countries classified according to the SITC 10 *sections* (one-digit code). The second (Y_{13}) is also the "Hirschman coefficient" of concentration applied (by Michaely) to the exports of forty-four countries classified according to the SITC 150 *groups* (three-digit code). These two indices have been chosen because they involve two different degrees of aggregation. Values of both indices are given in columns Y_9 and Y_{13} of Appendix Table 1. The correlation coefficient (r) between commodity export concentration index (Y_9) and population (X_2) is —.41, and the coefficient between the same index (Y_9) and GNP (X_1) is —.08. The scatter diagrams of Figure 9 show these relations. The former coefficient is relatively high, indicating that the degree of association between commodity export concentration (Y_9) and population size in particular, is quite apparent. Tests of significance indicate that this correlation is significant at the .05 and .01 levels. One can suggest,

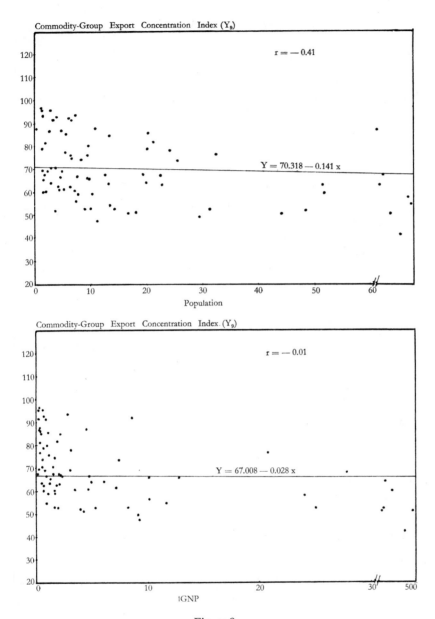

Figure 9
Scatter diagrams: Commedity-group export concentration and size.

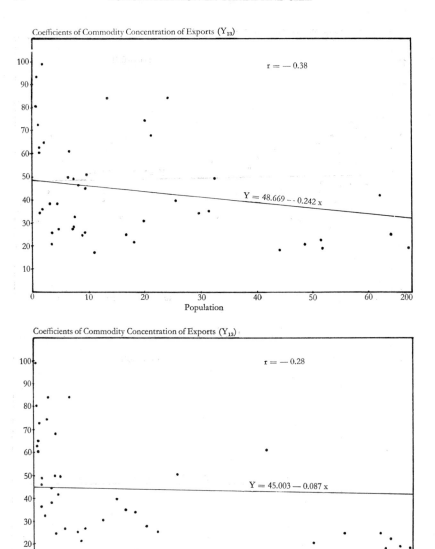

Figure 10
Scatter diagrams: Commodity export concentration and size

therefore, with reasonable confidence, that there is a tendency for
commodity concentration of exports (Y_9) to decrease as country size
(particularly population) increases. This is in line with a priori reasoning.

When the second index of concentration is used, some significant
correlation is also achieved. The coefficient of correlation (r) between
commodity export concentration index (Y_{13}) and population (X_2) is
—.38, and the coefficient between the same index of concentration
(Y_{13}) and GNP (X_1) is —.29. The scatter diagrams of Figure 10 show
these relations. Both coefficients are negative and relatively high, suggesting a tendency for commodity concentration of exports (Y_{13}) to
decrease as country size (in terms of both population and GNP) increases. If one may place some confidence in these coefficients, since
both of them are significant at the 0.05 level, they show that small
countries tend to have a higher commodity export concentration than
large countries. There is here, therefore, reasonable support for the
view that country size and commodity concentration of exports are
inversely related to each other.

The four correlation coefficients computed here are all negative, and
three of them can be taken with some confidence. Formal correlation
analysis, therefore, does provide reasonable support for the view that
small countries tend to have higher commodity export concentration
than large countries.

The rankings of the median commodity export concentration also
provide similar support for the view that there is an inverse relation
between size and commotidy export concentration. When the seventy-
eight countries (of the Coppock sample) are ranked in increasing order
of population size, the median commodity export concentration(Y_9)
is 78.0 for the first quartile, 67.9 for the second, 65.6 for the third,
and 61.5 for the fourth quartile. Thus a declining trend is revealed,
indicating that commodity export concentration and size (in terms of
population) are inversely related to each other. When the countries
(75 of the 78) are ranked in increasing order of GNP size, a similar
declining trend is also revealed. The median commodity export concentration (Y_9) is 80.3 for the first quartile, 66.7 for the second, 66.4
for the third, and 55.3 for the fourth. This result also demonstrates
that commodity export concentration and country size in terms of
GNP are also inversely related to each other. These trends are given
in Table 19.

When the forty-four countries (of the Michaely sample) are ranked

Table 19

Relation between Size of Country (Population, GNP) and Commodity-Group Export Concentration (Y$_9$)

GROUPS OF COUNTRIES Countries Ranked in Increasing Order of Population Size (Quartiles)	Number of Countries	Average Population (million)	Median Commodity-Group Export Concentration
I	20	2.04	78.0
II	20	6.02	67.9
III	20	14.02	65.6
IV	18	113.93	61.5
Countries Ranked in Increasing Order of GNP Size (Quartiles)	Number of Countries	Average Population ($ billions)	Median Commodity-Group Export Concentration
I	19	0.405	80.3
II	19	1.35	66.7
III	19	4.04	66.4
IV	18	56.92	55.3

in increasing order of population size, the median commodity export concentration (Y$_{13}$) is 62.8 for the first quartile, 32.5 for the second, 44.6 for the third, and 24.8 for the fourth. There is here an unsteady tendency for the median concentration to fall as population size increases. The third quartile has a higher median than the second, but the first quartile has the highest median, and the fourth quartile has the lowest median. The inverse association of the former correlation analysis, between commodity concentration of exports (Y$_{13}$) and population size, can be observed from these rankings. When the countries (41 out of 44) are ranked in increasing order of GNP size, a declining trend, between commodity export concentration and GNP size, is also observed. The median commodity export concentration (Y$_{13}$) is 61.7 for the first quartile, 49.6 for the second, 28.9 for the third, and 24.8 for the fourth. The inverse association between commodity export concentration and GNP size is revealed. The degree of concentration decreases as country size (in terms of GNP) increases. These results are given in Table 20.

The view that small countries have higher commodity export concentration than large countries finds some support here. The four correlation coefficients are all negative, one is very low and can be

Table 20

Relation between Size of Country (Population, GNP) and Commodity Concentration of Exports (Y$_{13}$)

GROUPS OF COUNTRIES Countries Ranked in Increasing Order of Population Size (Quartiles)	Number of Countries	Average Population (million)	Median Commodity Concentration of Exports
I	11	1.33	62.8
II	11	6.45	32.5
III	11	15.65	44.6
IV	11	60.15	24.8
Countries Ranked in *Increasing Order of* *GNP Size* *(Quartiles)*	*Number* *of* *Countries*	*Average* *GNP* *($ billion)*	*Median* *Commodity* *Concentration* *of Exports*
I	10	0.42	61.7
II	10	1.94	49.6
III	10	6.09	28.9
IV	11	67.39	24.8

ignored, but three are significant statistically and can be taken with some confidence; and most of the rankings of median commodity export concentration reveal a declining trend. An inverse association can be, therefore, assumed to exist between commodity export concentration and size in terms of both population and, to a lesser extent, GNP.

B. *Commodity Concentration of Imports and Size*

Is there, in general, any observable association between commodity concentration of imports and size of country? Is it plausible to assume, as we did with commodity exports, that there is an inverse relation between size and commodity import concentration? It might be expected that the smaller the country and the more specialized production is, the more would be the need for a larger variety of imported products. In other words, this will argue for a positive association between size and commodity import concentration, the smaller the country the less concentrated are commodity imports expected to be. Or it might be argued, particularly in those countries where the production of export commodities depends in the main on imported products, that an inverse association exists between size and commodity concentration of imports. The smaller the country, the more specified production and exports are, and, consequently, the more concentrated would imports be. It has also been claimed by Kuznets that "since imports are assumed to reflect the diversity of gaps between domestic supplies and total consumption and investment needs, there need be no significant association between the concentration or diversity of the commodity composition of imports and size of country."[1]

Which of these claims do the facts support? The index used here as a measure of the degree of concentration of commodity imports is also the Hirschman coefficient of concentration (applied by Michaely) to the imports of forty-four countries classified according to the SITC 150 *groups* (three-digit code). The values of this index are given in column Y_{14} of Appendix Table 1. The index is correlated to size of country in terms of both population and GNP. The correlation coefficient (r) between commodity concentration of imports (Y_{14}) and population (X_2) is —.10, and between the same index (Y_{14}) and GNP (X_1) is —.13. Both of these coefficients are very low, and both are not significant at any level of confidence. This indicates that the association between commodity import concentration and size of country, in terms of population and GNP, is very weak or hardly existent. The diagrams of Figure 11 show these relations. It should be remembered that similar coefficients for commodity export concentration were relatively higher and could also be taken with some confidence. This demonstrates that the association between commodity export concentration and size is stronger than the association (if any) between commodity import concentration and size. When the forty-four countries are ranked in increasing order of population size, the median commodity import concentration (Y_{14}) is 19.1 for the first quartile, 19.7 for the second, 21.5 for the third, and 23.5 for the fourth. Unlike the inverse and very weak relationship indicated by the formal correlation analysis, these medians show a positive association between commodity import concentration and population size. As country size, in terms of population, increases, commodity concentration of imports increases. The range in the medians, however, is not wide which suggests that the association between size and commodity concentration of imports is weak, if not nonexistent. When the countries (41 out of 44)

---

[1] Simon Kuznets, *op. cit.*, *Economic Development and Cultural Change*, Vol. XIII, No. 1, Part II, October 1964, p. 54.

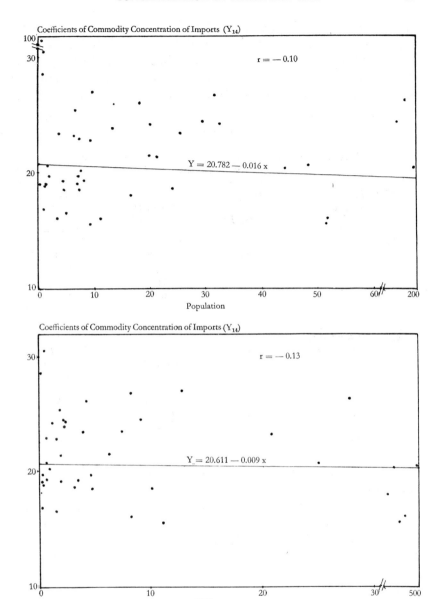

Figure 11
Scatter diagrams: Commodity import concentration and size.

are ranked in increasing order of GNP size, no trend is revealed. The median commodity import concentration (Y_{14}) is 20.0 for the first quartile, 23.4 for the second, 22.5 for the third, and 20.4 for the fourth. The first and last quartiles have almost the same median concentration, and the second quartile has a slightly higher median than the third. Table 21 shows these relations.

Table 21

Relation between Size of Country (Population, GNP) and Commodity Concentration of Imports (Y_{14})

Countries Ranked in Increasing Order of Population Size (Quartiles)	Number of Countries	Average Population (millions)	Median Commodity Concentration of Imports
I	11	1.33	19.1
II	11	6.45	19.7
III	11	15.65	21.5
IV	11	60.15	23.5

Countries Ranked in Increasing Order of GNP Size (Quartiles)	Number of Countries	Average GNP ($ billions)	Median Commodity Concentration of Imports
I	10	0.42	20.0
II	10	1.94	23.4
III	10	6.09	22.5
IV	11	67.39	20.4

Results of the formal correlation analysis and of the rankings of the median commodity import concentration, fail to reveal a strong association between commodity concentration of imports and size. The correlation coefficients are very low and insignificant, and rankings of medians do not indicate any observable and significant pattern. Therefore, no relationship can be assumed to exist between commodity import concentration and size.

If one were to accept the results of this and the preceeding sections, then one would expect the ratio of commodity concentration of exports to imports to be inversely (and perhaps strongly) associated with size. The ratio of commodity export concentration (Y_{13}) to commodity import concentration (Y_{14}) would decline as size (particularly population) increases. Column Y_{15} of Appendix Table 1 gives the values of the ratio of commodity concentration of exports to imports.

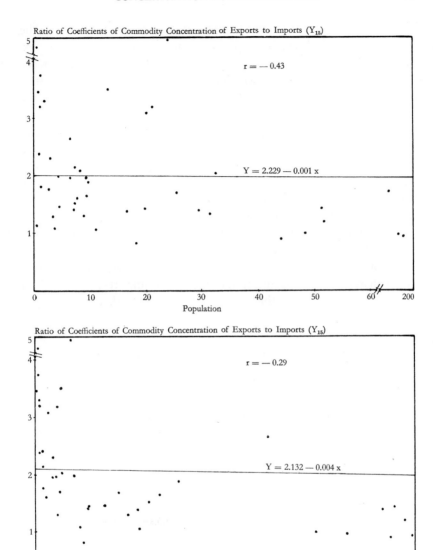

Figure 12
Scatter diagrams: Commodity concentration of exports to imports and size

This index (Y_{15}) is correlated to population size and GNP size. The correlation (r) between the ratio of commodity concentration of exports (Y_{15}) and population (X_2) is —.427, and the coefficient between the same index (Y_{15}) and GNP (X_1) is —.295. Figure 12 shows these relations. Both of these coefficients are negative, and as expected, the correlation between the index (Y_{15}) and population is the higher of the two. In fact the coefficient of —.427 is the highest correlation coefficient found in measuring the association between concentration in international trade and size. It should also be mentioned that tests of significance indicate that both coefficients can be taken with some confidence. The former and higher coefficient is significant at the 0.05 and 0.01 levels, and the latter is significant at the 0.05 level.

The rankings of the median ratio of commodity concentration of exports to imports, reveal the same inverse association. When the forty-four countries are ranked in increasing order of population size the median ratio of concentration of exports to imports (Y_{15}) is 2.4 for the first guartile, 1.6 for the second, 1.9 for the third, and 1.3 for the

Table 22

Relation between Size of Country (Population, GNP) and Ratio of Commodity Concentration of Exports to Imports (Y_{15})

GROUPS OF COUNTRIES Countries Ranked in Increasing Order of Population Size (Quartiles)	Number of Countries	Average Population (millions)	Median Ratio of Concentration of Exports to Imports
I	11	1.33	2.4
II	11	6.45	1.6
III	11	15.65	1.9
IV	11	60.15	1.3

Countries Ranked in Increasing Order of GNP Size (Quartiles)	Number of Countries	Average GNP ($ billions)	Median Ratio of Concentration of Exports to Imports
I	10	0.42	2.8
II	10	1.94	2.2
III	10	6.09	1.4
IV	11	67.39	1.3

fourth. Thus an unsteady declining tendency is revealed. The ratio of concentration of exports to imports (Y_{15}) tends to decrease as population size increases. When the countries (41 out of 43) are ranked in increasing order of GNP size, the same declining pattern is revealed. The median ratio of concentration of exports to imports (Y_{15}) is 2.8 for the first quartile, 2.2 for the second, 1.4 for the third, and 1.3 for the fourth. The ratio of commodity concentration of exports to imports decreases steadily as GNP size increases. Table 22 gives these relations.

Both correlation analysis and the median trend indicate an inverse relationship between the ratio of commodity concentration of exports to imports (Y_{15}) and country size in terms of population and GNP. The median ratios decline steadily as population size and GNP size increase, and both correlation coefficients are negative and statistically significant. This result is of some interest. Since the correlation coefficients here are higher than the coefficients found between commodity export concentration and (particularly population) size, it suggests that the commodity concentration of imports must have increased as size (particularly population) increases. This implies that it may be more likely perhaps to assume that commodity import concentration is positively associated with size.

C. Geographic Concentration of Exports and Size

It has also been suggested by Kuznets that "Given the dominance in world trade of large countries and of developed countries, and the dominance of the latter even in the trade of underdeveloped countries, geographic concentration, i.e., concentration of a country's foreign trade in a few, or perhaps one or two, sources of imports and destinations of exports, should be most conspicuous in the case of small countries, and particularly those with low per capita product; and such concentration might be less prevalent in the foreign trade of large countries, particularly those with high per capita income."[1] This is one of the arguments suggesting (in this case) an inverse association between size of country and geographic concentration in foreign trade. Others, like Hirschman,[2] have also argued for an inverse association between geographic concentration and size of country by assuming that there is a positive association between geographic concentration

---

[1] Simon Kuznets, *op. cit.*, p. 36.
[2] Albert O. Hirschman, *National Power and Structure of Foreign Trade, op. cit.*

of exports and commodity concentration of exports, i.e., the geographic concentration of exports is stronger the stronger the commodity concentration of exports.[1] And since small countries generally have a rather strong commodity concentration of exports, they are expected, as a result, to have a rather strong geographic concentration of exports. Hence, the inverse association between size of country and geographic concentration of exports. The implication being that small countries, on account of their high commodity export concentration, may find it more convenient to rely on a few export markets. A case, however, can be made for the opposite point of view; a small country with a strong commodity concentration of exports would be forced, as if to compensate for this limited diversity, to distribute her exports among as many countries as possible, thus making for a low geographic export concentration.

Let us see what the general picture is. Three different indices measuring country and regional concentration of exports are utilized for this purpose. Each will be separately correlated to size of country in terms of both population and GNP. The first (Y_{10}) is a country-export concentration index, i.e., the 'Hirschman Coefficient' applied to the export of each of eighty countries to all other countries; the second (Y_{11}) is a regional export concentration index, i.e., also the 'Hirschman Coefficient' applied to the International Monetary Fund regional classification; and the third (Y_{12}) is the percent of exports to the region receiving most of the country's exports, the regions and percentages being those used by the International Monetary Fund. The values of these indices, computed by Coppock for a sample of eighty-three countries, are given in columns Y_{10}, Y_{11}, and Y_{12} of Appendix Table 1.

The correlation coefficient (r) between country-export concentration index (Y_{10}) and population (X_2) is $-.24$, and the coefficient between the same index (Y_{10}) and GNP (X_1) is $-.21$. Both coefficients are negative and of similar strength and the former coefficient is significant at the 0.05 level. If one could place any confidence in them, they do suggest that the larger the country, in terms of population size at least, the lower is the country-export concentration. Size of country and country-export concentration are inversely related to each other. Figure 13 shows this relation.

---

[1] It has already been mentioned that this positive association between commodity and geographic concentration of exports has been borne out by the Michaely study. See Michael Michaely, *Concentration in International Trade, op. cit.,* particularly pp. 18-25.

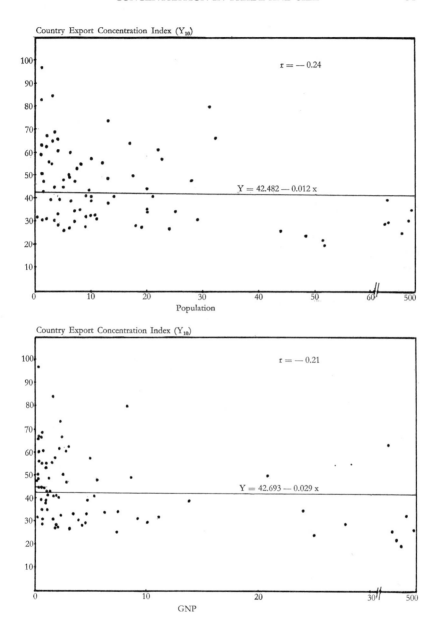

Figure 13
Scatter diagrams: Country export concentration and size.

The rankings of the median country-export concentration show the same inverse association between country export concentration and size of country, in terms of both population and GNP. When the eighty countries of the sample are ranked in increasing order of population size, the median country-export concentration index (Y_{10}) is 55.5 for the first quartile, 42.1 for the second, 40.7 for the third, and 33.1 for the fourth. Thus a steady declining trend is revealed, demonstrating that country-export concentration and population size are inversely associated. The smaller the country, in terms of population size, the stronger is its country-export concentration, i.e., the stronger is its tendency to rely on a fewer export markets. When the countries (77 out of 80) are ranked in increasing order of GNP size, a similar declining pattern is also revealed. The median country-export concentration (Y_{10}) is 50.6 for the first quartile, 41.0 for the second, 40.7 for the third, and 31.9 for the fourth. Thus the inverse association is also observed between size of country (in terms of GNP size) and country-export concentration. The smaller the country, in terms of GNP size, the stronger is the tendency to rely on fewer export markets. Table 23 gives these results.

Both formal correlation analysis and the pattern of the median

Table 23

Relation between Size of Country (Population, GNP) and Country Export Concentration (Y_{10})

GROUPS OF COUNTRIES Countries Ranked in Increasing Order of Population Size (Quartiles)	Number of Countries	Average Population (millions)	Median Country Export Concentration
I	20	2.04	55.5
II	20	6.02	42.1
III	20	13.33	40.7
IV	20	74.01	33.1
Countries Ranked in Increasing Order of GNP Size (Quartiles)	Number of Countries	Average GNP ($ billions)	Median Country Export Concentration
I	19	0.405	50.6
II	19	1.35	41.0
III	19	3.48	40.7
IV	20	51.69	31.9

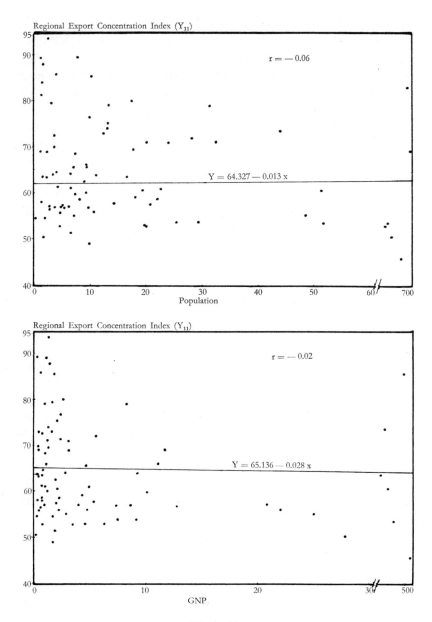

Figure 14
Scatter diagrams: Regional export concentration and size.

analysis, indicate an inverse association between country-export concentration and size of country in terms of population and GNP. Such a conclusion supports the view that geographic concentration of exports (as measured in terms of country-export concentration) is more conspicuous in the case of small countries and less prevalent in the case of large countries.

The second measure, the regional export concentration index (Y_{11}), also shows an inverse (but very weak) relationship between size of country and regional concentration of exports. The correlation coefficient (r) between regional export concentration index (Y_{11}) and population (X_2) is —.06, and between the same index (Y_{11}) and GNP (X_1) is —.02. Both coefficients are very low and both are not statistically significant. This indicates that the association between regional export concentration (unlike country export concentration) and size of country in terms of population and GNP is very weak or nonexistent. Figure 14 shows this relation.

The rankings of the median regional export concentration reveal also a similar weak relationship between regional export concentration and size of country in terms of population and GNP. When the eighty-three countries are ranked in increasing order of population size, the median regional export concentration (Y_{11}) is 68.7 for the first quartile, 59.8 for the second, 65.9 for the third, and 58.1 for the fourth. Although the declining trend is not systematic, the tendency for the median concentration to decrease as population size increases is apparent. The first quartile has the highest median and the fourth quartile the lowest median. When the countries (80 out of 83) are ranked in increasing order of GNP size, almost the same pattern is observed. The median regional export concentration (Y_{11}) is 62.3 for the first quartile, 68.9 for the second, 59.9 for the third, and 56.9 for the fourth. The declining trend is also not consistent (the second quartile has a higher median concentration than the first), but the tendency for the median concentration to decrease as GNP size increases is apparent. These results are given in Table 24.

Correlation analysis and rankings of median regional export concentration do not indicate any significant association between regional concentration of exports and country size in terms of both population and GNP. The correlation coefficients are negative but are not statistically significant, and the rankings show only a mild tendency towards increasing concentration as size of country decreases. The view that the geographic concentration of exports (as measured in terms of

Table 24

*Relation between Size of Country (Population, GNP) and Regional
Export Concentration (Y$_{11}$)*

GROUPS OF COUNTRIES Countries Ranked in Increasing Order of Population Size (Quartiles)	Number of Countries	Average Population (millions)	Median Regional Export Concentration
I	21	2.05	68.7
II	21	6.17	39.8
III	21	14.06	65.9
IV	20	105.01	58.1
Countries Ranked in Increasing Order of GNP Size	*Number of Countries*	*Average GNP ($ billions)*	*Median Regional Export Concentration*
I	20	0.425	62.3
II	20	1.365	68.9
III	20	3.615	59.9
IV	20	51.96	56.9

regional export concentration) is more conspicuous in the case of small countries does not find significant support here.

The third measure of geographic concentration, the percent of exports to region receiving most of country's exports (Y_{12}), also reveals an inverse relationship between size of country (particularly in terms of GNP size) and geographic concentration of exports (as measured by this index). The correlation coefficient (r) between the concentration index (Y_{12}) and population (X_2) is —.03, and between the same index (Y_{12}) and GNP (X_1) is —.23. Both coefficients are negative, but only the latter is significant at the 0.05 level and can be taken with some confidence, the former is too low and statistically insignificant. Only with respect to the latter coefficient (where GNP is used for size) is an inverse association suggested between geographic export concentration (as measured by this index) and country size. Figure 15 shows this relation.

The rankings of the median concentration index (Y_{12}) indicate also an inverse (but not systematic) relationship between geographic concentration of exports (as measured by this index) and country size in terms of both population and GNP. When the eighty-three countries are ranked in increasing order of population size, the median index (Y_{12}) is 60.1 for the first quartile, 50.0 for the second, 56.0 for the

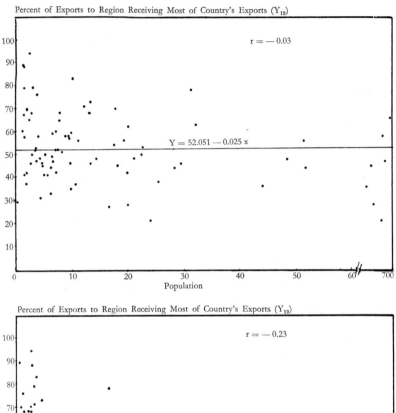

Figure 15
Scatter diagrams: Exports to region receiving most exports and size

third, and 46.5 for the fourth. The declining trend is not consistent, but the tendency for the median concentration to decrease as population size increases is observable. The third quartile has a higher median than the second, but the first quartile has the highest median and the fourth quartile the lowest median. When the countries (80 of the 83) are ranked in increasing order of GNP size, the same pattern is almost observed. The median concentration index (Y_{12}) is 50.5 for the first quartile, 60.0 for the second, 47.5 for the third, and 46.0 for the fourth. The declining trend is also not consistent (the second quartile has a higher median concentration than the first quartile), but the tendency toward the decrease in the median concentration as GNP size increases is also observable. Table 25 gives these relations.

Table 25

Relation between Size of Country (Population, GNP) and % of Exports to Region receiving most of Country's Exports (Y_{12})

GROUPS OF COUNTRIES Countries Ranked in Increasing Order of Population Size (Quartiles)	Number of Countries	Average Population (millions)	Median % Of exports to Region
I	21	2.05	60.1
II	21	6.17	50.0
III	21	14.06	56.0
IV	20	105.01	46.5
Countries Ranked in Increasing Order of GNP Size (Quartiles)	Number of Countries	Average GNP ($ billions)	Median % Of Exports to Region
I	20	0.425	50.5
II	20	1.365	60.0
III	20	3.615	47.5
IV	20	51.96	46.0

The view that geographic concentration of exports (measured in terms of the percent of exports to region receiving most of country's exports) is more conspicuous in the case of small countries, does not find unqualified support here. The correlation coefficients are both negative, only one is statistically significant and can be taken with some confidence, and the rankings of the median concentration show an unsteady decreasing tendency as size of country increases.

To *conclude*, simple correlation analysis between concentration indices and size of country in terms of population and GNP, and comparisons of the median concentration for the quartiles of the countries ranked with reference to size of country, together, suggest the following results: an inverse association can perhaps be assumed to exist between size (in terms of population and GNP) and commodity export concentration; no significant association is found to prevail between size and commodity import concentration, although import concentration showed a tendency to increase as population size increased; and only a weak inverse association can be assumed to exist between size (in terms of population and GNP) and geographic export concentration. This latter association was weaker than the association between size and commodity export concentration. Therefore, the view that the effect of size on geographic export concentration is more conspicuous than its effect on commodity export concentration, does not find strong support in this analysis. Both commodity and geographic concentration of exports do tend to decrease as size (in terms of population and GNP) increases. Some of the correlation coefficients of these relationships are statistically significant and can be taken with some confidence, and the rankings of the median concentration, more often than not, reveal a declining pattern. There is therefore some support, but not unqualified support, for the claim that commodity and geographic concentration of exports are generally more conspicuous in the case of small countries and less prevalent in the case of large countries.

2. Three-Variable Analysis: Cross-Classifications and Correlations

The purpose of this section is to find out whether the nature of the association between concentration in international trade and size, as revealed in the first part of this Chapter, is influenced by the level of economic development and by the degree of involvement in foreign trade. It is suggested in the literature that concentration in trade is, perhaps, more dependent on economic development than on the mere size of a country. The more developed a country is, the more diversified are its exports and also its imports. Hence, one can argue for an inverse association between concentration in trade and economic development. Such an association may perhaps be significant enough to affect and even alter the direction of the association between concentration in trade and size. Multi-variant analysis, with degree of concentration in trade as the dependent variable, and with size and degree of development as independent variables, will indicate the extent to which this is true.

It has also been observed (see Chapter IV of this investigation) that the degree of dependence on foreign trade and size of country are inversely related to each other. Dependence-on-trade has a tendency to decrease as country size increases. It is, therefore, also relevant to find out whether the degree of dependence on foreign trade has any influence on the association between concentration and size. The effect of a country's degree of dependence on foreign trade may be such as to change the nature of the association between concentration and size. Multi-variant analysis, with degree of concentration in trade as the dependent variable and with size and degree of dependence on trade as the independent variables, will indicate the extent to which this is possible.

Two methods of analysis will be used—a cross-classification method of analysis, and multiple-correlation analysis, with two independent variables. Both methods already described can be subjected to the same interpretation, with the former being a crude alternative of the latter. An example of the cross-classification method may still be helpful.

It has been alleged, as previously mentioned, that the association between concentration-in-trade and size may change if the degree of development is taken into account. Cross-classifying concentration indices by size and by economic development will demonstrate whether this allegation is true or not. Namely, countries are ranked in increasing order of size and divided into thirds; countries in each of the thirds are ranked in increasing order of degree of development and divided into thirds; and, then, the median value of the concentration index is calculated for the countries in each of the nine cells. Comparison of these median values across any row, down any column, or diagonally will reveal the manner in which concentration-in-trade changes as size and/or economic development change, and will, thus, provide an answer to the allegation concerning the impact of economic development on the association between size and concentration-in-trade.

The multiple-correlation analysis does not require explanation. It is formal multiple-correlation analysis with concentration-in-trade as the dependent variable, and size and economic development or dependence-on-trade as the independent variables. Analysis is restricted only to variables included in the cross-classification method. Hence, the multiple-correlation analysis will include two independent variables only. The standard multiple regression equations, multiple correlation coefficients, and standard deviations will be computed.

Export concentration is only considered since data on imports utilized in this study are not wide enough to permit such method of analysis. Commodity export concentration (Y_9) and country export concentration (Y_{10}) are selected and separately related to size of country (population, GNP) and degree of development (Y_{23}), and to size of country and degree of dependence-on-trade (Y_{16}). The relationship between export concentration, size, and economic development will be considered first.

A. *Export Concentration, Development, and Size*

This is mainly an analysis of the effect of economic development on the association between commodity export concentration and size, and between geographic export concentration and size. Commodity export concentration medians (Y_9) classified by size (GNP and population) and by economic development (Y_{23})[1], indicate an inverse association between size and commodity export concentration, and also an inverse sssociation between economic development and commodity export concentration. Table 26 shows these results. The median values of commodity export concentration observe a declining directional pattern across any row, down any column, and also diagonally. This pattern is observed in both population and GNP breakdowns. The level of economic development, in other words, does not seem to alter the inverse association between size and commodity export concentration. See Table 26.

This is contrary to Michaely findings, referred to previously, which suggested that size did not have a significant impact on commodity export concentration in the case of the 'developed' countries. Michaely reported, for example, 'small-developed' countries as having lower commodity export concentration than 'large-underdeveloped' countries.[2] The results here do not support such a conclusion. The 'develo-

---

[1] Data on economic development limit the size of the sample and as a result, only a two-by-two breakdown (small vs. large) is permitted, when export concentration is classified by size and by economic development.

[2] M. Michaely, *op. cit.*, Table II, p. 729.

ed-small' countries show regularly higher concentration medians than the 'underdeveloped large' countries. The inverse association between size and commodity export concentration is observed, regardless of the level of economic development.

Table 26

Commodity Export Concentration Medians (Y_9) by Size (GNP) and by Degree of Development (Y_{23})

	Small Countries	Large Countries	TOTAL
Underdeveloped Countries	75.8 *Range* (52.8-95.6) n = 11	67.9 *Range* (63.2-76.1) n = 3	75.9 *Range* (52.8-95.6) n = 13
Developed Countries	70.6 *Range* (69.3-96.4) n = 3	62.1 *Range* (47.3-92.1) n = 12	64.0 *Range* (47.3-96.4) n = 15
TOTAL	74.9 *Range* (52.8-96.4) n = 14	63.3 *Range* (47.3-92.1) n = 15	65.7 *Range* (47.3-96.4) n = 29

Commodity Export Concentration Medians (Y_9) by Size (Population) and by Degree of Development (Y_{23})

	Small Countries	Large Countries	TOTAL
Underdeveloped Countries	87.7 *Range* (52.8-96.4) n = 8	63.4 *Range* (52.1-85.6) n = 8	74.9 *Range* (52.1-96.4) n = 16
Developed Countries	67.8 *Range* (60.8-92.1) n = 6	59.9 *Range* (47.3-65.5) n = 7	64.0 *Range* (47.3-92.1) n = 13
TOTAL	75.0 *Range* (52.8-96.4) n = 14	63.2 *Range* (47.3-85.6) n = 15	65.7 *Range* (47.3-96.4) n = 29

Formal multiple-correlation analysis, with size (X_1 or X_2) and economic development (Y_{23}) as the two independent variables, provides the same results. Multiple regression equations indicate an inverse association between commodity export concentration (Y_9) and size (X_1 and X_2), and also an inverse association between commodity export concentration and economic development (Y_{23}). The two multiple regression equations, with the coefficients of multiple correlation (R), and the standard deviations are given below:

$$Y_9 = -0.2618X_1 - 0.0075Y_{23} + 76.399$$
$$(.1699) \qquad (.0067) \qquad (3.090) \qquad R = .474$$

$$Y_9 = -0.2252X_2 - 0.0118Y_{23} + 79.465$$
$$(.1167) \qquad (.0056) \qquad (3.507) \qquad R = .511$$

It is worth noting that the two R-values here are considerably higher than the simple correlation coefficients between commodity export concentration (Y_9) and size. These r-values, as shown previously, were approximately zero ($-.03$ and $-.01$ respectively). When size (X_1 and X_2) was paired with economic development higher R-values were yielded. This could be interpreted as evidence, perhaps that commodity export concentration is dependent more on the level of economic development than on the size of the country. This interpretation should be taken cautiously since the standard deviations of the economic development (Y_{23}) coefficients are not small enough to accept these coefficients.

The cross-classification method of analysis applied to geographic export concentration yields a similar pattern as commodity export concentration. Geographic export concentration medians (Y_{10}) classified by size and by economic development (Y_{23}) indicate an inverse association between size and geographic export concentration, and also an inverse association between economic development and geographic export concentration. See Table 27 for these results. The median values of geographic export concentration observe, in the population breakdown, a declining trend across any row, down any column, and also diagonally. In the GNP breakdown, this directional pattern is not observed. The level of economic development, however, with one exception, does not seem to alter the inverse association between size and geographic export concentration.

Multiple-correlation analysis, with geographic export concentration (Y_{10}) as the dependent variable, and with size and economic development (Y_{23}) as the independent variables, also reveals an inverse association between geographic export concentration and size. The association between geographic concentration and economic development is negative only when economic development is paired with GNP (X_1); when economic development is paired with population (X_2), the association between geographic export concentration and eco-

Table 27

Country-Export Concentration Medians (Y_{10}) by Size (GNP) and by Degree of Development (Y_{23})

	Small Countries	*Large Countries*	TOTAL
Underdeveloped Countries	*43.4* Range (27.7-96.9) n = 11	*62.4* Range (59.9-84.4) n = 3	53.0 Range (27.7-96.9) n = 14
Developed Countries	50.2 Range (29.3-57.5) n = 3	*32.8* Range (19.9-63.8) n = 12	33.6 Range (19.9-63.8) n = 15
TOTAL	45.9 Range (27.7-96.9) n = 14	34.2 Range (19.9-84.4) n = 15	40.7 Range (19.9-96.9) n = 29

Country-Export Concentration Medians (Y_{10}) by Size (Population) and by Degree of Development (Y_{23})

	Small Countries	*Largh Countries*	TOTAL
Underdeveloped Countries	55.0 Range (27.7-96.9) n = 8	42.0 Range (24.3-57.5) n = 8	46.0 Range (24.3-96.9) n = 16
Developed Countries	44.2 Range (32.1-84.4) n = 6	31.3 Range (19.9-63.8) n = 7	34.2 Range (19.9-84.4) n = 13
TOTAL	49.7 Range (27.7-96.9) n = 14	35.1 Range (19.9-63.8) n = 15	40.7 Range (19.9-96.9) n = 29

nomic development turns out to be positive. However, the standard deviations of the economic development (Y_{23}) coefficients are as large as the coefficients themselves. Hence, these coefficients cannot be accepted. The coefficients of GNP (X_1) and population (X_2) are, on the other hand, acceptable. The multiple regression equations below give these relationships with the relevant coefficients and standard deviations.

$$Y_{10} = -0.623X_1 + 0.008Y_{23} + 48.073$$
$$(.2198) \quad (.0086) \quad (3.995) \quad R = .501$$
$$Y_{10} = -0.482X_2 - 0.002Y_{23} + 54.542$$
$$(.1493) \quad (.0072) \quad (4.484) \quad R = .549$$

Both of these R-values are higher than the simple correlation coefficients ($-.24$ and $-.21$ respectively) between geographic export concentration (Y_{10}) and size (in terms of population and GNP). It is worth noting that the R-value of .549 is the highest correlation coefficient yielded by multiple-correlation analysis.

Table 28

Commodity-Export Concentration Medians (Y_9) by Size (GNP) and by Dependence on Trade (Y_{16})

DEPENDENCE ON TRADE	GNP COMMODITY-EXPORT CONCENTRATION MEDIANS			
	LOWEST THIRD	MIDDLE THIRD	HIGHEST THIRD	TOTAL
LOWEST THIRD	78.0 *Range (54.5-86.6)* n = 8	67.4 *Range 51.2-87.0)* n = 6	57.7 *Range (41.6-76.1)* n = 11	64.0 *Range (41.6-87.0* n = 25
MIDDLE THIRD	77.6 *Range (67.7-95.7)* n = 8	66.6 *Range (50.4-93.5)* n = 10	*52.8* *Range (50.5-65.5)* n = 7	67.6 *Range (50.4-95.7* n = 25
HIGHEST THIRD	*87.6* *Range (60.2-96.4)* n = 9	69.3 *Range (52.1-84.9)* n = 9	64.6 *Range (47.3-85.3)* n = 7	66.7 *Range (47.3-96.4* n = 25
TOTAL	78.9 *Range (54.5-96.4)* n = 25	67.4 *Range (51.2-93.5)* n = 25	59.9 *Range (41.6-92.1)* n = 25	66.7 *Range (41.6-96.4* n = 75

Commodity-Export Concentration Medians (Y_9) by Size (Population) and by Dependence on Trade (Y_{16})

DEPENDENCE ON TRADE	POPULATION COMMODITY-EXPORT CONCENTRATION MEDIANS			
	LOWEST THIRD	MIDDLE THIRD	HIGHEST THIRD	TOTAL
LOWEST THIRD	*81.8* *Range (62.5-86.6)* n = 4	67.4 *Range (54.5-80.1)* n = 5	63.2 *Range (41.6-87.0)* n = 16	64.0 *Range (41.6-87.0* n = 25
MIDDLE THIRD	70.2 *Range (60.1-95.7)* n = 10	59.2 *Range (52.8-93.5)* n = 6	63.3 *Range (50.5-85.6)* n = 9	67.6 *Range (50.5-95.7* n = 25
HIGHEST THIRD	70.6 *Range (52.1-96.4)* n = 11	64.6 *Range (47.3-92.1)* n = 14	*Range* n = 0	66.7 *Range (47.3-96.4* n = 25
TOTAL	70.6 *Range (52.1-96.4)* n = 25	65.5 *Range (47.3-93.5)* n = 25	63.2 *Range (41.6-87.0)* n = 25	66.7 *Range (41.6-96.4* n = 75

B. *Export Concentration, Dependence on Trade, and Size*

The purpose of this section is to assess the impact of dependence-on-trade on the association between commodity export concentration and size, and between geographic export concentration and size. The analysis is also based on a cross-classification method of analysis, and on multiple-correlation analysis, with two independent variables.

Commodity export concentration medians (Y_9) classified by size (GNP and population) and by dependence on trade (Y_{16}), indicate an inverse association between size and commodity export concentration. A declining directional pattern is observed in the median values across any row, and also diagonally. No such directional pattern is observed however in the median values down any column. See Table 28 for these results. These patterns imply an inverse association between size and commodity export concentration, and also imply the absence of any association between dependence on trade and commodity export concentration. Dependence on trade has no observable impact on the association between commodity export concentration and size, since the same declining pattern is observed regardless of the degree of dependence on trade.

Results of formal multiple-correlation analysis provide similar conclusions. Multiple regression equations, with commodity export concentration (Y_9) as the dependent variable, and with size and dependence-on-trade (Y_{16}) as the independent variables, indicate an inverse association between commodity export concentration and size. The association between commodity export concentration and dependence on trade is positive when dependence on trade is paired with population (X_2), and becomes negative when dependence on trade is paired with GNP (X_1). The standard deviations of the dependence-on-trade coefficients are, however, too large to make them acceptable.

$$Y_9 = -0.028X_1 + 0.002Y_{16} + 66.891$$
$$ (.044) \qquad (.095) \qquad (5.82) \qquad R = .084$$
$$Y_9 = -0.162X_2 - 0.113Y_{16} + 76.383$$
$$ (.045) \qquad (.092) \qquad (5.05) \qquad R = .431$$

The first R-value is nearly zero, and is not much higher than the value of the simple correlation coefficient $(-.03)$ between commodity export concentration and size. Dependence-on-trade, in other words, has no impact on the nature of the association between commodity export concentration and size (in terms of population). When dependence on trade is paired with GNP a higher R-value (.431) is yielded. Taking both results together, one can suggest that the degree of dependence on trade does not seem to have an appreciable influence on the nature of the association (if any) between commodity export concentration and size.

We finally consider the influence of dependence-on-trade on the association between geographic export concentration and size. Applying, first, the cross classification method of analysis to geographic export concentration, yields a similar pattern as that yielded by commodity export concentration. Geographic export concentration medians (Y_{10}) classified by size (both population and GNP) and by degree of dependence on trade (Y_{16}), indicate an inverse association between geographic export concentration and size, and no association between dependence-on-trade and geographic export concentration. In both population and GNP breakdowns, a declining directional pattern is observed in the median concentration values across any row, and also diagonally. No such pattern is, however, observed in the median values down any column. See Table 29. These patterns can be interpreted as evidence of an inverse association between size and geographic concentration of exports, and also as evidence of the lack of any association between dependence-on-trade and geographic export concentration. As with commodity export concentration, dependence on trade does not show any observable influence on the association between geographic export concentration and size. The declining pattern in the median concentration values is observed, regardless of the degree of dependence on trade.

Formal multiple-correlation analysis provides somewhat different results. Multiple regression equations, with geographic export concentration (Y_{10}) as the dependent variable, and with size and dependence-on-trade (Y_{16}) as the independent variables, yield multiple correlation coefficients (R-values of .179 and .161) that are lower than the simple correlation coefficients ($-.24$ and $-.21$) between geographic export concentration and size yielded by simple correlation analysis.

$$Y_{10} = -0.023X_1 + 0.087Y_{16} + 38.361$$
$$\quad\quad (.036) \quad\quad (.078) \quad\quad (3.94) \quad\quad R = .179$$
$$Y_{10} = \quad 0.006X_2 + 0.099Y_{16} + 37.170$$
$$\quad\quad (.041) \quad\quad (.083) \quad\quad (4.57) \quad\quad R = .161$$

These equations also indicate a positive association between geographic export concentration and dependence on trade, although the cross-

Table 29

Country-Export Concentration Medians (Y_{10}) by Size (GNP) and by Dependence on Trade (Y_{16})

DEPENDENCE ON TRADE	GNP COUNTRY-EXPORT CONCENTRATIONS MEDIANS			
	LOWEST THIRD	MIDDLE THIRD	HIGHEST THIRD	TOTAL
LOWEST THIRD	44.6 *Range* (28.6-55.9) n = 8	40.6 *Range* (28.0-61.6) n = 8	34.3 *Range* (26.6-57.5) n = 10	40.6 *Range* (26.6-61.6) n = 26
MIDDLE THIRD	55.0 *Range* (34.9-68.6) n = 9	33.4 *Range* (26.7-66.6) n = 9	39.8 *Range* (19.9-80.2) n = 8	41.7 *Range* (19.9-80.2) n = 26
HIGHEST THIRD	44.7 *Range* (30.8-96.9) n = 9	57.5 *Range* (26.9-84.4) n = 9	32.1 *Range* (26.0-49.1) n = 7	41.0 *Range* (26.9-96.9) n = 25
TOTAL	47.6 *Range* (28.6-96.9) n = 26	41.0 *Range* (26.7-84.4) n = 26	33.6 *Range* (19.9-80.2) n = 25	40.7 *Range* (19.9-96.9) n = 77

Country-Export Concentration Medians (Y_{10}) by Size (Population) and by Dependence on Trade (Y_{16})

DEPENDENCE ON TRADE	POPULATION COUNTRY-EXPORT CONCENTRATION MEDIANS			
	LOWEST THIRD	MIDDLE THIRD	HIGHEST THIRD	TOTAL
LOWEST THIRD	46.3 *Range* (28.6-55.9) n = 4	50.2 *Range* (32.5-55.4) n = 5	34.8 *Range* (26.6-61.6) n = 16	41.0 *Range* (26.6-61.6) n = 25
MIDDLE THIRD	53.0 *Range* (31.0-68.6) n = 10	40.7 *Range* (27.7-47.4) n = 7	26.7 *Range* (19.9-80.2) n = 9	41.7 *Range* (19.9-80.2) n = 26
HIGHEST THIRD	44.7 *Range* (30.6-96.9) n = 11	39.8 *Range* (26.0-73.6) n = 14	35.1 n = 1	20.2 *Range* (26.0-96.9) n = 26
TOTAL	47.7 *Range* (28.6-96.9) n = 25	40.7 *Range* (26.0-73.6) n = 26	34.8 *Range* (19.9-80.2) n = 26	40.7 *Range* (19.9-96.9) n = 77

classification method of analysis failed to provide such evidence. Thus, when size (both X_1 and X_2) was paired with dependence-on-trade, the R-values became lower than the simple correlation coefficients with size as the only independent variable. It seems, then, that the degree of dependence on trade does have some influence on the association between geographic export concentration and size. This suggestion should also be taken cautiously since the standard deviations of the dependence-on-trade coefficients are as large as the coefficients themselves, and the positive association, therefore, between dependence on trade and geographic concentration cannot be accepted.

To *conclude*, the three-variable analysis of export concentration, with economic development and size as the two independent variables, reveals an inverse relationship between export concentration (both commodity and geographic) and size, and also an inverse relationship between export concentration and economic development. The cross-classification method of analysis indicates that the inverse relationship between concentration (both commodity and geographic) and size is maintained regardless of the level of economic development. The multiple-correlation analysis provides the same results and also suggests that the association between export concentration and economic development is, perhaps, stronger than the association between export concentration and size.

The three-variable analysis of export concentration, with dependence-on-trade and size as the two independent variables, reveals that there is no apparent relationship between dependence-on-trade and export concentration (both commodity and geographic), and that the influence of dependence-on-trade on the association between size and export concentration cannot be discerned. The cross-classifications do not indicate any pattern between dependence-on-trade and export concentration, and the multiple-correlation analysis does not yield more significant results than those yielded by the two-variable relationships.

CHAPTER FOUR

DEPENDENCE ON TRADE AND SIZE

The economic reasons that suggest a significant inverse association between size of country and dependence on foreign trade are several. These reasons, already discussed in the literature[1], relate to the limited extent of the domestic market of small countries, and to the resulting impediments to division of labor and utilization of large-scale production; to the lack of diversity in natural resources and the resulting concentration in economic activity; and to the relatively lower transportation costs for a small country, with its small area, to and from its boundaries than for a larger country. As if to compensate for, or to take advantage of, these factors small countries invariably show a tendency to depend more heavily on international trade than large countries. An inverse association, in other words, between size of country (as represented by population size and GNP size) and degree of dependence on foreign trade, is generally expected to exist.

Empirical illustrations supporting this inverse association have already been provided by Kuznets. One such illustration relates imports and exports to national income plus imports for each of fifty-three countries for the year 1938-39. The rank correlation between size of country, as measured by population, and the ratio of exports to total product plus imports is —0.44; that between population size and the import ratio is —0.56. Both coefficients are statistically significant at a demanding level of confidence, and suggest that, by and large, the smaller the country, the larger the ratio of exports or imports to total product.[2] Another illustration is also provided by Kuznets and derived from data prepared by Woytinsky[3] on per capita income and per capita foreign trade for sixty countries, for the year 1949. By arranging the thirty countries with the higher per capita incomes by decreasing size of population, and averaging the per capita incomes and the per capita foreign trade levels for successive groups of five countries, Kuznets

---

[1] See Simon Kuznets, "Economic Growth of Small Nations", *op. cit.*; and Charles P. Kindleberger, *Foreign Trade and the National Economy*, New Haven, Yale University Press, 1962, pp. 32-36.

[2] Simon Kuznets, "Economic Growth of Small Nations," *op. cit.*, p. 19.

[3] See W.S. & E.S. Woytinsky, *World Commerce and Governments*, Twentieth Century Fund, 1955, Table 25.

found out that "with one exception, the ratio of foreign trade to national income rises as the average size of population declines—and the
result would be the same if foreign trade were related to national income or to gross national product plus imports." It was also found
that "there is no clear association between the ratio of foreign trade
to income and per capita income."[1] Calculating the same ratio for the
thirty countries with lower per capita income, most of them underdeveloped, gives also the same relationship, namely, a rise in the ratio
of foreign trade to national income as population size declines. But
it was observed that the association is not as regular and the range not
as pronounced as among the more developed countries. This finding
suggests that foreign trade by the less developed countries is subject
to the more accidental influences of availability of world-wide marketable resources, and thus some of the larger nations, as a result, may
be as heavily engaged in foreign trade as, or even more than, the
smaller units.[2] It also suggests an important qualification to the association between size and dependence on foreign trade. As is the case
with the relation between size and commodity and geographic concentration of exports, it seems that the effect of 'size' on dependence
on foreign trade is relatively unimportant among the under-developed
countries. One can argue, on the basis of these results, that it is not
'size' which is the important determinant of the degree of dependence
on foreign trade; it is rather the level of the country's economic development. It is thus possible for some of the large (underdeveloped)
countries to be equally and/or more dependent on foreign trade than
the small (underdeveloped) countries.

Another important qualification suggested by similar findings is
that there may be an upper limit beyond which the degree of dependence on foreign trade stops to increase despite a decline in population size. This is evident in the foreign trade ratios, also prepared by
Kuznets[3] for two different time periods (1938-39 and 1950-54), where
the rise in these ratios associated with a decline in population size

---

[1] Simon Kuznets, *op. cit.*, pp. 19-20. For a summary of findings refer to Table
1(A), p. 19.

[2] *Ibid.*, p. 20 Table 1(B) gives summary of calculations.

[3] See his *Six Lectures on Economic Growth*, Illinois, The Free Press of Glencoe,
1959, Table 10, p. 96. The foreign trade ratio for each country was calculated by
dividing the sum of commodity exports and imports by the sum of national income
and imports (all in current prices), and then the ratios for the separate countries
were averaged (unweighted arithmetic means) for the successive countries in the
arrays.

ceases once the ratios reach certain high levels. In the 1938-39 period, for example, the highest ratio of 0.38 is reached for the group of countries with an average population of 3.7 million, and the ratio remains the same, even though average population drops to 1.5 millions. This pattern is more strongly revealed in the 1950-1954 data, where the average foreign trade ratio reaches a maximum of 0.41 for the group of countries with an average population of 10.4 million, and remains the same even when the average population per country drops to 0.8 million. Such results have prompted Kuznets to conclude: "Apparently, under prevailing political, institutional, and economic conditions the proportion of total available product that can be secured from foreign trade has an upper limit and the proportion of output that must be secured from sources within the domestic boundaries has a corresponding lower limit."[1] If true, this generalization would imply that small countries cannot rely indefinitely on foreign trade as an escape from their 'smallness'. There seems to be a limit to the amount of goods and services that can be made available to a country through international trade. Once this limit is reached, the desired goods and services, if to be obtained at all, would have to come from domestic sources.

This chapter, in its two parts, is an attempt to find out the extent to which these generalizations and qualifications are true, and to provide more extensive evidence on the direction and magnitude of the association between dependence on trade and size of country. The *first* part, which involves a two-variable analysis, interprets the nature of the association between size and dependence on trade. Simple correlation anlysis will again be utilized, with population and GNP (representing size of country) as the independent variables, and the indices measuring the degree of dependence on trade as the dependent variables. The dependent variables will also be ranked with reference to population and GNP, i.e., countries will be grouped in quartiles, and the medians for the quartiles of the countries ranked in increasing order of size, will indicate whether any systematic relationship exists between size of country and dependence on trade. The *second* part involves three-variable relationships and utilizes, also, two methods of analysis—a cross-classification method of analysis, and formal multiple-correlation analysis, with two independent variables. This part has the purpose of investigating whether the association between depen-

---

[1] *Ibid.*, p. 98.

dence-on-trade and size of country is influenced by economic growth and development. Indices measuring dependence-on-trade are the dependent variables, and size and economic growth, or size and economic development, are the two independent variables.

1. Two-Variable Analysis: Patterns and Correlations

Three different aspects of involvement in international trade are considered—Foreign trade (exports and imports of goods and services) proportions; Export proportions; and foreign capital and donations proportions.[1] Five variables are used as indicators of these aspects of dependence on trade. Two variables measure the foreign trade proportions, one measures the export proportions, and two measure the capital and donations proportions. Each one of the three aspects will be separately analyzed. Simple correlations between these five dependence-on-trade variables and size of country represented by population and GNP, and comparisons of the median dependence-on-trade for the quartiles of the countries ranked with reference to size, will help in interpreting the significance of the association between size of country and degree of dependence on foreign trade.

A. Foreign Trade Proportions and Size

Does the size of a country have any effect on the proportions of foreign trade to national product? Is there any systematic association between size of country and foreign trade proportions? Do the facts support the view that this proportion is expected to rise as size of country declines? Two indices measuring foreign trade proportions are used, and both are correlated to size of country in terms of population size and GNP size. The first index (Y_{16}) expresses exports plus imports (both goods and services) of a sample of eighty countries as a percentage of gross national product. The second (Y_{17}) expresses the same exports plus imports per capita. Values of these indices (prepared by Coppock) are given in columns Y_{16} and Y_{17} of Appendix Table 1.

The correlation coefficient (r) between foreign trade as percent of GNP (Y_{16}) and population (X_2) is $+.01$, and between the same index (Y_{16}) and GNP (X_1) is $-.34$. The scatter diagrams of Figure 16 show these relations. One of the coefficients is positive and approximately

---

[1] These proportions are explained later on in this chapter and in Appendix B.

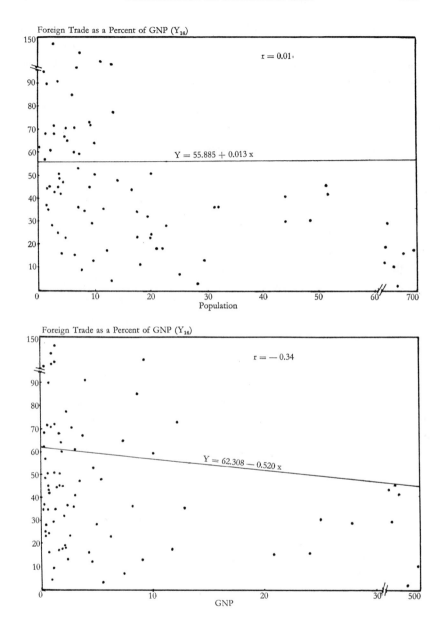

Figure 16
Scatter diagrams: Foreign trade proportions and size

zero and can thus be ignored, but the other index (when size is represented by GNP) is relatively high, and can be taken with confidence since it is significant at both the .05 and .01 levels. So only in this latter case can it be claimed, with reasonable amount of confidence, that there is an inverse association between foreign trade proportions (i.e., trade as % of GNP) and country size. When size is represented by population no association exists.

The rankings of the median foreign trade proportions, provide some evidence of a tendency of foreign trade proportions to decrease as country size increases, i.e., of an inverse association between size of country and foreign trade proportions. When the eighty countries are ranked in increasing order of population size, the median foreign trade proportion (Y_{16}) is 53.8 for the first quartile, 56.4 for the second, 35.2 for the third, and 18.5 for the fourth. The second quartile has a slightly higher median proportion than the first quartile, but the last two quartiles (and particularly the fourth) have significantly lower medians than the first two. An unsteady declining trend between foreign trade ratios and population size is thus observed. When the eighty countries are ranked in increasing order of GNP size, a similar pattern is revealed. The median foreign trade proportion (Y_{16}) is 44.0 for the first quartile, 45.0 for the second, 38.7 for the third, and 32.9 for the fourth. The first two quartiles have almost the same median ratios, but the third and fourth quartiles show respectively lower medians. Thus the inverse association between foreign trade proportions and GNP size is also observed. The median foreign trade ratios tend to decline as GNP size increases. Table 30 shows these relations.

Correlation analysis and the rankings of the median foreign trade proportions do not provide unqualified support for the claim that foreign trade proportions (exports plus imports of goods and services as percent of GNP) tend to decline as country size (represented by both population and GNP) increases. The inverse association (revealed by formal correlation analysis) is statistically significant and can be taken with reasonable confidence only when size is represented by GNP. The correlation coefficient shows the wrong sign and is approximately zero when population is used for size. And the rankings of the median trade proportions for both measures of size observe only an unsteady declining tendency.

When the second index (Y_{17}) is used, the results are not any more significant, and the claim for an inverse relationship between foreign trade involvement and size of country does not find any support. The

Table 30

Relation between Size of Country (Population, GNP) and Foreign Trade as %
of GNP (Y₁₆)

GROUPS OF COUNTRIES *Countries Ranked in Increasing Order of Population Size (Quartiles)*	*Number of Countries*	*Average Population (millions)*	*Median Foreign Trade Ratio*
I	20	2.23	53.8
II	20	6.29	56.4
III	20	14.23	35.2
IV	20	105.01	18.5
Countries Ranked in Increasing Order of GNP Size (Quartiles)	*Number of Countries*	*Average GNP ($ billions)*	*Median Foreign Trade Ratio*
I	20	0.425	44.0
II	20	1.365	45.0
III	20	3.615	38.7
IV	20	51.96	32.9

correlation coefficient (r) between foreign trade per capita (Y_{17}) and population (X_2) is —.06, and between the same index (Y_{17}) and GNP (X_1) is +.03. Figure 17 shows these relations. One of these coefficients is negative and one is positive, and both are very low and cannot be taken with any confidence. Contrary to expectations, therefore, the association between foreign trade ratios (per capita) and size of country is almost nonexistent. It should be remembered that the correlation coefficient between foreign trade per capita and GNP size is positive. While one cannot place any confidence in such a low coefficient, it nevertheless suggests that foreign trade per capita does not decrease as GNP size increases. Small countries (in terms of GNP size) do not necessarily have higher foreign trade per capita ratios than large countries.

The rankings of the median foreign trade per capita ratios reveal the same pattern of association as in the correlation analysis. When the eighty-three countries are ranked in increasing order of population size, the median foreign trade per capita (Y_{17}) is 111.5 for the first quartile, 146.0 for the second, 91.3 for the third, and 43.4 for the fourth. The second quartile has a higher median foreign trade ratio than the first quartile, but the last two quartiles have lower medians,

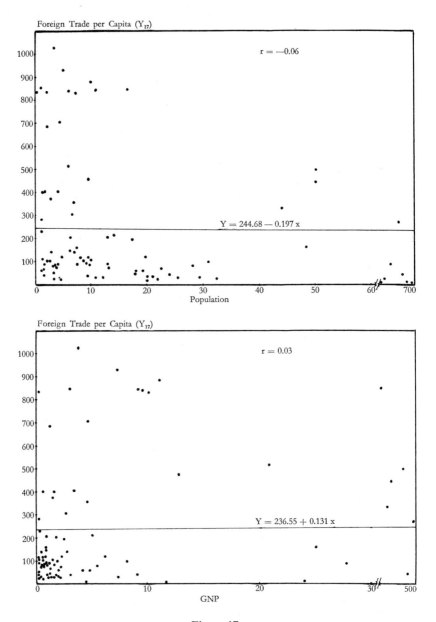

Figure 17
Scatter diagrams: Foreign trade per capita and size.

respectively, than the first two quartiles. The trend is not systematic, but a declining tendency can be observed. Foreign trade per capita ratios tend to decrease as population size increases. When the countries (80 out of 83) are ranked in increasing order of GNP size, a positive unsteady association is revealed between foreign trade (per capita) ratios and GNP size. The median foreign trade per capita (Y_{17}) is 97.9 for the first quartile, 92.4 for the second, 119.9 for the third, and 389.4 for the fourth. The median ratio of the second quartile is slightly lower than the first quartile, but the medians of the last two quartiles (and particularly the fourth) are, respectively, higher than the medians of the first two quartiles. Foreign trade per capita ratios show an unsteady increasing tendency, but nevertheless a tendency, to increase as GNP size increases. This is contrary to a priori reasoning, and does not support the contention, already referred to, that small countries generally have a higher dependence on foreign trade. These results are summarized in Table 31.

Formal correlation analysis and the rankings of the median foreign trade per capita fail to indicate a consistent association between foreign trade per capita and size of country. Results of correlation analysis are not significant, and median analysis reveals two tendencies: a tendency

Table 31

Relation between Size of Country (Population, GNP) and Foreign Trade per Capita (Y_{17})

GROUPS OF COUNRTIES Countries Ranked in Increasing Order of Population Size (Quartiles)	Number of Countries	Average Population (millions)	Median Foreign Trade Capita
I	21	2.05	111.5
II	21	6.17	146.0
III	21	14.06	91.3
IV	20	105.01	43.4
Countries Ranked in Increasing Order of GNP Size (Quartiles)	Number of Countries	Average GNP ($ billions)	Median Foreign Trade per Capita
I	20	0.425	97.9
II	20	1.365	92.4
III	20	3.615	119.9
IV	20	51.96	389.4

of foreign trade per capita to increase as GNP size increases, and a tendency of foreign trade per capita to decrease as population size increases. One cannot claim, therefore, that there is an inverse relationship between foreign trade per capita and country size. In fact a tendency of foreign trade per capita to increase as GNP size increases is observed. Hence, it can be claimed, at least, that small countries (in terms of GNP size) do not necessarily have higher foreign trade per capita ratios than large countries.

Comparisons of the median foreign trade proportions (both Y_{16} and Y_{17}) for the quartiles of the countries ranked with reference to size may be adequate to reveal the nature of the directional pattern that exists between size and foreign trade proportions. They do not suffice, however, to verify the Kuznets contention that there may be an upper limit beyond which the degree of dependence on foreign trade stops to increase despite of decline in population size. Countries were, for this purpose arrayed (in descending order of population size) in

Table 32

Relation between Size of Country (Population) and Foreign Trade Proportions (Y_{16}, Y_{17})

Countries Ranked in Descending Order of Population Size	Number of Countries	Average Population (millions)	Average Foreign Trade Ratio (Y_{16})
I	10	181.9	0.22
II	10	28.1	0.23
III	10	17.7	0.30
IV	10	10.8	0.56
V	10	7.6	0.60
VI	10	5.0	0.49
VII	10	3.1	0.62
VIII	10	1.4	0.57
Countries Ranked in Descending Order of Population Size	Number of Countries	Average Population (millions)	Average Foreign Trade Per Capita (Y_{17})
I	13	148.2	154
II	10	23.3	48
III	10	15.5	182
IV	10	9.8	278
V	10	7.0	287
VI	10	4.5	430
VII	10	2.7	271
VIII	10	1.2	298

eight groups, and the ratios (both the foreign trade ratio and the foreign trade per capita) for the separate countries were averaged (unweighted arithmetic means) for the successive groups of countries in the arrays. Table 32 shows the results. Both of these ratios do not fail to indicate the tendency of small countries to depend more heavily on trade. The average foreign trade ratio (Y_{16}) for example, rises steadily from 0.22 to 0.60 as the average population per country falls from 181.9 million to 7.6 million. The same is also true of the average foreign trade per capita ratio (Y_{17}). With one exception, the trade per capita ratio rises from \$ 154 to \$ 430 as the average population per country declines from 148 million to 4.5 million. It is, nevertheless, evident from both of these ratios that the increase in the degree of dependence on trade associated with a decline in population size stops once the ratios reach a certain maximum level. The average foreign trade ratio (Y_{16}) reaches the high level of 0.60 for the group of countries with an average population of 7.6. Beyond this level, the ratio does not follow a rising trend; in fact, it decreases slightly to 0.57 despite the drop in the average population to 1.4 million. A similar pattern is also revealed by the average foreign trade per capita ratio (Y_{17}). This ratio reaches a maximum of \$ 430 for the group of countries with an average population of 4.5 million, and then declines when the average population declines 1.2 million. While crude, these results do provide some support for the generalization that there is an upper limit to the total available product that can be secured from foreign trade. The inverse relationship between size of country and dependence on trade ceases once the foreign trade proportions of a country reach certain high levels.

B. *Export Proportions and Size*

The association between foreign trade proportions and country size did not turn out to be as strong as one would have expected. Foreign trade proportions did show a general tendency to decline as country size, particularly population, increases. The inverse correlation coefficients, however, were not all statistically significant, and in one case a positive tendency was even observed. It is, perhaps, more likely that export proportions alone would correlate better with size of country than did foreign trade proportions. In can be argued, for example, that foreign trade proportions which include both exports and imports are not significantly related to size because imports are not significantly

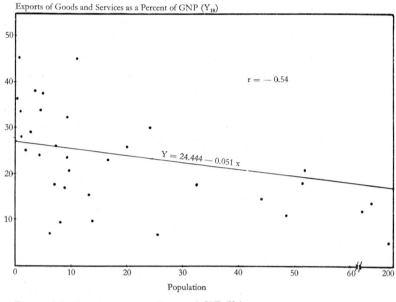

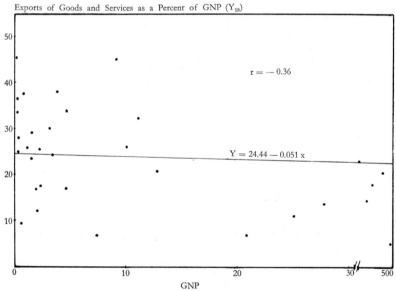

Figure 18
Scatter diagrams: Export proportions and size.

related to size. Imports, perhaps, depend more on the degree of industrialization and level of economic development of the country rather than on its mere size. Export proportions, therefore, are expected to be more strongly associated with size of country than are foreign trade proportions. The a priori case for an inverse association between export proportions and size seems convincing.

To measure the magnitude of the association between exports and country size, the index expressing the exports of goods and services as percent of gross national product is correlated to size of country as represented by both population and GNP. This index (Y_{18}) is the unweighted averages of the ratios of exports of goods and services to gross national product for the years 1950-1956. Values of these ratios, computed by Michaely for a sample of thirty-two countries, are given in column Y_{18} of Appendix Table 1.

The correlation coefficient (r) between exports as percent of GNP (Y_{18}) and population (X_2) is —.54, and between the same index (Y_{18}) and GNP (X_1) is —.36. The scatter diagrams of Figure 18 show these relationships. Both coefficients, as anticipated, are negative and quite high. In fact, the correlation coefficient (—.54) between export ratios and population size is the highest correlation coefficient found in measuring the association between size of country and any single dependent variable considered in this investigation. This coefficient is significant at the .05 and .01 levels, and the coefficient between export ratios and GNP size is significant at the .05 level. One can say, therefore, with reasonable confidence, that size of country (particularly when represented by population size) and export proportions are inversely related to each other. There is a strong tendency for export proportions (i.e., exports of goods and services as percent of GNP) to decrease as country size increases. This tendency, it needs scarcely be repeated, is appreciably stronger than the tendency for the foreign trade proportions (both exports and imports) to decrease as country size increases. Such a difference implies that the association between import proportions and size of country is fairly weak.

The rankings of the median proportions reveal, as in the formal correlation analysis, the same inverse association between exports of goods and services as percent of GNP and size of country in terms of both population and GNP. When the thirty-two countries are ranked in increasing order of population size, the median export ratio (Y_{18}) is 31.4 for the first quartile, 21.8 for the second, 23.2 for the third, and 14.1 for the fourth. Thus a declining trend is indicated. The pattern is not very systematic. The third quartile has a slightly higher median export ratio than the second quartile, but the first quartile has the highest median and the fourth quartile the lowest. The inverse pattern between export proportions and population size is nevertheless observed. When the same countries are ranked in increasing order of GNP size, a similar pattern is revealed. The median export ratio (Y_{18}) is 25.6 for the first quartile, 20,5 for the second, 29.1 for the third, and 14.1 for the fourth. A declining (but not systematic) tendency is indicated. The fourth quartile has the lowest median export ratio, and the second quartile has the lower median than the first quartile, but the third quartile has a higher median than the first two quartiles. Table 33 gives these relations. The inverse association between export ratios and GNP size is apparent.

Table 33

Relation between Size of Country (Population, GNP) and Exports of Goods and Services as % of GNP (Y_{18})

GROUPS OF COUNTRIES Countries Ranked in Increasing Order of Population Size (Quartiles)	Number of Countries	Average Population (millions)	Median Goods & Services Export Ratio
I	8	1.93	31.4
II	8	7.03	21.8
III	8	16.16	23.2
IV	8	71.93	14.1
Countries Ranked in Increasing Order of GNP Size (Quartiles)	Number of Countries	Average GNP ($ billions)	Median Goods & Services Export Ratio
I	8	0.45	25.6
II	8	2.25	20.5
III	8	7.98	29.1
IV	8	88.41	14.1

Both correlation analysis and the rankings of the median export ratios (and particularly the former) indicate a significant inverse association between export proportions and size of country in terms of population and GNP. Small countries, in other words, are expected to have higher export ratios than large countries. This result is understandable since small countries may find it necessary to rely more heavily on exports as an escape from their smallness and as a compensation for their limited domestic markets.

C. *Foreign Capital Proportions and Size*

Do small countries also show a tendency to depend more heavily than large countries on foreign capital and donations? Are there e-conomic reasons that suggest a relationship between size of country and extent of dependence on foreign capital and donations? If small countries are likely to rely more heavily on foreign trade, and if, as a result of this trade involvement, they tend to depend on foreign capital and donations to finance their trade, then one can argue for an inverse association between foreign capital and donations proportions and size of country. The larger the country, the less would be the need to depend on foreign capital and donations.

Do the facts support this line of argument? In order to measure the degree of dependence on foreign capital and donations, and to inter-pret the association between foreign capital proportions and size of country, two indices were constructed and each separately correlated to size of country in terms of both population and GNP. The first index (Y_{19}) expresses foreign capital as percent of gross national product; it is the unweighted averages for the years 1953-1958 of the ratios of foreign capital (private capital and official and banking long-term cap-ital) to gross national product. The second index (Y_{20}) expresses both foreign capital and donations as percent of GNP; it is also the un-weighted averages for the same period of the ratios of foreign capital donations (private and official) to gross national product. The values of these indices, computed for a sample of sixty-five countries, are given in columns Y_{19} and Y_{20} of Appendix Table 1.

The correlation coefficient (r) between foreign capital as percent of GNP (Y_{19}) and population (X_2) is $-.20$, and between the same index (Y_{19}) and GNP (X_1) is $-.19$. The scatter diagrams of Figure 19 show these relations. Both coefficients are negative and of similar strength, and both suggest that there is a tendency for foreign capital propor-tions to decline as country size increases. Both coefficients, however, cannot be taken with much confidence since both of them are below the .05 level of significance. These results suggest, therefore, that the dependence of small countries on foreign capital is not as pronounced as their dependence on exports.

The rankings of the median foreign capital proportions indicate

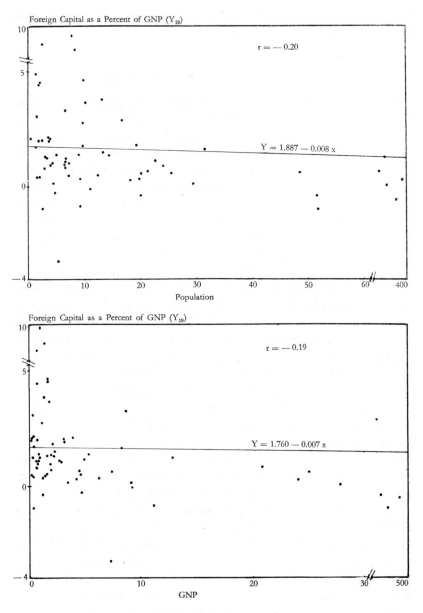

Figure 19
Scatter diagrams: Foreign capital proportions and size.

the same inverse pattern between foreign capital and size of country in terms of both population and GNP. When the sixty-five countries are ranked in increasing order of population size, the median foreign capital ratio (Y_{19}) is 2.01 for the first quartile, 1.04 for the second, 1.66 for the third, and 0.58 for the fourth. Thus a declining trend (though not systematic) is observed. The third quartile has a slightly higher median ratio than the second quartile, but the first quartile has the highest median, and the fourth quartile the lowest. An inverse association between foreign capital proportions and population size can be thus inferred. When the same countries are ranked in increasing order of GNP size, a steady declining pattern is revealed. The median foreign capital ratio (Y_{19}) is 1.87 for the first quartile, 1.36 for the second, 1.24 for the third, and 0.33 for the fourth. The inverse association between foreign capital ratios and GNP size is readily apparent. Foreign capital proportions tend to decline as GNP size increases. Table 34 gives these relations.

Formal correlation analysis and the rankings of the median foreign capital proportions both indicate an inverse pattern between size of country (as represented either by population or GNP) and foreign capital as percent of GNP. The degree of dependence on foreign capital tends to decrease as size of country increases. Small countries show a

Table 34

Relation between Size of Country (Population, GNP) and Foreign Capital as % of GNP (Y_{19})

GROUPS OF COUNTRIES *Countries Ranked in Increasing Order of Population Size (Quartiles)*	*Number of Countries*	*Average Population (millions)*	*Median Foreign Capital Ratio*
I	16	1.94	2.01
II	16	5.43	1.04
III	16	12.02	1.66
IV	17	69.99	0.58
Countries Ranked in Increasing Order of GNP Size	*Number of Countries*	*Average GNP ($ billions)*	*Median Foreign Capital Ratio*
I	16	0.40	1.87
II	16	1.32	1.36
III	16	3.46	1.24
IV	17	44.85	0.33

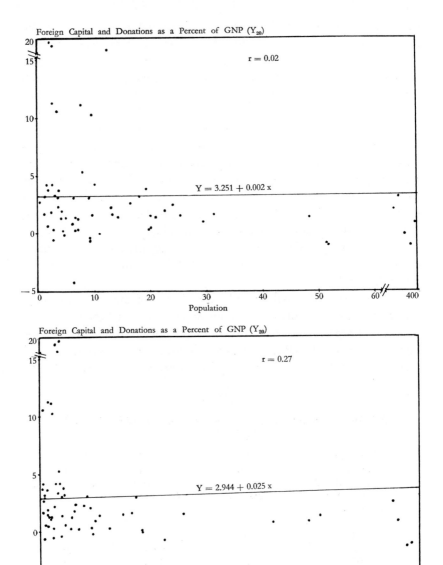

Figure 20
Scatter diagrams: Foreign capital and donations proportions and size.

tendency to depend somewhat more heavily than large countries on foreign capital. It should be cautioned, however, that the correlation coefficients, while negative, are not statistically significant and cannot be taken with much confidence, and that the median anlysis does not indicate a steady declining pattern. It can be suggested, therefore, that the tendency of small countries to depend more heavily than large countries on foreign capital is not as pronounced and as apparent as their tendency to depend on exports.

When the second index (Y_{20}), representing the dependence on foreign capital and donations is used, different results are yielded. The inverse pattern disappears. The correlation coefficient (r) between foreign capital and donations as percent of GNP (Y_{20}) and population (X_2) is $+.02$, and between the same index (Y_{20}) and GNP (X_1) is $+.27$. The scatter diagrams of Figure 20 show these relations. Both coefficients are no longer negative. The former is too low to be taken with any confidence, but the latter is significant at the .05 level and hence can be taken with some confidence. This result suggests that there is a tendency for capital and donations proportions to increase (and not to decrease) as size of country (in terms of GNP) increases. This implies, since Y_{20} includes both foreign capital and *donations* for the same sample of countries, that the association between donations and size of country, unlike the association between foreign capital and size of country, is more likely to be positive rather than negative. This is an interesting proposition, and the a priori case for it appears, perhaps, convincing if one does not abstract from the non-economic (mainly political and strategic) factors that generally govern the behavior of foreign aid.

The rankings of the median capital and donations ratios do not indicate any systematic pattern between capital and donations proportions and size of country in terms of population and GNP. When the countries (63 of the 65) are ranked in increasing order of population size, the median capital and donations ratio (Y_{20}) is 3.32 for the first quartile, 1.30 for the second, 2.41 for the third, and 1.40 for the fourth. Thus no steady directional tendency is revealed. The first quartile has the highest median, and the fourth quartile has a lower median than the third, but the second quartile has the lowest median of all. This absence of a clear trend, since an inverse pattern between capital proportions (only) and size of country has already been suggested, is further evidence of the weak association between donations and country size as represented by population. When the same countries are ranked in increasing order of GNP size, a non-consistent yet declining pattern is revealed. The median capital and donations ratio (Y_{20}) is 2.89 for the first quartile, 3.82 for the second, 1.88 for the third, and 0.90 for the fourth. The second quartile has a higher median than the first quartile, but the last two quartiles have consecutively lower medians than the first two quartiles. Unlike correlation analysis which yielded a rather significant positive association between capital and donations ratios and GNP size, median analysis indicates an unsteady declining tendency. Table 35 shows these relations.

Table 35

Relation between Size of Country (Population, GNP) and Foreign Capital and Donations as % of GNP (Y_{20})

GROUPS OF COUNTRIES Countries Ranked in Increasing Order of Population Size (Quartiles)	Number of Countries	Average Population (millions)	Median Foreign Capital & Donations Ratio
I	16	1.94	3.32
II	16	5.62	1.30
III	16	12.76	2.41
IV	15	71.94	1.40
Countries Ranked in Increasing Order of GNP Size (Quartiles)	*Number of Countries*	*Average GNP ($ billions)*	*Median Foreign Capital & Donations Ratio*
I	16	0.40	2.89
II	16	1.32	3.82
III	16	3.46	1.88
IV	15	48.49	0.90

Correlation analysis and the rankings of the median foreign capital and donations proportions do not suggest that small countries are likely to rely more heavily than large countries on foreign capital and donations. The median analysis does not reveal any clear pattern, and the correlation analysis, in one case, suggests the opposite, namely, a positive association between foreign capital and donations proportions and country size. In view of previous results, this further suggests a relatively more significant association between dependence on foreign donations and country size.

2. THREE-VARIABLE ANALYSIS: CROSS-CLASSIFICATIONS AND CORRELATIONS

It has been contended that the association between dependence on trade and size of country is not as significant nor as consistent among the underdeveloped countries as it is among the developed countries. This implies that the impact of 'size' on the degree of dependence on trade is relatively unimportant among the underdeveloped countries. and suggests, therefore, that a country's level of economic development (and possibly rate of economic growth) should be given due consideration when interpreting the association between dependence on trade and size of country. It is possible for the level of economic development to have such an influence on the degree of dependence on foreign trade as to offset the association between dependence on trade and size. It can be argued, for example, that a significant positive association between economic development and dependence on trade (i.e., an increase in the level of development leading to an increase in the degree of dependence on trade) may make it possible for large developed countries to have higher trade proportions then small but less developed countries. Or it could also be argued, if the association between size and dependence on trade is not reliable among the underdeveloped countries, that some of the large underdeveloped countries may be equally, or even more, dependent on foreign trade than some of the small underdeveloped countries. In either case, the inverse association between dependence on trade and size would have been altered.

The purpose of this part, then, is to find out whether the (direction or magnitude of the) association between size and dependence on trade, described in the first part of this chapter, is affected by the level of economic development and the rate of economic growth. Multivariant analysis, with dependence-on-trade as the dependent variable, and with size and economic development, or with size and economic growth as the two independent variables, will help provide an answer to this question. As in other chapters, two methods of analysis are used: a cross-classification method of analysis, and multiple-correlation analysis, with two independent variables. One measure of dependence-on-trade, foreign trade as percent of GNP (Y_{16}), is selected for this purpose[1] and is separately related to size of country (population

---

[1] Other measures of dependence-on-trade, e.g., Y_{18}, achieved better results in the two-variable analysis. Y_{16} is however chosen because it represents a larger sample of eighty countries.

and GNP) and degree of economic development (Y_{23}), and to size of country and rate of economic growth (Y_{21}). The relationship between dependence-on-trade, economic development, and size is analyzed first.

A. *Dependence on Trade, Economic Development, and Size*

This is mainly an analysis of the impact of the level of economic development on the association between dependence on trade and size of country. Dependence-on-trade medians (Y_{16}) classified by size of country (both population and GNP) and by economic development

Table 36

Dependence on Trade Medians (Y_{16}) by Size (GNP) and by Degree of Development (Y_{23})

	Small Countries	*Large Countries*	TOTAL
Underdeveloped Countires	50.7 *Range* (29.0-98.9) n = 12	28.1 *Range* (15.5-28.8) n = 3	48.4 *Range* (15.5-98.9) n = 15
Developed Countries	68.2 *Range* (60.8-127.4) n = 3	44.8 *Range* (23.1-100.6) n = 12	53.3 *Range* (23.1-127.4) n = 15
TOTAL	57.1 *Range* (29.0-127.4) n = 15	41.9 *Range* (15.5-100.6) n = 15	49.4 *Range* (15.5-127.4) n = 30

Dependence on Trade Medians (Y_{16}) by Size (Population) and by Degree of Development (Y_{23})

	Small Countries	*Large Countries*	TOTAL
Underdeveloped Countries	46.6 *Range* (15.5-95.0) n = 8	40.4 *Range* (28.1-98.9) n = 8	46.6 *Range* (15.5-98.9) n = 16
Developed Countries	68.2 *Range* (53.3-127.4) n = 7	41.9 *Range* (23.1-100.6) n = 7	57.0 *Range* (23.1-127.4) n = 17
TOTAL	60.8 *Range* (15.5-127.4) n = 15	41.9 *Range* (23.1-100.6) n = 15	49.4 *Range* (15.5-127.4) n = 30

(Y_{23}), reveal an inverse association between size and dependence on trade, and a positive association between economic development and dependence on trade. Table 36 shows these results. The dependence-on-trade medians decrease as size increases, and they increase as development increases. The 'small' countries repeatedly show higher dependence on trade medians than the 'large' countries, and the 'developed' countries show higher dependence on trade medians than the 'underdeveloped' countries. This pattern is equally apparent with both population and GNP breakdowns. On account of the inverse association between size and dependence on trade, and the positive association between economic development and dependence on trade, the category of 'small-developed' countries shows the highest dependence on trade median, and the category of 'large-underdeveloped' countries shows the lowest dependence on trade median. This pattern is observed in both population and GNP breakdowns. Also observed is the inverse association between size and dependence on trade regardless of the level of economic development. The inverse association between size and dependence on trade is revealed by moving horizontally across 'rows' of equal levels of development (true for both population and GNP), and also by moving diagonally (true for both population and GNP). The inverse association between size and dependence on trade does not change with the level of economic development. 'Small' countries, whether 'developed' or 'underdeveloped', show higher dependence on trade medians than 'large' countries. It could have been possible, for example, for the category of 'large-developed' countries to have a higher dependence on trade median than the category of the 'small-underdeveloped' countries, and thus the inverse association between size and dependence on trade would have been offset. The cross-classifications do not indicate such a result, which means that the positive association between economic development and dependence on trade is not significant enough to alter the inverse association between size and dependence on trade.[1] This conclusion does not support the contention, already referred to, that it is possible for the level of economic development to offset the inverse association between

---

[1] That the association between development and dependence on trade is not as strong as the association between size and dependence on trade is also implied in the following observation: The positive association between development and dependence on trade is revealed, in the cross-classifications, by moving vertically and by moving diagonally in southwesterly direction, but *not* by moving in southeasterly direction. This pattern is observed in both population and GNP breakdowns.

size and dependence on trade. Nor do these cross-classifications support the argument that the association between size and dependence on trade is neither regular nor significant among the underdeveloped countries. The impact of 'size' on dependence on trade does not seem to be any different among countries of different levels of development.

Formal multiple-correlation analysis, with size and economic development as the two independent variables, seems to provide similar results. Multiple regression equations, given below, show an inverse association between dependence-on-trade (Y_{16}) and size of country (X_1 and X_2), and a positive association between dependence-on-trade (Y_{16}) and economic development (Y_{23}):

$$Y_{16} = -0.7555X_1 + 0.0164Y_{23} + 54.7130$$
$$\qquad (.328) \qquad (.013) \qquad (6.01) \qquad R = .412$$
$$Y_{16} = -0.5216X_2 + 0.0035Y_{23} + 61.5769$$
$$\qquad (.232) \qquad (.011) \qquad (6.94) \qquad R = .404$$

The positive association between dependence-on-trade and economic development is very weak, and both Y_{23} coefficients are not acceptable since the standard deviations are at least as large as the coefficients themselves. The standard deviations of the X_1 and X_2 coefficients are relatively smaller. They are not small enough to accept these coefficients too, but they are, perhaps, sufficient to suggest that the relationship between economic development and dependence on trade is too weak to have any impact on the association between dependence on trade and size.

Three-variable analysis (cross-classifications and multiple-correlations) of dependence on trade, with economic development and size as the two independent variables, suggests a very weak positive association between dependence on trade and economic development, a relatively more acceptable negative association between dependence on trade and size, and provides no support for the contention that it is possible for the country's level of economic development to offset the association between dependence on trade and size. This conclusion, to repeat, is contrary to the qualifications (referred to earlier in this chapter) suggesting either that the impact of 'size' on dependence on trade is umimportant among the underdeveloped countries, or that the association between economic development and dependence on trade could be strong enough to alter the inverse relationship between size and dependence on trade.

B. *Dependence on Trade, Economic Growth, and Size*

The same questions posed with respect to the analysis of dependence on trade, economic development, and size will be repeated here. The cross-classification method of analysis, and multiple-correlation analysis, with economic growth and size as the two independent variables, will interpret the impact of economic growth on the relationship between dependence on trade and size. This analysis, in other words, is similarly concerned with finding out whether the same association between size and dependence on trade will be maintained regardless of the country's rate of economic growth. The same (Y_{16}) of dependence on trade, and index (Y_{21}) of rate of economic growth are selected for this purpose.

Table 37

Dependence on Trade Medians (Y_{16}) by Size (GNP) and by Economic Growth (Y_{21})

	Small Countries	*Large Countries*	TOTAL
Low Economic Growth	*62.5* *Range (44.8-127.4)* n = 8	*35.5* *Range (15.5-73.5)* n = 7	*51.0* *Range (15.5-127.4)* n = 15
High Economic Growth	*48.4* *Range (29.0-98.9)* n = 7	*44.8* *Range (28.1-100.6)* n = 8	*45.9* *Range (28.1-100.6)* n = 15
TOTAL	*57.1* *Range (29.0-127.4)* n = 15	*41.9* *Range (15.5-100.6)* n = 15	*49.4* *Range (15.5-127.4)* n = 30

Dependence on Trade Medians (Y_{16}) by Size (Population) and by Economic Growth (Y_{21})

	Small Countries	*Large Countries*	TOTAL
Low Economic Growth	*67.5* *Range (15.5-127.4)* n = 8	*41.9* *Range (23.1-64.2)* n = 7	*51.0* *Range (15.5-127.4)* n = 15
High Economic Growth	*53.3* *Range (34.6-95.0)* n = 7	*36.9* *Range (28.1-100.6)* n = 8	*45.9* *Range (28.1-100.6)* n = 15
TOTAL	*60.8* *Range (15.5-127.4)* n = 15	*41.9* *Range (23.1-100.6)* n = 15	*49.4* *Range (15.5-127.4)* n = 30

Dependence-on-trade medians (Y_{16}) classified by size of country (population and GNP) and by rate of economic growth (Y_{21}), reveal an inverse pattern between size and dependence on trade, and also an inverse pattern between economic growth and dependence on trade. 'Small' countries (in terms of both population and GNP) have higher dependence-on-trade medians than 'large' countries, and countries with 'low' rates of economic growth have higher dependence-on-trade medians than countries with 'high' rates of economic growth. See Table 37. A declining directional pattern is observed in the median values across any row, down any column (with one exception), and also diagonally (in southeasterly and northeasterly directions). Regardless of the rate of economic growth, the inverse relationship between dependence on trade and size is observed. Apparently the rate of economic growth does not seem to alter the nature of the association between size of country and degree of dependence on trade.

Multiple-correlation analysis, with dependence on trade (Y_{16}) as the dependent variable, and with size $(X_1$ and $X_2)$ and economic growth (Y_{21}) as the two independent variables, also supports the same conclusion, namely, that economic growth does not seem to affect the association between size and dependence on trade. The relevant regression equations, given below, yield R-values not higher than the simple correlation coefficients between dependence on trade and size alone. When size was paired with rate of economic growth, the correlation

$$Y_{16} = -0.5173X_1 - 0.4995Y_{21} + 64.9055$$
$$\phantom{Y_{16} =} (.269) \qquad (1.79) \qquad (9.95) \qquad R = .342$$
$$Y_{16} = 0.0280X_2 - 0.6500Y_{21} + 59.0520$$
$$\phantom{Y_{16} =} (.257) \qquad (1.93) \qquad (10.36) \qquad R = .069$$

coefficients did not increase. There is, therefore, hardly any relationship between economic growth and dependence on trade. The economic growth (Y_{21}) coefficients are negative, but their standard deviations are higher than the coefficients themselves, and they cannot be accepted. Hence, economic growth does not apparently influence the relationship between dependence on trade and size of country. It should also be noted that, unlike the cross-classifications, the multiple correlations indicate a positive (not negative) association between dependence-on-trade (Y_{16}) and population (X_2). The standard deviation of this coefficient, however, is large, and this positive relationship is not statistically significant.

The three-variable analysis (cross-classification and multiple-correlations) of dependence on trade, with economic growth and size as the two independent variables, does not, therefore, suggest that the rate of economic growth has an impact on the association between dependence on trade and size. An inverse association between dependence on trade and economic growth is observed, but it is not statistically significant, and hence, it cannot influence the relationship between dependence on trade and size.

CHAPTER FIVE

ECONOMIC GROWTH, DEVELOPMENT, AND SIZE

Is the economic structure of small nations so different from those of large nations that one should, as Kuznets has asked, "devise variants of a theory of economic growth for the many small national units different from those for the few large ones"? Or can one hope to establish significant general features of modern economic growth by treating countries of different size "as comparable and equivalent units"?[1] Should one assume that "the alternatives open to small countries in the contemporary world are much more narrowly circumscribed than those open to large countries"?; and that "so much theorizing about growth... assumes a large closed economy model that it is important... to differentiate sharply between the growth process in a large closed economy and in a small open economy"?; and that "the study of development could be enriched if we make a distinction between 'large' and 'small' underdeveloped countries"?[2] Empirical evidence analyzed here may throw some light on these questions and may help assess the significance of the factor of size in economic growth and economic development.

Data on rates of economic growth over long periods compiled by François Perroux[3] demonstrate that the rate of increase of real income per head of population, in terms of ten-year averages over periods stretching generally from 1860 to 1950, does not seem to have been affected in any particular way by the size of any of the nations examined. Leduc and Weiller who analyzed these findings conclude that "It would therefore seem that the 'size of nations' cannot be considered responsible for notable differences in the observed rates of growth... and that it is quite certain that small size does not imply either slowness or irregularity of progress. Nor, on the other hand, is small size a sufficient reason for rapid and steady progress."[4] The authors also

---

[1] Simon Kuznets, *Six Lectures on Economic Growth*, Illinois, The Free Press of Glencoe, 1959, p. 90.

[2] William G. Demas, *op. cit.*, pp. 39-42.

[3] See his "Matériaux Pour une Analyse de la Croissance Economique", *Cahiers de l'I.S.E.A.*, Series de No. 8, p. 43.

[4] G. Leduc and J. Weiller, "The Size of the Economy and its Relations to Stability and Steady Progress: II," in E. A. G. Robinson, ed., *Economic Consequences of the Size of Nations, op. cit.*, pp. 204-5.

make further remarks concerning other aspects of economic growth which seem to imply that economic development has its own inevitable laws, regardless of the size of the country. They suggest, for instance, that "structural changes which accompany economic growth also seem to follow similar patterns in all countries (notably the progressive transfer of manpower from agriculture to industry and later to tertiary activities) irrespective of their size"; that "the size of a nation has nothing to do with the relative order of magnitudes as regards either the ratio of capital formation to national product or the ratio of capital stock to national product"; and that "It also seems proved—both for 'large' countries...—and for 'small' countries... that the acceleration of the rate of growth of population precedes that of the rate of increase of real *per caput* income."[1] A similar conclusion as to the significance of size in economic growth is also reached by Kuznets who suggests that "The pattern of economic growth of countries should also display, regardless of the wide difference in size, considerable similarities: a shift from agriculture toward other sectors in the economy; a shift from family and individual firms toward corporations; similar trends in the capital formation proportions; and so on"; and that while the factor of size may contribute to international differences in income levels, "it is not in and of itself so crucial that it must be included as a dominant factor in any initial review and discussion of the characteristics of modern economic growth."[2]

What does the empirical evidence analyzed in this chapter indicate? Does the size of a country have any influence on its rate of economic growth and general level of wellbeing? Is there, in other words, any significant association between the size of a country and its rate of economic growth and level of economic development? Is 'smallness' in and of itself necessarily an impediment to economic growth and progress? The two parts of this chapter are an attempt to answer these questions. The *first* part interprets the magnitude of the association between size of country and economic growth and development. Simple correlation analysis will be utilized, with size of country (represented by population and/or GNP) as the independent variable, and the indices measuring growth and development (five such indices have been chosen for this purpose) as the dependent variables. These dependent variables will also be ranked with reference to size of country to determine whether any pattern exists. Both these procedures will

---

[1] *Ibid.*, p. 206.

[2] Simon Kuznets, *Six Lectures on Economic Growth, op. cit.*, pp. 90-91.

indicate the nature and magnitude of the association between size of country and economic growth and development. The *second* part, based on three-variable relationships, examines whether the association between size of country and economic growth and development is influenced by the degree of dependence on trade and by the concentration of exports. These are relevant questions to investigate since it has been observed, in two preceding chapters, that some observable pattern exists between size of country and both dependence on trade and export concentration. For this purpose, two methods of analysis are used—a cross-classification method of analysis, and formal multiple-correlation analysis with two independent variables. Economic growth and development indices will be the dependent variables, and size and dependence on trade, or size and export concentration, will be the two independent variables.

1. Two-Variable Analysis: Patterns and Correlations

The economic development and growth variables considered here are five: two indices measure rates of economic growth, one index measures the rate of growth of export proceeds, and two indices measure levels of economic development. The association between each one of these indices and size of country in terms of population and/or GNP will be separately analyzed. Formal correlation analysis, to repeat, and comparisons of the median indices of economic growth and development for the quartiles of the countries ranked in increasing order of size of country, will be used for the purpose of interpreting the strength and direction of the association between size of country and economic growth and development. The indices measuring economic growth will be considered first.

A. *Economic Growth Rates and Size*

The purpose of this section, therefore, is to investigate whether the size of a country has any influence on the rate of economic growth. It will try to find out whether the rate of economic growth changes with a change in the size of country, and, more specifically, whether small size constitutes an impediment to economic progress. The indices considered here are three. The first (Y_{21}) is the percent increase in GNP per year, i.e., average annual rates of growth of gross national product for the years 1951 to 1957, adjusted for price changes for each of thirty countries. The second index (Y_{22}) is the average increase in per capita GNP per year for the years 1951 to 1957, in absolute terms (U.S. Dollars), also adjusted for price changes for each of thirty-one countries. The third (Y_{25}) which measures the growth of exports may not be an economic growth index proper. It is the logarithmic rates of growth of exports, i.e., slope of least-squares line through logarithms of annual export proceeds of each of eighty-three countries for the years 1946 to 1958. The values of these three indices computed by Coppock, are given respectively in columns Y_{21}, Y_{22} and Y_{25} of Appendix Table 1. The indices are separately correlated to size of country in terms of both population and GNP.

The correlation coefficient (r) between the percent increase in GNP per year (Y_{21}) and population (X_2) is +.17, and between the some index (Y_{21}) and GNP (X_1) is +.04. The scatter diagrams of Figure 21 show these relations. Both coefficients are very low which suggests that the association between the rate of growth of GNP and size of country in terms of both population and GNP is almost nonexistent. Both coefficients are positive but both of them are well below the .05 level of significance and cannot be taken with any confidence. Rates of growth of GNP and country size are not strongly related.

The rankings of the median rates of growth of GNP also reveal a similar lack of association between rates of growth of GNP and size of country in terms of both population and GNP. When the thirty countries are ranked in increasing order of population size, the median rate of growth of GNP per year (Y_{21}) is 3.0 for the first quartile, 6.4 for the second, 4.4 for the third, and 5.8 for the fourth. Thus no systematic pattern is revealed. The first quartile has the lowest median growth rate, but the second quartile has the highest. No association between growth rates of GNP and population size is observed. When the same countries are ranked in increasing order of GNP size, also no pattern is indicated. The median rate of growth of GNP per year (Y_{21}) is 6.4 for the first quartile, 4.1 for the second, 4.6 for the third, and 5.4 for the fourth. The first quartile has the highest median rate, and the second quartile the lowest. Thus no systematic directional tendency is revealed, i.e., no association between growth rates of GNP per year and GNP size is observed. Table 38 gives these relations.

Results of formal correlation analysis and of the rankings of the median growth rates of GNP, for a sample of thirty countries, do not indicate that any significant relationship exists between rates of growth of GNP per year and size of country in terms of both population and

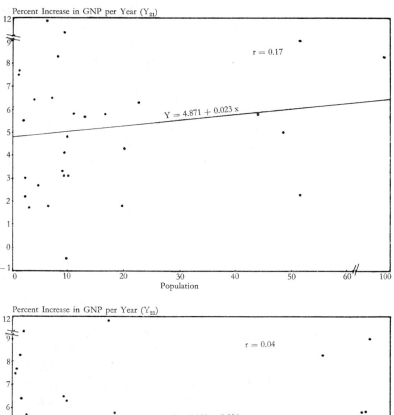

Figure 21
Scatter diagrams: Increase in GNP and size.

Table 38

Relation between Size of Country (Population, GNP) and % Increase in GNP per Year, 1951-1959 (Y_{21})

GROUPS OF COUNTRIES Countries Ranked in Increasing Order of Population Size (Quartiles)	Number of Countries	Average Population (millions)	Median Increase in GNP per Year
I	7	2.07	3.0
II	7	6.60	6.4
III	8	10.21	4.4
IV	8	43.24	5.8
Countries Ranked in Increasing Order of GNP Size (Quartiles)	Number of Countries	Average GNP ($ billions)	Median Increase in GNP Per Year
I	7	0.47	6.4
II	7	1.33	4.1
III	8	5.39	4.6
IV	8	33.60	5.4

GNP. The correlation coefficients are low and non-significant, and the medians do not indicate any systematic relationship. The rates of economic growth of small countries are not necessarily lower than those of large countries. Size of country does not seem to have any marked effect on the rate of growth of GNP.

When the second index (Y_{22}) of economic growth is considered, a similar result is obtained. The correlation coefficient (r) between the increase in per capita GNP per year (Y_{22}) and population (X_2) is $-.08$, and between the same index (Y_{22}) and GNP (X_1) is $+.12$. The scatter diagrams of Figure 22 show these relations. Both coefficients again are very low. They have different signs, but they are well below the .05 level of significance and cannot be taken with any confidence. Apparently, there is no strong association between size of country and annual increase in per capita GNP.

The rankings of the median increase in per capita GNP also fail to reveal a steady pattern in the growth rate of per capita GNP as country size in terms of both population and GNP increases. When the thirty-one countries of the sample are ranked in increasing order of population size, the median increase in per capita GNP (Y_{22}) is 10.8 for the first quartile, 22.8 for the second, 8.6 for the third, and 21.1 for

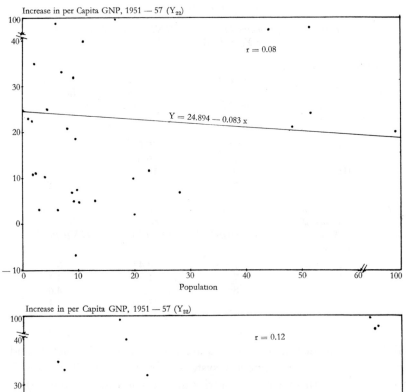

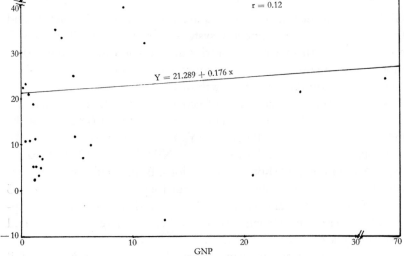

Figure 22
Scatter diagrams: Increase in per capita GNP and size.

the fourth. The pattern is not consistant, and no directional tendency is noticeable. The third quartile has the lowest median increase and the second quartile has the highest. When the same countries are ranked in increasing order of GNP size, a similar unsteady pattern between increase in per capita GNP and size is also observed. The median increase in per capita GNP (Y_{22}) is 14.6 for the first quartile, 5.8 for the second, 28.3 for the third, and 24.0 for the fourth. The second quartile shows the lowest median increase and the third quartile shows teh highest median, but the last two quartiles show considerably highre medians than the first two. The difference between the medians of the first and last quartiles is also sizeable. There is, therefore, a tendency for the median increase in per capita GNP to rise as GNP size increases. Small countries (in terms of GNP) tend to have lower average rates of increase in per capita GNP than large countries. Table 39 shows these relations.

Formal correlation analysis and the rankings of the median growth rates of per capita GNP with reference to size of country for a sample of thirty-one countries, fail to reveal any significant association between growth rates of per capita GNP and size of country in terms of population and GNP. Both correlation coefficients are low and well

Table 39

Relation between Size of Country (Population, GNP) and Increase in per Capita GNP, 1951-1957 (Y_{22})

GROUPS OF COUNTRIES Countries Ranked in Increasing Order of Population Size (Quartiles)	Number of Countries	Average Population (millions)	Median Increase in Per Capita GNP
I	8	2.38	10.85
II	8	7.60	22.80
III	8	12.46	8.65
IV	7	48.24	21.20
Countries Ranked in Increasing Order of GNP Size (Quartiles)	Number of Countries	Average GNP ($ billions)	Median Increase in Per Capita GNP
I	8	0.53	14.65
II	8	1.65	5.85
III	8	6.85	28.35
IV	7	36.81	24.00

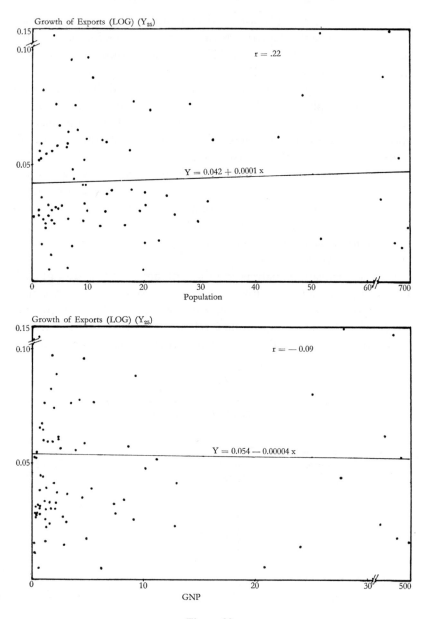

Figure 23
Scatter diagrams: Growth of exports and size.

below the .05 level of significance, and the median rankings did not indicate any steady pattern. An unsteady increasing tendency was, in one case, observed, but it cannot be claimed that size of country has a noticeable effect on the growth rate of per capita GNP.

The third index (Y_{25}) considered here measures the rate of growth of export proceeds. This is not a proper economic growth indicator, but since exports have been found to be reasonably associated with size, it may be worthwhile to investigate whether the growth of exports is in any way affected by the size of country. The correlation coefficient (r) between the logarithmic rates of growth of exports (Y_{25}) and population (X_2) is $+.22$, and between the same index (Y_{25}) and GNP (X_1) is $-.09$. The scatter diagrams of Figure 23 show these relations. Both coefficients are low which is indicative of a weak relationship between growth of exports and size of country in terms of both population and GNP, and they have two different signs. Both coefficients are also below the .05 level of significance. The relationship between size of country and growth of exports cannot be taken with much confidence.

Comparisons of the median growth of exports (Y_{25}) for the quartiles of the countries ranked with reference to size of country, fail to indicate any directional pattern. When the eighty-three countries are ranked in increasing order of population size, the median growth of exports (Y_{25}) is .028 for the first quartile, .048 for the second, .039 for the third, and .036 for the fourth. The first quartile has the lowest median logarithmic rate, the second quartile has the highest, and the fourth quartile has a lower rate than the third. No association is thus observed between growth of exports and population size. When the countries (80 of the 83) are ranked in increasing order of GNP size, also no directional pattern is revealed. The median growth of exports (Y_{25}) is .031 for the first quartile, .041 for the second, .046 for the third, and .038 for the fourth. The first and fourth quartiles have almost the same median values, and the middle two quartiles have similar median values too. The median growth of exports does not change systematically with a change in size of GNP. Growth of exports and GNP size are not associated. Table 40 gives these relations.

Findings of correlation analysis and of the comparisons of the median growth of exports for a sample of eighty-three countries, do not indicate any significant association between growth of exports and size of country as represented either by population or GNP. The correlation coefficients are low and not significant, and the median growth of ex-

Table 40

Relation between Size of Country (Population, GNP) and Growth of Exports: Log. (Y_{25})

GROUPS OF COUNTRIES Countries Ranked in Increasing Order of Population Size (Quartiles)	Number of Countries	Average Population (millions)	Average Growth of Exports
I	21	2.05	0.028
II	21	6.17	0.048
III	21	14.06	0.039
IV	20	105.01	0.036
Countries Ranked in Increasing Order of GNP Size	Number of Countries	Average GNP ($ billions)	Average Growth of Exports
I	20	0.425	0.031
II	20	1.365	0.041
III	20	3.615	0.046
IV	20	51.96	0.038

ports for the quartiles of the countries ranked with reference to size of country do not observe a steady directional pattern. It cannot therefore be claimed that size of country (in terms of both population and GNP) has any marked effect on the rates of growth of export proceeds.

B. Levels of Economic Development and Size

It may also be pertinent not only to inquire whether the pace of economic growth differs for countries of different size, but also whether the level of economic development itself differs with size of country. How do the levels of economic development of large and small countries compare with each other? Does the size of a country have any effect on its economic wellbeing? In attempting to answer these questions, two indices measuring economic development will be correlated to size of country as represented by population only.[1] The first index (Y_{23}) is the average per capita gross national product (in U.S. dollars) for each of thirty countries, for the years 1951 to 1957, adjusted for

---

[1] In analyzing the relationship between levels of economic development and size, GNP will not be used as an independent variable, since this implies correlating GNP per capita with GNP. Such a procedure would have been biased. In the event that population is randomly distributed with respect to GNP, this would have in effect correlated GNP with itself.

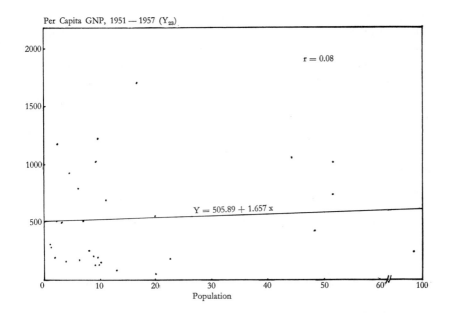

Figure 24
Scatter diagram: Per capita GNP and size.

price changes. The second index (Y_{24}) is the per capita gross national product in 1957 (in U.S. dollars) for each of eighty countries. These two indices are considered, although both of them measure per capita GNP, since they involve different numbers of countries and since one is a seven-year average adjusted to price changes, while the other is not.

The correlation coefficient (r) between per capita GNP for the years 1951-1957 (Y_{23}) and population (X_2) is $+.08$. The scatter diagram of Figure 24 shows this relation. This coefficient of correlation is very low and well below the .05 level of significance, which is indicative of a weak association between per capita GNP and size of country as represented by population size. Large countries (population wise) do not necessarily have higher per capita GNP than small countries. This is not a surprise, since some of the poorest countries in the world are lagre countries in terms of population.

Comparisons of the median per capita GNP (Y_{23}) for the quartiles of the thirty countries ranked with reference to population size, indicate a positive unsteady pattern. When the thirty countries are ranked in increasing order of population size, the median per capita GNP

(Y_{23}) is 302.0 for the first quartile, 252.0 for the second, 439 for the third, and 487.5 for the fourth. Unlike formal correlation analysis, something of a pattern emerges here. There is a tendency for per capita GNP to increase as population size increases. The first quartile has a higher median than the second quartile, but the last two quartiles have consecutively higher medians than the first two. Large countries (in terms of population) tend to have higher per capita GNP than small countries. One must mention, though, that the difference in median values of the first and last quartiles is not substantial. Table 41 shows these relations.

Table 41

Relation between Size of Country (Population) and per Capita GNP,
1951-1957 (Y_{23})

GROUPS OF COUNTRIES *Countries Ranked in Increasing Order of Population Size (Quartiles)*	*Number of Countries*	*Average Population (millions)*	*Median Per Capita GNP*
I	7	2.16	302.0
II	7	7.16	252.0
III	8	11.14	439.0
IV	8	43.68	487.5

Formal correlation analysis reveals a very weak association between per capita GNP (the 1951-1957 average adjusted for price changes) and population size. When the median per capita GNP is, however, compared for the quartiles of the countries ranked in increasing order of population size, something of an increasing pattern emerges. Per capita GNP shows a tendency to increase as population size increases. But the difference between the medians is not very large, and the positive association, therefore, between per capita GNP and population size remains not very significant.

When the second measure of economic development is used (the per capita GNP in 1957 for each of eighty countries) a similar picture is revealed. The correlation coefficient (r) between per capita GNP in 1957 (Y_{24}) and population (X_2) is $+.12$. The scatter diagram of Figure 25 shows this relation. The coefficient between GNP per capita and population size is, again, positive and fairly low. It is also below the .05 level of confidence, which is indicative again of the weak associ-

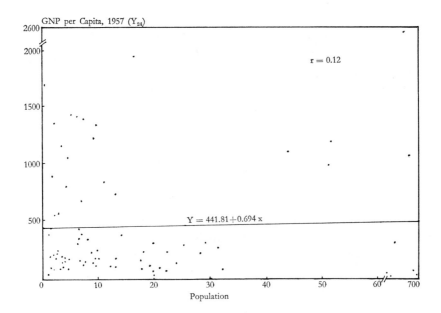

Figure 25
Scatter diagram: GNP per capita and size.

ation between GNP per capita and population size. Large countries, in terms of population, do not necessarily have higher GNP per capita than small countries.

The rankings of the median GNP per capita with reference to population size indicate the same relationship, as in formal correlation analysis, between GNP per capita and population size. When the eighty countries are ranked in increasing order of population size, the median GNP per capita (Y_{24}) is 233.0 for the first quartile, 320.0 for the second, 173.5 for the third, and 241.5 for the fourth. Thus, no directional pattern emerges here. The second quartile has the highest median GNP per capita; the third quartile has the lowest median; and the difference between the medians of the first and last quartiles is negligible. There is no association between GNP per capita and population size. Large countries, in terms of population, do not necessarily have higher GNP per capita levels than small countries. Table 42 shows these relations.

Correlation analysis reveals a very weak association between level of economic development (GNP per capita in 1957 for eighty countries) and population size. The same lack of association was revealed,

Table 42

Relation between Size of Country (Population) and GNP per Capita,
1957 (Y_{24})

GROUPS OF COUNTRIES Countries Ranked in Increasing Order of Population Size	Number of Countries	Average Population (millions)	Median GNP Per Capita
I	20	3.23	233.0
II	20	6.29	320.0
III	20	14.23	173.5
IV	20	105.01	241.5

too, when the median GNP per capita levels were compared for the quartiles of the countries ranked in increasing order of population size. It can thus be concluded that levels of economic development have nothing to do with, or are not influenced by, size of country in terms of population.

2. THREE-VARIABLE ANALYSIS: CROSS-CLASSIFICATIONS AND CORRELATIONS

The three-variable analysis has the purpose of examining the extent to which the association between economic development (or growth) and size of country, interpreted in the first part of this chapter, is influenced by the country's dependence on trade and concentration of exports. Since some observable pattern has been indicated (see previous two chapters) between size of country and both dependence on trade and export concentration, it becomes relevant to inquire whether the nature of the association between size of country and economic development (or growth) will change with a change in dependence on trade or a change in export concentration. Multivariant analysis, with economic development (or growth) indices as the dependent variables, and with size and dependence on trade, or with size and export concentration as the two independent variables, will indicate the nature of the association between economic development (or growth) and export concentration, and will also indicate the impact of dependence on trade and export concentration on the association between size and economic development (or growth).

Similar to previous chapters, two methods of analysis will be used: the cross-classification method of analysis, and formal multiple-correlation analysis with two independent variables. Correlation analysis includes only those variables used by the cross-classification analysis.

A. *Economic Development and Size*

There are three factors that are considered here for their impact on the association between economic development and size; they are— dependence on trade, commodity export concentration, and geographic export concentration. The relationship between economic development and size[1] and each of these three factors will be separately analyzed. Economic development will be treated as the dependent variable, and size and each of these factors as the two independent variables. The average per capita gross national product (Y_{23}) is chosen as the index of economic development since it is a seven-year average adjusted for price changes, and since it yielded the best results in simple correlation analysis.

1. *Economic Development, Dependence on Trade, and Size*

This is mainly an analysis of the effect of dependence on trade on the association between economic development and size. An inverse pattern has been already indicated to exist between size and dependence on trade. Is this pattern strong enough to influence the association between economic development and size? Economic development me-

Table 43

Degree of Development Medians (Y_{23}) by Size (Population) and by Dependence on Trade (Y_{16})

	Small Countries	*Large Countries*	TOTAL
Low *Dependence* *on Trade*	194.0 *Range* (162.0-252.0) n = 5	*645.5* *Range* (185.0-1713.0) n = 10	252.0 *Range* (162.0-1713.0) n = 15
High *Dependence* *on Trade*	509.5 *Range* (123.0-1172.0) n = 10	*151.0* *Range* (47.0-688.0) n = 5	494.0 *Range* (47.0-1172.0) n = 15
TOTAL	302.0 *Range* (123.0-1172.0) n = 15	423.0 *Range* (47.0-1713.0) n = 15	362.5 *Range* (47.0-1713.0) n = 30

[1] Similar to the procedure adopted in the two-variable analysis, only population will be used here as a measure of size. See previous footnote.

dians (Y_{23}) classified by size (population) and by dependence on trade (Y_{16}), do not reveal a steady pattern between dependence on trade and economic development. The economic development medians do not observe any steady pattern across all rows, down all columns, nor diagonally. See Table 43. These results are in line with the two-variable analysis, where no significant association was yielded between economic development and population size. It is now further revealed that such a relationship does not seem to be offset by a change in the degree of dependence on trade.

Formal multiple-correlation analysis, with economic development (Y_{23}) as the dependent variable, and with size (X_2) and dependence on trade (Y_{16}) as the two independent variables, yields similar results. The multiple regression equation shows a positive coefficient between economic development (Y_{23}) and size (X_2), and also a positive coefficient between economic development and dependence on trade (Y_{16}). The equation is given below.

$$Y_{23} = 2.1978X_2 + 1.0399Y_{16} + 439.8339$$
$$(4.37) \qquad (3.39) \qquad (225.32) \qquad R = .101$$

The standard deviations of the X_1 and Y_{16} coefficients are not, however, small enough to make the coefficients acceptable. Therefore, the association between economic development and population (X_2) is not statistically significant, and so is the association between economic development and dependence on trade. This is also revealed by the fact that the R-value here is not substantially higher than the correlation coefficient yielded by simple correlation analysis. The degree of dependence on trade does not seem to leave a significant impact on the association between economic development and size. It should be, nevertheless, noted that while the association between economic development and dependence on trade is not significant, the coefficients of this association are positive. Dependence on trade, therefore, may not be a strong vehicle of economic development, it is at least not an impediment to it. This result is of relevance to small countries where dependence on trade is relatively more predominant.

2. *Economic Development, Commodity Export Concentration, and Size*

Commodity export concentration is also relatively more predominant in the economies of small nations. It is equally relevant, therefore, to analyze the effect of commodity export concentration on the association between economic development and size. Is there any relationship between commodity export concentration and economic development? Economic development medians (Y_{23}) classified by size (population) and by commodity export concentration (Y_9), fail to indicate any steady pattern between economic development and size, but do indicate a steady negative pattern between economic development and commodity export concentration. The median values of economic development do not observe a steady pattern across all rows nor diagonally. See Table 44. This is again in line with the two-variable ana-

Table 44

Degree of Development Medians (Y_{23}) by Size (Population) and by Commodity-Export Concentration (Y_9)

	Small Countries	*Large Countries*	TOTAL
Low Commodity-Export Concentration	358.0 *Range* (203.0-513.0) n = 2	*620.0* *Range* (86.0-1713.0) n = 12	532.5 *Range* (86.0-1713.0) n = 14
High Commodity-Export Concentration	300.0 *Range* (123.0-1172.0) n = 12	*190.0* *Range* (47.0-1713.0) n = 3	252.0 *Range* (47.0-1713.0) n = 15
TOTAL	300.0 *Range* (123.0-1172.0) n = 14	423.0 *Range* (47.0-1713.0) n = 15	302.0 *Range* (47.0-1713.0) n = 29

lysis where no significant association was indicated between economic development and population. The inverse relation between economic development and commodity export concentration is however steady, since the medians do observe one directional inverse pattern down all columns, and also diagonally. It remains to be seen, from formal correlation analysis, whether this inverse relationship between economic development and commodity export concentration is expected to have an appreciable influence on the relationship between economic development and size.

Formal multiple-correlation analysis indicates that neither the association between economic development and size, nor between economic development and commodity export concentration are acceptable. Multiple regression equation, with economic development (Y_{23}) as the dependent variable, and with size (X_2) and commodity export concentration (Y_9) as the two independent variables, yields a positive coefficient between economic development and size, and yields a negative coefficient between economic development and commodity export concentration. The standard deviations of these coefficients are not small enough to accept the association between economic development and size, nor between economic development and commodity export concentration. However, unlike the association between economic development and dependence on trade, the coefficient between economic development and commodity export concentration is negative. While this association is not statistically significant, one cannot say that commodity export concentration is not capable, perhaps, of imparting an adverse influence on economic development.

$$Y_{23} = 1.4397X_2 - 12.6522Y_9 + 1435.709$$
$$\quad\quad (4.08) \quad\quad (6.04) \quad\quad\quad (448.70) \quad\quad R = .394$$

It seems, therefore, that both the cross-classifications and multiple correlations suggest that the relationship between economic development and population size, and that between economic development and commodity export concentration are not significant. There is, however, some evidence that commodity export concentration, unlike dependence on trade, could have an adverse effect on economic development. This result should be of importance to small countries since commodity export concentration is relatively more conspicuous among small countries. The practical consequences of this are also quite significant. This implies, perhaps, that measures designed to reduce commodity export concentration may enhance the economic development of small countries.

3. *Economic Development, Geographic Export Concentration, and Size*

Geographic export concentration is also generally more prevalent among small countries than among large ones. It is, therefore, also relevant to examine the impact of geographic export concentration on the association between economic development and size. What is the nature of the association between geographic export concentration and economic development? Is it significant enough to influence the relationship between economic development and size? Economic development medians (Y_{23}) classified by size (population) and by geographic export concentration(Y_{10}), indicate an unsteady positive pattern between economic development and size, and a steady negative pattern between economic development and geographic export concentration.

Table 45

*Degree of Development Medians (Y₂₃) by Size (Population) and by
Country Export Concentration (Y₁₀)*

	Small Countries	*Large Countries*	TOTAL
Low Country- Export Concentration	513.0 *Range* (203.0-1042.0) n = 5	*688.0* *Range* (47.0-1234.0) n = 9	620.0 *Range* (47.0-1234.0) n = 14
High Country- Export Concentration	298.0 *Range* (123.0-1172.0) n = 9	*169.0* *Range* (86.0-1713.0) n = 1	190.0 *Range* (86.0-1713.0) n = 15
TOTAL	300.0 *Range* (123.0-1172.0) n = 14	423.0 *Range* (47.0-1713.0) n = 19	302.0 *Range* (47.0-1713.0) n = 29

Again, no steady pattern between economic development and size is observed across all rows nor diagonally. This supports previous results where no significant relationship was yielded between economic development and size. The inverse pattern between economic development and geographic export concentration is, however, steady. The development medians observe a declining pattern down any column and also diagonally. See Table 45 for these results. This pattern may not be strong enough to leave an impact on the association between economic development and size. What do multiple-correlations show?

Formal multiple-correlation analysis also reveals that the relationship between economic development and size, and the relationship between economic development and geographic export concentration are both not statistically significant. Regression equation, with economic development (Y_{23}) as the dependent variable, and with size (X_2) and geographic export concentration (Y_{10}) as the two independent variables, yields a positive coefficient between economic development and size, and a negative coefficient between economic development and geographic export concentration. But both standard deviations are very high. Therefore, both relationships are not statistically acceptable. The R-value yielded here is nearly the same as the one yielded by simple correlation analysis. Geographic export concentration does not seem to have any impact on the association between economic development and size.

$$Y_{23} = 0.7540X_2 - 1.8560Y_{10} + 604.851$$
$$(4.92) \qquad (5.53) \qquad (303.36) \qquad R = .104$$

Both cross-classifications and multiple correlations reveal that the relationship between economic development and population size, and between economic development and geographic export concentration are not significant. With respect to the latter relationship, the cross-classifications showed an inverse pattern, but correlation analysis did not yield acceptable results. There is no evidence, therefore, that geographic export concentration could have any significant effect on economic development. This conclusion should be of importance to small countries since they tend to have relatively higher geographic export concentration than large countries. Geographic export concentration is not necessarily an obstacle to economic development and measures designed to reduce geographic export concentration need not help the economic development of small countries.

4. *Conclusions*

The three-variable analysis of the relationship between economic development and size suggests the following conclusions: (a) There is no steady association between economic development and size. The cross-classifications did not reveal steady directional patterns, nor did multiple correlations yield significant coefficients between economic development and size. This is in line with results of two-variable analysis. (b) There is no strong association between economic development and dependence on trade. The cross-classifications failed to indicate a steady pattern, and multiple correlation did not yield acceptable coefficients. A tendency for economic development to increase with an increase in dependence on trade was, however, observed. Dependence on trade, therefore, is not necessarily an obstacle to economic development. (c) There is also no strong association between economic development and commodity export concentration. The cross-classifications indicated a steady inverse pattern, but multiple correlations did not yield significant coefficients between economic development and commodity export concentration. There was, however, some evidence that commodity export concentration could perhaps have an adverse effect on economic development. (d) Finally, there is also no strong association between economic development and geographic export concentration. The cross-classifications indicated a steady inverse pattern, but the multiple correlations yielded non-significant result between economic development and geographic export concentration. There is no evidence, therefore, that geographic export concentration should be an obstacle to economic development.

B. *Economic Growth and Size*

Analysis here will be similar to the previous section since the same factors, namely, dependence on trade, commodity export concentration, and geographic export concentration, are considered for their impact on the association between economic growth and size. The relationship between economic growth and size and each of these factors is separately analyzed. Economic growth is treated as the dependent variable, and size and each of these factors as the two independent variables. The percent increase in GNP per year (Y_{21}) is used as the index of economic growth. It is a seven-year average of annual rates of growth of gross national product adjusted for price changes. It also yielded relatively better results (compared to the other economic growth indices) in the simple correlation analysis.

1. *Economic Growth, Dependence on Trade, and Size*

This three-variable analysis can be justified on similar grounds as the analysis of the relationship between economic development, dependence on trade, and size. Since a relatively apparent pattern has been established between dependence on trade and size, it becomes relevant to inquire whether this pattern is strong enough to leave an impact on the association between growth and size. Economic growth medians (Y_{21}) classified by size (GNP and population) and by dependence on trade (Y_{16}), indicate an unsteady negative pattern between economic growth and dependence on trade. The median values of economic growth observe (with one exception) a rising directional pattern across any row and also (with one exception) diagonally. There is, therefore, an unsteady tendency for economic growth medians to increase with size, regardless perhaps of the degree of dependence on trade. The median values also observe (with one exception) a declining directional pattern down any column and diagonally. There is, therefore, a tendency, unsteady but nevertheless a tendency, for economic growth medians to decline with an increase in the degree of dependence on trade. See Table 46 for these results. Hence the cross-classification analysis indicates that there is a weak positive pattern between economic growth and size, and a weak negative pattern between econom-

Table 46

*Economic Growth Medians (Y_{21}) by Size (GNP) and by Dependence
on Trade (Y_{16})*

| | *Small
Countries* | *Large
Countries* | TOTAL |
|---|---|---|---|
| *Low Dependence
on Trade* | 6.4
Range (3.3-9.8)
n = 5 | 5.4
Range (−.5-9.8)
n = 10 | 5.8
Range (−.5-8.9)
n = 15 |
| *High Dependence
on Trade* | 4.2
Range (.7-7.7)
n = 10 | 5.8
Range (−.5-11.4)
n = 5 | 4.3
Range (.7-11.4)
n = 15 |
| TOTAL | 4.8
Range (.7-9.8)
n = 15 | 5.8
Range (−.5-11.4)
n = 15 | 5.2
Range (−.5-11.4)
n = 30 |

*Economic Growth Medians (Y_{21}) by Size (Population) and by Dependence
on Trade (Y_{16})*

| | *Small
Countries* | *Large
Countries* | TOTAL |
|---|---|---|---|
| *Low Dependence
on Trade* | 5.5
Range (1.8-8.3)
n = 5 | 5.8
Range (−.5-9.8)
n = 10 | 5.8
Range (−.5-9.8)
n = 15 |
| *High Dependence
on Trade* | 3.6
Range (.7-11.4)
n = 10 | 4.8
Range (3.1-5.8)
n = 5 | 4.3
Range (.7-11.4)
n = 15 |
| TOTAL | 4.1
Range (.7-11.4)
n = 15 | 5.7
Range (−.5-9.8)
n = 15 | 5.2
Range (−5.-11.4)
n = 30 |

ic growth and dependence on trade. Due to this latter result, it is not
likely that dependence on trade will influence the association between
economic growth and size. Let us see what the multiple correlations
show.

Formal multiple-correlation analysis, with economic growth (Y_{21})
as the dependent variable, and with size (X_1 and X_2) and dependence
on trade (Y_{16}) as the two independent variables, provides similar results. The two multiple regression equations show positive coefficients
between economic growth and size, and negative coefficients between
economic growth and dependence on trade. The standard deviations
of all these coefficients are higher than the coefficients themselves.

Therefore, neither the relationship between economic growth and size, nor between economic growth and dependence on trade, are statistically acceptable. Also observed are the two low R-values yielded by these equations. See the two equations below.

$$Y_{21} = 0.0026X_1 - 0.0065Y_{16} + 5.6020$$
$$(.036) \qquad (.023) \qquad (1.50) \qquad R = .067$$
$$Y_{21} = 0.0231X_2 - 0.0072Y_{16} + 5.2763$$
$$(.027) \qquad (.022) \qquad (1.29) \qquad R = .186$$

Both of these multiple-correlation coefficients are not any higher than the coefficients yielded by simple-correlation analysis. Apparently, dependence on trade does not seem to have any influence on the association between economic growth and size, and neither size nor dependence on trade are important factors in economic growth. These results are of significance to small countries who normally depend more heavily on trade as an escape from their smallness. In a previous chapter it was suggested that dependence on trade is not an important source of extra economic instability. It is now further suggested that dependence on trade is not an important factor in economic growth.

2. Economic Growth, Commodity Export Concentration, and Size

Commodity export concentration is relatively more prevalent among small countries than among large ones. It is, therefore, relevant to find out whether commodity export concentration has any effect on the association between economic growth and size. What kind of a relationship exists between economic growth and commodity export concentration? Does the same relationship hold between economic growth and size regardless of the country's commodity export concentration? Economic growth medians (Y_{21}) classified by size (GNP and population) and by commodity export concentration (Y_9), indicate an unsteady positive pattern between economic growth and size, and an unsteady positive pattern between economic growth and commodity export concentration. The median values of economic growth observe a rising directional pattern across any row and also diagonally only in the population breakdown. Such a pattern disappears in the GNP breakdown. Therefore, the relationship between economic growth and size is not steady. There is, nevertheless, a tendency for economic growth to increase with an increase in size, and there is also evidence, in the case of the population breakdown, that this positive tendency is not offset by commodity export concentration.

Table 47

Economic Growth Medians (Y_{21}) by Size (GNP) and by Commodity-Export Concentration (Y_9)

	Small Countries	Large Countries	TOTAL
Low Commodity-Export Concentration	4.1 *Range* (3.1-5.7) n = 4	5.8 *Range* (−.5-9.0) n = 10	5.3 *Range* (−.5-9.0) n = 14
High Commodity-Export Concentration	*6.0* *Range* (.7-9.8) n = 10	*3.1* *Range* (1.8-11.4) n = 5	*5.5* *Range* (.7-11.4) n = 15
TOTAL	5.2 *Range* (.7-9.8) n = 14	5.8 *Range* (−.5-11.4) n = 15	5.5 *Range* (−.5-11.4) n = 29

Economic Growth Medians (Y_{21}) by Size (Population) and by Commodity-Export Concentration (Y_9)

	Small Countries	Large Countries	TOTAL
Low Commodity-Export Concentration	4.9 *Range* (3.3-6.5) n = 2	5.3 *Range* (−.5-9.0) n = 12	5.3 *Range* (−.5-9.0) n = 14
High Commodity-Export Concentration	*4.8* *Range* (.7-11.4) n = 12	*8.3* *Range* (4.3-9.8) n = 3	*5.5* *Range* (.7-11.4) n = 15
TOTAL	4.8 *Range* (.7-11.4) n = 14	5.7 *Range* (−.5-9.8) n = 15	5.5 *Range* (−.5-11.4) n = 29

The median values of economic growth do not, likewise, observe a steady pattern down all columns nor diagonally. Hence, the relationship between economic growth and commodity export concentration is fairly weak. The overall tendency is mildly positive, but no steady pattern can be said to exist between economic growth and commodity export concentration. See Table 47 for these results. It should be apparent that the cross-classification analysis does not reveal any significant relationship between economic growth and size, nor between economic growth and commodity export concentration. It is clear, therefore, that commodity export concentration is not likely to influence the association between economic growth and size, and that neither size nor commodity export concentration are important factors in economic growth. Consequently, small countries, who may encounter relatively high commodity export concentration, neet not be handicapped, as a result, in their economic growth.[1]

3. *Economic Growth, Geographic Export Concentration, and Size*

Geographic export concentration is also relatively more common among small countries. It is likewise relevant to find out whether geographic export concentration has any impact on the association between economic growth and size. Is there any relationship between economic growth and geographic concentration? What do the facts show? Economic growth medians (Y_{21}) classified by size (GNP and population) and by geographic export concentration (Y_{10}) reveal an unsteady positive pattern between economic growth and size, and a steady positive pattern between economic growth and geographic export concentration. The median values of economic growth observe a rising directional pattern across all rows, but such a positive pattern is not observed diagonally. The positive pattern between economic growth and size is not maintained regardless of geographic export concentration. The association between economic growth and size is not strong. There is, however, a tendency, unsteady but nevertheless a tendency, for economic growth to increase with an increase in size.

The median values of economic growth observe, on the other hand, a steady positive pattern down all columns and also diagonally. This implies that the positive association between economic growth and geographic export concentration is perhaps more significant than the positive association between economic growth and size. Regardless of country size, economic growth medians seem to increase with an increase in geographic export concentration. There is, therefore, a steady positive pattern between economic growth and geographic export concentration. See Table 48 for these results. These cross-classifications indicate an unsteady positive relationship between economic growth and size, and a steady positive relationship between economic growth and geographic export concentration. It is not therefore clear that geographic export concentration may not influence the association between economic growth and size. The positive association between economic growth and geographic export concentration may not be

---

[1] Multiple regression equations are not available for this and the following section. Results of the cross-classifications do, perhaps, suggest that it is not likely for multiple-correlation analysis to provide entirely different conclusions.

Table 48

Economic Growth Medians (Y_{21}) by Size (GNP) and by Country-Export Concentration (Y_{10})

	Small Countries	Large Countries	TOTAL
Low Country-Export Concentration	4.3 Range (3.3-8.3) n = 3	5.0 Range (−.5-9.0) n = 11	4.6 Range (−.5-9.0) n = 14
High Country-Export Concentration	5.5 Range (.7-9.8) n = 11	6.1 Range (1.8-11.4) n = 4	5.7 Range (.7-11.4) n = 15
TOTAL	5.1 Range (.7-9.8) n = 14	5.8 Range (1.8-11.4) n = 15	5.5 Range (.7-11.4) n = 29

Economic Growth Medians (Y_{21}) by Size (Population) and by Country-Export Concentration (Y_{10})

	Small Countries	Large Countries	TOTAL
Low Country-Export Concentration	3.3 Range (2.7-8.3) n = 5	5.0 Range (−.5-9.0) n = 9	4.6 Range (−.5-9.0) n = 14
High Country-Export Concentration	5.5 Range (.7-11.4) n = 9	5.8 Range (3.1-9.8) n = 6	5.7 Range (.7-11.4) n = 15
TOTAL	4.8 Range (.7-11.4) n = 14	5.7 Range (−.5-9.8) n = 15	5.5 Range (−.5-11.4) n = 29

fairly significant, but it is perhaps sufficient to suggest that geographic export concentration is not necessarily an impediment to economic growth. This conclusion is also of relevance to small countries who normally find it more appropriate on account of the limited diversity of their exports, to concentrate on few export markets for their exports.

4. *Conclusions*

The three-variable analysis of the relationship between economic growth and size suggests the following results: (a) There is no strong association between economic growth and size. The cross-classifications did not indicate a steady directional pattern, and multiple correlations did not yield significant coefficients between economic growth and size. A mild tendency for economic growth to increase with size was, however, observed. (b) There is no signification relationship between economic growth and dependence on trade. The classifications failed to indicate a steady directional pattern, and the correlations did not yield acceptable coefficients between economic growth and dependence on trade. The R-values were very low. Dependence on trade, therefore, is not an important factor in economic growth. (c) There is also no significant association between economic growth and commodity export concentration. Only an unsteady positive pattern was revealed by classification analysis. Commodity export concentration, therefore, is not necessarily an obstacle to economic growth. (d) Finally, the classification analysis indicated a steady positive pattern between economic growth and geographic export concentration. This positive pattern may not be statistically significant, it is, nevertheless, sufficient to suggest that geographic export concentration is not at least an obstacle to economic growth.

PART TWO

CHAPTER SIX

SIZE AND GROWTH OF THE LEBANESE ECONOMY

The purpose of this Chapter is to analyse the implications of the size of the Lebanese economy on its structure and economic performance. One distinguishing feature which characterizes the Lebanese economy is the preponderance of trade and services over all other sectors of economic activity. Such a preponderance, it will be argued, is to a large measure a consequence of the 'smallness' of Lebanon. Discussion will therefore center around an analysis of this special feature and its implications on the economic growth of Lebanon.

1. Lopsided[1] Structure

That Lebanon is predominantly a country of trade and services reflects itself in the 'lopsided' distribution of its national product. A breakdown of the total national product by sector,[2] given in Table 49 below, shows that agriculture and industry combined generate, as a rule, less than one third of national product; while the 'services' producing sectors generate the remaining two-thirds; hence the 'lopsidedness' referred to above which is unique to Lebanon.

The pattern and quality of the country's resource endowments and the size of its economy should have left their impact on this unique feature. Lebanon is not well endowed with agricultural and mineral resources. The physiogeographic structure of the country is such (i.e., there are no wide valleys or plains) that, more often than not, resort is made to cultivate lands which are not generally fit (had it not been for the extensive use of terracing so predominant in Lebanon) for cultivation. As a result, it is estimated that the bulk of agricultural income emanates from land the productivity of which has been greatly improved by irrigation, terracing or both. The same is the case with

---

[1] Some may object to the word 'lopsided' since it may imply a 'defective' structure. It is used here only to refer to the unsymmetrical or one-sided distribution of national income.

[2] A Warning regarding these series is in order. Income estimates come from three different sources. Therefore, their comparability has to be cautiously interpreted since it cannot be assumed that these different sources used similar statistical methods in arriving at their estimates.

Table 49

Net National Product, by Sector: 1950-1966
(At Current Factor Cost)
(in Percentages)

SECTOR	1950	1951	1952	1953	1954	1955	1956	1957	1958	1959	1960	1961	1962	1964	1965	1966
Agriculture	19.7	19.4	19.3	18|9	18.0	16.2	16.3	15.8	16.5	14.6	14.1	14.1	14.2	11.9	11.6	11.4
Industry	13.5	13.5	13.9	13.7	13.2	12.7	12.9	12.5	13.6	12.2	12.1	12.1	11.7	12.8	13.1	13.2
Construction	4.1	3.2	4.3	4.0	4.7	4.3	3.5	2.7	2.8	3.3	3.5	3.5	3.4	5.6	5.7	6.0
Transportation	4.1	4.2	4.0	4.3	4.7	5.4	5.5	5.3	4.3	4.0	3.9	4.0	4.7	8.1	8.2	8.0
Trade	28.8	31.0	29.4	29.3	29.6	28.8	31.2	27.5	31.8	32.0	32.0	31.4	32.1	30.8	30.6	40.6
Finance & Insurance	3.8	4.2	4.5	4.3	4.5	5.1	5.6	6.0	7.0	6.3	6.3	6.4	6.5	3.4	3.4	3.6
Real Estate	9.2	8.9	8.8	8.6	8.8	8.4	9.2	9.2	11.7	11.0	11.0	11.1	10.8	7.8	7.6	7.3
Government	6.9	5.9	5.7	6.1	5.8	6.0	6.7	7.2	8.5	8.0	7.8	7.7	8.2	7.7	8.0	8.2
Services	9.6	9.5	9.5	10.5	10.6	12.0	11.3	9.8	7.8	8.9	9.2	9.2	9.1	10.6	11.3	11.5

Source: Based on Appendix Table 2 on net national product by sector, 1950-1966. Percentages for years 1964-1966 are based on gross domestic product estimates.

mineral resources; the country has hardly any significant quantities of mineral ores to talk about. It can thus be said that almost all natural resources which are prerequisites for the development of a sound agricultural and industrial base, and therefore which are basic to the production of 'goods' in general, are either deficient or completely lacking in Lebanon. To compensate for the general paucity of natural resources required for the development and sustained growth of agriculture and industry, Lebanon has been generously endowed with natural resources which lend themselves to the production and promotion of 'services'. These resources have generally been put to good advantage and have already left their distinguishing and now almost indelible mark on the basic structure of the economy. Foremost among them are Lebanon's central geographic location, and the attractiveness and variety (within a small area) of its climatic conditions. The former attribute has made Lebanon, and particularly Beirut, the hub of the Middle East—a busy trade and financial center with relatively well developed transport, banking and allied facilities. The latter has led to the development and improvement of touristic attractions which are partly responsible for the almost monopolistic position Lebanon enjoys as an educational, health and estivage center for the region.

These natural endowments have also left their indelible imprint on the Lebanese character. This imprint has been of such a magnitude that not only are the country's natural resources more conducive to the development and promotion of 'services', but also and even more forcefully are its human resources. It is commonly held now that the country's real economic advantage is not in its natural but in its human resources. The Lebanese have as a result become noted for their outgoing disposition, their capacity to emulate, and their mercantile attitude. These traits made possible an early contact with western civilization and the adoption of skills which promote further specialization in trade and services. It should be noted also that while these human attributes have contributed significantly to the growth of the 'services' producing sectors, they have been at the same time major impediments to the growth of the 'goods' producing sectors. The quality of the human resources is, therefore, one of the main factors which has been responsible for the unique structure of the Lebanese economy. The mercantile orientation and the Lebanese attitude to business, an attitude which considers industrial and agricultural pursuits less lucrative, are partly responsible for channelling heavy investments (away from agriculture and industry) into real estate and commercial projects. While profitable to the investor, some of these projects are unproductive (in the sense that they constitute only a transference of wealth) and involve an element of social waste. Reference is here made both to villa building and other forms of wasteful ostentaion which directly use up the country's real resources, and also to investment in land or securities for speculative or wealth-holding purposes. These heavy investments have helped to create a large class of middlemen, speculators, administrators and a variety of caterers. The mentality, values, and business conduct of this class should invite considerable comment from other social scientists. The entrepreneurial talents, however, wasted in these unproductive pursuits which do nothing more than the transfer of wealth, must not escape the economist. These factors, though non-economic in nature, should be given due importance when accounting for the special economic structure of the country. They have not only misdirected (and often misused) the country's capital resources into speculative and unproductive investments; more importantly, they have inculcated into the Lebanese an unsavouring attitude towards traditional vocations, and have been instrumental in transforming the attributes of the national character of the people. Ethical and moral values, as a result, are undergoing noticeable change. Material achievements are more and more being prized, and often with some contempt to other achievements. Beirut and now almost the whole country are 'being swept over by a spiteful catering attitude, that stops at nearly nothing in its quest for material gain'.[1] The average Lebanese, and particularly the young, resists employment in traditional handicrafts and agriculture. He would rather be a simple city clerk than acquire a vocation and work in a rural area. This psychological factor has contributed significantly to the prevalent scarcity of skilled and semi-skilled workers, and such a scarcity is undoubtedly a major obstacle to the growth of the industrial and agricultural sectors—an obstacle which will be intensified as the requirements of a balanced economic growth increases the demand for a skilled and a more technically prepared labor force. It has also contributed to the already sizeable phenomenon of the migration of rural (and generally unskilled) workers to Beirut. This is a serious problem since

---

[1] For this and other implications of Lebanon's special structure see Yusif A. Sayigh, "Lebanon: Special Economic Problems Arising from a Special Structure", *Middle East Economic Papers*, 1957, Economic Research Institute, American University of Beirut, pp. 60-88; and Elias S. Saba, "The Implications of the Foreign Sector in the Lebanese Economy", *Middle East Economic Papers*, 1962, *op. cit.*, pp. 140-154.

it has implied a neglect and often desertion of agricultural land, and has created additional unemployment and related problems in the urban centers.

2. Increasing Lopsidedness

What makes this special economic structure so important to Lebanon is the current tendency of the lopsidedness to increase, and therefore the indication that it is likely to become a permanent distinguishing feature of the country's economic structure. It is also an indication of the fact that attempts so far (if any) to correct the 'lopsidedness' have not been effective. The sectoral shares of agriculture, industry, and services (given in the Table below) give full support to this. Both industry and agriculture have declined in relative importance, while the 'services' sector has increased. Three-year moving averages of the relative share of the agricultural sector (as percent of net national product) have declined steadily from 19.5 percent to 11.6 percent between 1950 and 1966. Similarly with the percentage share of the industrial

Table 50

Origins of Net National Product, 1950-1966
(At Current Factor Cost)

	Net National Product (LL million)	Agriculture	Industry	Services
		Percentage of Net National Product; Three-Year Moving Averages		
1950	1,042			
1951	1,086	19.5	13.6	66.9
1952	1,115	19.2	13.7	67.1
1953	1,168	18.7	13.6	67.7
1954	1,256	17.7	13.2	69.1
1955	1,374	16.8	12.9	70.2
1956	1,417	16.1	12.7	71.2
1957	1,503	16.2	13.0	70.8
1958	1,325	15.6	12.8	71.6
1959	1,570	15.1	12.6	72.3
1960	1,671	14.3	12.1	73.6
1961	1,707	14.1	12.0	73.9
1962	1,788	13.4	12.2	74.4
1964	3,200	12.6	12.5	74.9
1965	3,523	11.6	13.0	75.3
1966	3,867			

Source: Table 2 on Net National Product, by sector, 1950-1966 in Statistical Appendix.

sector. Three-year moving averages of the relative share of industry showed a slight tendency to decline (with the exception of the last three years) from 13.6 percent to 13.0 percent between 1950 and 1966. Whereas, the three-year moving averages of the relative importance of 'services' have increased steadily, from around 67 percent to over 75 percent between 1959 and 1966.[1] This is a significant tendency which has evidenced further the existing disparity between the 'services' producing and 'goods' producing sectors, and has accentuated the country's already noted dependence on 'services'. At the turn of the last decade, industry and agriculture comprised around 33 percent of net national product, and 'services' provided the remaining 67 percent. By the beginning of this decade, the share of industry and agriculture had dropped to 26 percent, and that of 'services' had risen to 74 percent. This disparity is unquestionably wide and unique to Lebanon. And the fact that it has had a clear directional tendency to rise makes it even more significant. A closer look at past trends in the rates of economic growth of the various sectors may suggest a further future increase in the dependence on services, unless drastic measures are implemented to accelerate the expansion in the goods producing sectors to such an extent that their share will ultimately increase not only in absolute but also in relative terms. It must be noted, however, that even when such measures are successfully implemented, it may not be possible, and in fact may prove detrimental to the whole economy, to alter its basic structure. Trade has always been the traditional activity of the Lebanese; and, "most of the institutional set up around him, especially in the field of banking is geared towards trade, and particularly international trade. To him, agriculture and industry are, at best, secondary fields of investment. This mentality appears to be typically Lebanese, and it may be a mistake to attempt to alter it basically."[2] Realizing this, all efforts should still be made to encourage an expan-

---

[1] That it is unique to Lebanon is supported by data on twenty eight countries ranging from industrialized advanced countries to underdeveloped countries, where it was observed that twenty three have a higher value of goods production and only five show a higher value of services production. The countries where the production of goods is greater than the production of services had an average for the whole group of about two thirds goods and one third services. Of the five 47 to 53 percent. The fifth, Lebanon, was the only country where about two thirds of the total value of production relates to services and only one third to goods. See Albert Y. Badre, "The National Income of Lebanon," *op. cit.*, pp. 32-34.

[2] Paul J. Klat, "The Future of Economic Development in the Arab World," *Middle East Economic Papers, 1956*, Economic Research Institute, American University of Beirut, 1957, p. 61.

sion in the production of goods, if only to stop the current decline in their relative importance, and, if possible, to reverse it. A reversal of these declining trends, in view of the country's limited domestic market, and the maldistribution of income which imposes further limitations of its own on the market, is imparative. Without it, all attempts to compensate for the country's smallness and to improve its prospects for a sustained and a more balanced economic growth may be fruitless.

3. Disparity in Economic Growth Rates

A look at the behavior of current rates of econmic growth of the different sectors, provides further reasons for the expanding discrepancy between the goods producing and the services producing sectors. Net National income between 1950 and 1966 has been growing at annual rates which vary between 3 percent and 10 percent.[1] The average of these rates amounts to 5.5 percent and to 7.0 percent (if 1958 is excluded). Table 51 below gives a breakdown of these rates by

Table 51

Growth of Net National Product, 1950-1966
(At Current Factor Cost)

	Per Cent Per Annum Compounded	
Net National Product	5.5	7.0[1]
Agriculture	2.8	3.5
Industry	4.6	5.3
Construction	6.3	7.4
Transportation	6.9	9.7
Trade	6.3	8.5
Finance & Insurance	10.1	10.7
Real Estate	6.2	5.8
Government	7.4	7.7
Services	6.5	9.3

Source: Based on Appendix Table 3 on annual variations in net national product by sector, 1950-1966.
[1] Excluding the year 1958.

---

[1] This excludes the exceptional rates for the years 1958 & 1959 on account of the political troubles of 1958 and the resulting substantial decline in national income. See table 3 on annual variations in net national product by sector, 1950-1966, in Statistical Appendix.

sector. It can be roughly assumed, barring political crises, that national income in Lebanon has been growing at an average annual rate of at least 7 percent. And since the rate of population increases is estimated to be 2 percent per annum, this means that per capita incomes have been rising at an average annual rate of at least 5 percent. While relatively impressive, this rate of growth has not been equally distributed among the various sectors. A brief look at the accompanying table is sufficient to indicate that on the average the 'services' sectors have been growing considerably faster than the goods sectors. This difference is particularly pronounced in the case of the finance, transportation and trade sectors where compounded annual rates of growth (excluding 1958) were as high as 10.7, 9.7, and 8.5 percent respectively. All other remaining services sectors, as would also be apparent, registered also rates of growth which exceeded those of agriculture and industry. When all the services producing sectors are combined (Table 52), the

Table 52

Growth of Net National Product, 1950-1966
(At Current Factor Cost)

	Per Cent Per Annum Compounded	
Net National Product	5.5	7.0[1]
Agriculture	2.8	3.6
Industry	4.6	5.3
Services	6.9	8.5

Source: Based on Table 3 in Appendix.
[1] Excluding 1958.

disparity in the rates of growth will still be obvious. Services in general have been expanding at a rate which exceeds the expansion rate of the whole economy. Industry's rates of 4.6 percent or 5.3 percent (if 1958 is excluded) are both lower than the economy's rate of growth. Those of agriculture (at 2.8, and 3.6 percent) are still even lower. These set of rates should demonstrate clearly the significant disparity that exists between the rates of growth of the services and the goods producing sectors.

If these disproportionate growth rates are maintained, and there are no indicators so far to suggest that they will not, the skewed structure of the economy will be aggravated, and attempts to correct this trend, if at all successful, may prove to be quite strenuous. Among other things, such attempts would entail the diversion of large sums of capital into the goods producing sectors, by forcing artificial directions on investments. Artificial directives, in view of the Lebanese attitude to business and the traditional economic vocation of the country (which for centuries has been in trade and commerce and not in production), may not be feasible. The magnitude of the capital diversion involved will become apparent, once the rates of capital formation and their breakdown into sectors of economic activity are presented.

4. CAPITAL FORMATION AND DISPARITY IN CAPITAL/OUTPUT RATIOS

It has been estimated that investment, both public and private, amounts on the average to 14 percent of net national product (varying between 12 percent and 16 percent over the decade 1948-1957).[1] The private sector, according to these estimates, is the predominant source of this relatively high rate of capital formation. Private capital varied between 74 percent and 86 percent of total capital formation, and averaged around 81 percent over the decade. Public investments, on the other hand, amounted only to 19 percent of total capital formation, fluctuating between 14 percent and 26 percent of total investments over the decade. No breakdown of the sources (whether foreign or domestic) of this capital formation is available. It is however estimated[2] that about 80 percent of capital formation comes from domestic sources and about 20 percent from outside sources. Private foreign capital consists mainly of emigrant remittances and investment-seeking capital from the oil-producing neighbouring countries.

A breakdown of private capital formation into sectors (given in Table 53 below) demonstrates clearly that the services sectors are the major recipients of private capital investments.[3] On the average, their share amounted to 75.5 percent of private capital formation, varying

---

[1] These estimates were prepared by A. Y. Badre as quoted by Food and Agricultural Organization of the United Nations, *Lebanon: Country Report*, FAO Mediterranean Development Project, Rome, 1959, p. II 25. For a breakdown of investments into source (public or private) and sector of economic activity, see Appendix Table 4 on Capital Formation, 1948-1957.

[2] Food and Agricultural Organization of the United Nations, *op. cit.*, p. II 26.

[3] No breakdown into sectors of economic activity of public investment is available. But since they constitute only a minor portion of total capital formation, their exclusion may not distort the picture significantly.

Table 53

Private Capital Formation, by Sector
(1948-1957)

	Private Capital Formation (LL million)	Agriculture	Industry	Services
		(Percentage of Private Capital Formation)		
1948	97	6.2	15.5	78.3
1949	91	8.8	15.4	73.8
1950	130	9.2	17.7	73.1
1951	113	12.4	13.3	74.4
1952	128	11.7	11.7	76.3
1953	132	12.9	11.4	75.8
1954	140	14.3	10.7	73.0
1955	157	9.6	8.3	82.1
1956	176	12.5	13.6	73.9
1957	150	12.0	18.0	70.0
Mean		11.0	13.6	75.5

Source: Based on Appendix Table 4 on Capital Formation, 1948-1957.

between 70 percent and 82 percent over the 1948-1957 decade. Industry's share varied between 8 percent and 18 percent and averaged to less than 14 percent of total private investments. Agriculture's share was the lowest. It amounted to 11 percent of private investments, fluctuating between 6 and 14 percent. On the average, therefore, the services producing sectors receive three-fourths of total private investments,[1] and leave the goods producing sectors with the remaining one-fourth only. That the services sectors receive the bulk of private investments is both a reflection of and a reason for the relatively faster expansion that has taken place in these sectors. This is only normal in a services-biased economy where most of the institutions cater for the needs of services sectors. The unavailability of adequate specialized credit institutions to extend medium- and long-term capital for investment in industry and agriculture, and the almost complete lack of other credit facilities which help considerably in pooling savings funds and in channelling them into these sectors, are partly an outcome of this

---

[1] It should be mentioned that the bulk of the investment in 'services' has gone into real estate projects. It is estimated that such investments alone averaged to 54 *percent* (varying between 50 percent and 62 percent) of total private capital formation over the 1948-1957 decade. The remarkable construction boom the country is currently undergoing attests to this and to the fact that the construction industry is still the major recipient of capital investments.

bias and a likely cause of it.[1] A few of these deficiencies ought to be briefly mentioned.

To begin with, regular commercial banks, which in developed countries generally constitute a source of long term credit, do not in Lebanon undertake the issue of loans on longer than short term basis. These banks are also unequally distributed and heavily concentrated in Beirut. This places the less important urban centers and the rural areas at a disadvantage, and the people who need credit would have to resort to borrowing from landlords or money-lenders at high rates of interest. The non-existence of banking institutions in such places has also forced savings that might exist to be hoarded. Secondly, savings institutions are non-existent. There are no special savings banks in Lebanon to pool savings funds, and with the exception of a few banks which recently introduced certain savings devices, commercial banks do not generally consider it worthwhile to make a special effort to attract savings deposits. This is best reflected in the small ratio of savings deposits to total deposits. Thirdly, credit cooperatives, which usually constitute an important source of agricultural credit through the provision of a channel for farmers' savings and a way to mobilize capital for agricultural development, can practically be considered non-existent in Lebanon. The government, to be fair, promulgated various legislations for the purpose of spreading the cooperative movement. Such legislations have had no effect, however, on stimulating the formation of cooperatives. It seems that the social structure and the low saving capacity of most rural areas, do not help to overcome the individualistic and sectarian tendencies that presently impede the formation and spread of cooperative movements. Fourthly, capital markets in most developed economies serve as means for mobilizing long term capital funds. Lebanon's capital market is small and unorganized, and therefore cannot perform the expected role of pooling capital for long term investment. Corporations of good standing whose securities could be readily marketable, are only a handful in Lebanon. Private ownership is still the most predominant form of business, and the presence of many small firms is a clear feature of the economy. Finally,

---

[1] The only such specialized credit institution is the Agricultural, Industrial, and Real Estate Credit Bank, a partly government owned bank created in 1954. It may be of interest to note that this bank would not have been formed without government cooperation. Private capital accepted to participate only after the government had bought up 40 percent of its capital and guaranteed it a loan of LL 25 million. This provides an example of the difficulty of attracting capital into non-commercial enterprises.

the Agricultural, Industrial, and Real Estate Credit Bank, itself, has been criticized for being handicapped by major weaknesses and limitations, which have hindered its effectiveness in promoting an adequate flow of capital into the agricultural and industrial sectors.

The adverse effects of these institutional deficiencies must not be minimized. Experience of many countries shows that the growth and accumulation of capital have been practically parallel to the spread of adequate savings and specialized credit institutions. Lebanon's attempts so far to remedy this situation have only had meager beginnings. The high capital formation rate of 14 percent, and the disproportionately low share of the goods sectors of this capital (they receive only 25 percent as opposed to services' 75 percent), both strongly suggest that Lebanon's major problem is not the unavailability of capital, but that of channelling it into agriculture and industry. This still constitutes the main obstacle to a less lopsided economic structure.[1]

A related finding which points out another significant difference be-

Table 54

Capital-Output Ratios, by Sector
(1950-1957)

	Rate of Growth of NNP Per Cent Annum (Compounded)	Capital Formation as a Ratio of NNP Per Cent Per Annum	Capital-Output Ratio
Net National Product	5.39	13.96[a]	2.59
Agriculture	2.10	7.47[b]	3.56
Industry	4.29	11.17[b]	2.60
Services	7.33	16.20[b]	2.21

Source: Rates of growth of NNP are based on NNP figures already reported; Capital formation ratios are based on figures given in Table 4 in Statistical Appendix.

[a] Ratio of total capital formation (private & public) to NNP.

[b] Since no breakdown of public capital formation into sectors is available, these ratios are of private capital formation to NNP. This must understate the capital-output ratios but not significantly since public capital constitutes only a minor portion of total capital formation.

---

[1] For a detailed description of a suggested mechanism whereby the flow of capital into the goods producing sectors may be promoted, see Khalil Salem, *Credit and Economic Growth in Lebanon*, Unpublished Ph. D. Thesis submitted to the Department of Economics and Business Administration of Vanderbilt University, Nashville, Tennessee, July 1964.

tween the 'goods' and 'services' sectors must be noted. It seems that not only do the services producing sectors receive appreciably more private capital investments than do the goods producing sectors, they also enjoy relatively lower capital/output ratios. These ratios, reported in Table 54, have been computed from available data on rates of growth and capital formation of the various sectors. The capital/output ratio of the services sectors over the years 1950 through 1957 amounted to 2.21; those of the industrial and agricultural sectors for the same period were both higher at 2.60 and 3.56 respectively. This more favorable capital/output ratio of the 'services' sectors can also in part account, along with the fact that they receive a larger amount of capital investments, for the disparity in the expansion rates of the goods producing and services producing sectors.

5. MALDISTRIBUTION OF INCOME

The special economic structure of the country and the disparity in the rates of growth of the sectors, have helped considerably in augmenting the unequitable distribution of income among the various classes and geographic regions. It is true that the impressive expansion in the services sectors has enabled the country, despite its smallness and the general paucity of natural resources, to enjoy a standard of living which is 'substantially higher than anywhere else in either Asia or Africa with the exception of Israel and the Union of SouthAfrica.' But it is equally

Table 55

Income Distribution per Family

Maximum Annual Income/Family (L.L.)	Per Cent of Total Population		Cumulative Per Cent of Total Population	
	Churchill Study	IRFED Study	Churchill Study	IRFED Study
1,200	8	9	8	9
2,500	26	41	34	50
5,000	31	32	65	82
15,000	25	14	90	96
Over 15,000	10	4	100	100

Source: République Libanaise, Ministère du Plan, *Besoins et Possibilités de Développements du Liban*, (Mission IRFED), 1960-1961, Vol. 1, p. 94. The Churchill estimates are for the City of Beirut only (See his *The City of Beirut*, Economic Research Institute, American University of Beirut, 1954); The IRFED estimates are for the rural regions of the country.

true that the same expansion in services has also widened the discrepancy in the income levels of the various classes and geographic regions of the country. That the discrepancy in income levels is wide is supported by the following estimates on income distribution per family of five persons. Since it can be safely assumed that income per capita is around LL 1200 ($400), the above pattern of distribution suggests that at least half the population earns less than the average income per capita, and that only 18 percent earn more than the average income.[1] Figures on regional breakdown of income are not available. Sectoral shares of national income are, however, sufficient to indicate that the bulk of the national product arises in the commerce, finance and auxiliary sectors which are mostly located in Beirut. Income levels in Beirut are therefore expected to be much higher than elsewhere in the country. The extent to which the special economic structure of the country is responsible for this maldistribution of income is indicated by estimates (given in Table 56 below) on persons employed and national income per employed person by sector of economic activity. Agriculture which is estimated to employ slightly less than 50 percent of total number of persons employed, generates only 16 percent of the national product. Whereas, trade (with its auxiliary sectors of finance

Table 56

National Income and Employment, by Sector
(1957)

	National Income (Percentages)	Persons Employed (Percentages)	National Income Per Employed Person (L.L.)
Agriculture	16	49	1,082
Industry	13	12	3,500
Construction	3	7	1,242
Transportation	5	5	3,333
Commerce	31	12	8,849
Finance	6	0.4	45,500
Other Services	10	11	3,083
Government	7	4	6,750
Real Estate	9	n.a.	n.a.

Source: IRFED Mission, *Etude Préliminaire sur les Possibilités du Développement au Liban,* 1959-1960, Vol. I, p. I-I-33.

[1] These are now dated estimates. More recent and reliable studies on income distribution are unfortunately not available.

and transportation) employes only 17 percent of total number of persons employed and contributes around 42 percent of national income. The magnitude of the resulting unequitable distribution of income is more forcefully exposed by the almost unbelievable discrepancy in the incomes earned by persons employed in the different sectors. The income earned per employed person is lowest in the agricultural sector and highest in the finance sector. The disparity between these two sectors is so wide that a person employed in the finance sector earns on the average 45 times as much as a person employed in the agriculture sector. The maldistribution of income generated by such an incredible disparity is quite obvious.

The special structure of the economy, it has been observed, is also generating a "distributional pattern of income that favours entrepreneurs and capitalists rather than wage and salary earners. In trade, the share of wages and salaries amounts to only 10 percent of total income generated, compared with 36 percent in industry and 66 percent in construction. The share of profits and interest in the trade sector amounts to 85 percent of total income."[1]

6. MARKET LIMITATIONS AND DISECONOMIES OF SCALE

Income distribution considerations are of special significance to Lebanon, because an unequitably distributed income (such as Lebanon's) could be a major source of market limitation, and Lebanon's domestic market (without the added constraint of a maldistributed income) is already quite limited. The disparity in class and regional levels of income reflects itself in the flagrant difference in both the pattern and level of consumption of the different classes and regions of the country. Low and inelastic demands which characterize the low-income classes and regions are typical of the under-developed problems frequently talked about in the literature. Undoubtedly, a more equitable distribution of income will be effective in changing the pattern and raising the level of consumption of the less developed regions, and thus increasing aggregate demand and expanding the domestic market.

Another factor (not related to income distribution) that can also be a cause of restriction in the extent of the domestic market, is the imperfectly competitive structure that predominates in major sectors of the Lebanese economy. A cursory investigation of the main Lebanese

---

[1] See Elias S. Saba, "The Implications of the Foreign Sector in the Lebanese Economy," *op. cit.*, p. 152.

industries (textiles, confectionery, sugar...) is enough to bring out the fact that whatever competition exists between the few and unanonymous firms is of an imperfectly competitive variety. This question of the character of competition of the Lebanese market is of relevance here since an imperfectly competitive market structure could be considered to be both a consequence and a cause of market limitation. It is generally observed that it is easier to develop monopoly practices in small markets. Because a small market could only support a small number of firms, competition, if any, that could prevail is more likely to be monopolistic in nature. In a small country where competitors are relatively few in number and not total strangers to each other, the relationship between them tends to be more cooperative and less aggressive than it would be when competitors are many and anonymous.

Any measure that helps to expand the country's domestic market will do away with one of the main obstacles to sustained economic growth in Lebanon. In view of the country's disproportionate predominance of its services and trade sectors, and of the resulting need to promote the development of the commodity-producing sectors, such measures become basic to the country's general development. The expected increase in demand, attending a more equitable distribution of income, for example, is likely to induce an expansion in output, and such an expansion may make possible the adoption and operation of more efficient scales of plants in the country's main lines of production. All factors that may ultimately enable Lebanon to take advantage of economies of scale in her main industries, must be given due consideration. The importance of scale among the many factors that influence growth and productivity, in a small country like Lebanon, can be of considerable proportions. The lack of economies of scale may have handicapped the growth and efficiency of the agricultural and industrial sectors. Considering, however, some of the features already discussed in this Chapter, it could also be argued that it was not mainly the small size of the market, but a 'complex of factors', some related and some not related to size, that prevented the utilization of large scale production.

Experience of other countries, both large and small, with regard to the importance of economies of scale in explaining efficiency and growth, is not very clear. It may be interesting to mention briefly some of these cases. Switzerland provides a good example of an economy where the exceptionally high ratio of exports to domestic sales, and the high dependence on export markets, enabled the country to achieve the necessary economies of scale in her main industries. And this achievement, it is suggested, is one of the main factors that can explain the country's relatively high level of income per capita.[1] Belgium's example is different. Her dependence on export markets is not as high as Switzerland's, and those who have studied its efficiency were inclined to the view that the lack of economies of scale had not gravely handicapped the Belgian economy.[2] Discussion of the American case suggests that economies of scale form a part of the explanation of the efficiency of the American economy, but only a part. Other factors are immensely important in explaining the American situation.[3] Generalizing from the experience of India, it has been suggested that economic development, in some of its aspects, would be easier if a large and assured market were to be served.[4] The Italian case was found to be a good proof of the outstanding role of a large national market in the development of an efficient and well-balanced industrial and agricultural system. The comparative smallness of the Italian market, it is indicated, is of itself a serious obstacle to the development, on an adequate scale, of the process of industrialization, which is now a precondition of the country's general development. This is true not only of the backward region like the South, but also of the industrialized regions where, in the present phase of rapid technological process, the constraint of an insufficient domestic outlet is felt more and more keenly.[5]

Whatever the experience of other countries may suggest, it is believed that the smallness of the Lebanese market, and the resulting general lack of economies of scale, have had a considerable influence on both the pattern and pace of the country's general develpment. The prevalence of small and invariably very small firms, that can be observed in almost all sectors of economic activity, is by and large an outcome of the small domestic market.[6] While the presence of small

---

[1] See W. A. Jöhr and F. Kneschaurek, "Study of the Efficiency of a Small Nation: Switzerland," E. A. C. Robinson (ed.), *Economic Consequences of the Size of Nations*, London: Macmillan & Co., Ltd., 1960, pp. 54-77.

[2] L. Duquesne de La Vinelle, "Study of the Efficiency of a Small Nation: Belgium," *op. cit.*, pp. 78-92.

[3] S. Fabricant, "Study of the Size and Efficiency of the American Economy," *op. cit.*, pp. 35-53.

[4] C. N. Vakil and P. R. Brahmananda, "The Problems of Developing Countries, *op. cit.*, pp. 133-150.

[5] V. A. Marsan, "The Experience of Italy," *op. cit.*, pp. 151-167.

[6] It has also been suggested that the individualism of the Lebanese businessman could be a likely cause of this phenomonom. There is an abundance of proverbs

firms may not be a strong impediment in the services sectors, since the factor of scale is not as important in the production of services, it has undoubtedly been a major obstacle in industry and agriculture.

That the overwhelming majority of industrial firms in Lebanon is of an extremely small size is indicated by the following estimates. At least 51 percent of all establishments employed less than 10 persons; around 85 percent employed less than 25 persons; and 94 percent employed less than 50 persons. Only 6 percent of all establishments employed more than 50 persons.[1] For the sake of comparison it may be mentioned that in Switzerland, a country noted for the prevalence of very small firms, 82 percent (as opposed to Lebanon's 95 percent) of all industrial plants employ less than 50 workers. It should also be stated in this connection that the average size of the Lebanese industrial plant has not shown any strong tendency to increase. In 1955, an industrial plant employed on the average 18 workers, whereas in 1964 the average number of workers per plant had risen only to 21. For a detailed breakdown of the 1955 and 1964 industrial establishments and workers per establishment see Table 57 below. Projections prepared by IRFED Mission estimate that the number of workers employed by the industrial sector will increase from around 60,000 workers in 1959 to over 100.000 in 1975. If it is assumed that the average plant employs around 20 workers in 1975, the industrial sector will have in the neighbourhood of 2,000 additional plants, bringing the total to around 4,000 plants (employing more than five workers) by 1975. Of these, at least 2,000 would be plants employing less than 10 workers, and around 3,500 employing less than 25 workers.

These figures should reveal that the Lebanese industrial sector makes

---

playing up the wisdon and superiority of making business alone. The corporation as a result has had to grow slowly. The consequences in fragmentation and shortage of finance, in wasteful duplication, in inability to finance research, in the limitation of the life of firms to the lifetime of their owners, are too familiar for elaboration. See Y. A. Sayigh, *Economic Development of Lebanon – Its Prospects and Problems* (mimeographed), October 1955, p. 50.

[1] Extracted from La Direction Centrale de la Statistique, *Recensement de L'industrie Au Liban*, 1964. It should be noted that these figures understate the importance of small firms, since the census excluded plants employing less than five persons, and it is believed that there is a significantly large number of such firms in Lebanon. The figure for handicrafts and plants employing less than five persons is estimated to be around 8,550. See G. Siksek, B. J. Daouk, S. E. Baaklini, *Preliminary Assessment of Manpower Resources and Requirements in Lebanon*, American University of Beirut, Lebanon, 1960, p. 34. The Ministry of National Economy estimates the total number of industrial plants at 10,400, while the industrial census of 1964 covered only 2,098 plants of five workers and above.

Table 57

Growth of Manufacturing Industry, 1955-1964

	Number of Establishments		Number of Workers		Number of Workers per Establishment	
	1955	1964	1955	1964	1955	1964
Food Products	554	491	6,468	6,681	12	14
Beverages	74	43	1,040	1,556	14	36
Textiles	113	121	6,049	5,277	53	44
Footwear & Clothing	245	274	3,632	4,563	15	17
Wood Industry	71	82	755	1,962	11	24
Furniture	168	230	2,643	3,918	16	17
Paper & Paper Products	16	36	204	610	13	17
Printing & Allied Industries	108	185	1,660	3,798	15	21
Leather	45	154	937	1,112	21	21
Rubber Products	15	14	523	276	35	20
Chemical Products	37	54	630	1,425	17	26
Non-metallic Products	155	309	4,338	6,506	28	21
Metal Products	128	137	2,456	4,346	19	32
Trans. & Electrical Products	20	21	434	394	22	19
Miscellaneous	43	47	702	527	16	11
TOTAL	1,790	2,098	32,471	72,951	18	21

Source: Industrial Census of Lebanon, 1955, Table 2, p. 8; and La Direction Centrale de la Statistique Au Ministère du Plan, *Recensement de L'industrie Au Liban, Résultats Pour 1964,* pp. 24-35.

very modest use indeed, if any use at all, of the possibilities of large-scale production, and that these possibilities, judging by present trends, are not likely to be appreciably better in the future.

Some of the implications of this phenomenon ought to be high lighted. Small establishments predominate the industrial sector as far as number is concerned, but they provide a comparatively insignificant source of employment, cash receipts, and value added. While plants employing less than 10 workers comprise more than 51 percent of total number of plants, they employ less than 13 percent of total number of workers, and provide only 9 percent of total cash receipts and a similar percentage of total value added. In contrast, plants employing more than 50 workers are only around 7 percent of total number of plants, but employ 51 percent of the industrial labor force, and are responsible for 58 percent of total cash receipts and 57 percent of the total value added by all industrial establishments. If one were to define 'small' plants as those that employ less than 25 workers, 85 percent of Lebanon's total industrial plants will fall in this category, employing only 34 percent of the industrial labor force and generating respectively 25 percent and 27 percent of the cash receipt and value added of all industrial plants. This means that 85 percent of industrial plants (those employing less than 25 persons) generate only half the cash receipts and half the value added by 7 percent of plants (those employing more than 50 persons). This should demonstrate the disproportionately minor role 'small' establishments perform as sources of employment, cash receipts, and value added. For a breakdown of establishments, persons employed, cash receipts, and value added by size of establishment see Table 58 below. From the same Table the value added per

Table 58

Number of Establishments, Number of Persons employed, Cash Receipts, and Value added by Size of Establishment, 1964

Size of Establishment (Persons Employed)	Number of Establishments		Number of Persons Employed		Cash Receipts		Value Added	
	No.	%	No.	%	LL 1000's	%	LL 1000's	%
5- 9	1,078	51.4	5,297	12.9	77,334	9.0	28,846	9.2
10-24	693	33.0	8,571	20.9	140,668	16.3	54,549	17.5
25-49	187	8.90	6,171	15.0	142,991	16.6	52,050	16.7
50 and over	141	6.71	21,054	51.2	501,495	58.1	176,882	56.6
TOTAL	2,099	100	41,093	100	862,488	100	312,327	100

Source: La Direction Centrale de la Statistique Au Ministère du Plan, *Recensement de L'industrie Au Liban, Résultats Pour* 1964, pp. 24-35.

person employed in plants of different sizes can be computed. The results also indicat that the average value added per person employed rises as the average size of the establishment increases. The value added per person in plants of less than 10 workers amounted to LL 5,445, and increased regularly with the increase in the size of plants until it reached LL 8,400 for those employing more than 50 workers.

Small industrial plants therefore seem to be at a general disadvantage as sources of employment, cash receipts, value added, and also as far as productivity of workers are concerned. The repercussions of such observations are not likely to decline, if the average scale of plant does not expand, and if therefore the prospects of making modest use of large-scale production remain remote in the future.

As regards agriculture, the prevalence of very small units is even more observable. Excessive and often minute fragmentation of land is a reputable feature of Lebanese agriculture. 'It is not uncommon in Lebanon to find peasants owning just one terrace of vines or fruit trees or a small garden or even only a share of either. Sometimes the desire of equality in succession is carried so far that even a small grove is divided among the different heirs each getting a given number of trees.' It has been noted in this connection that in some cases 'heirs received one tree only, or even one branch of a tree. In Northern Lebanon, for example, a walnut tree was found to have as many as 14 owners. It is the *reductio ad absurdum* of private property.'[1] A notorious fragmentation of land impelled the Lebanese farmer to work against all odds in order to raise the productivity (which is already fairly high) of the small family farm. The modest growth in agricultural production has therefore been mainly due to intensification of agriculture, and not an expansion in cultivated area. The intensification was made possible by heavy investments in new terraces and in increased use of fertilizers. The small farmer has almost transformed the thin-soiled mountain slopes into prosperous fruit and vegetable gardens. Growth, as a result, has been highest in the production of fruits and vegetables (mainly citrus products and apples). 'He has built terraces to prevent erosion, dug ditches to canalize mountain streams for irrigation and planted trees to increase his income from the land. He has learnt the techniques of fruit farming and has made Lebanon famous for its high quality fruits.' In short, he has done almost all that could conceivably be done with the sparse and limited land resources as are available. 'On the whole, the small farmer in the mountain areas has a fairly decent standard of living.' In fact it is suggested that with his family he can make a comfortable living on a one acre farm.[2]

It must be mentioned that growth in other agricultural products

---

[1] Paul J. Klat, "Whither Land Tenure in the Arab World," *Middle East Economic Papers, 1955,* Economic Research Institute, American University of Beirut, p. 56.

[2] See George Hakim, "Land Tenure Reform," *Middle East Economic Papers, 1954,* op. cit., p. 86, who estimates that the net income per acre is around LL 6,400. This would place the per capita income of a small farmer (assuming an average family of five) at a higher level than the general per capita income of the whole country, even when supplementary income earnings, which are quite common in rural areas, are not considered.

(other than fruits and vegetables) has not been very impressive. Some in fact (e.g., wheat and barley) declined as land devoted to these products was reduced. Lebanon still remains an importer of these and other basic agricultural products. Only in the case of fruits and vegetables does the country have an export surplus. In almost all others, except in poultry and eggs where an appreciable expansion in production has recently taken place, the discrepancy between consumption and production remains substantially high.

With the indispensable requisites for the development of an efficient and well-balanced industrial and agricultural system almost completely lacking, Lebanon understandably has had to rely heavily on the production of services, where the question of scale is not as much of an impediment. Admittedly, this reliance has contributed significantly to the comparatively decent standard of living of the country. But it has also generated a defective economic structure which could be a major source of precariousness and instability. An extension of the small domestic market, and a possible achievement of the necessary economies of scale in the country's industries, could be instrumental in correcting the defective structure. Extending the local market (through a more equitable distribution of income, and a more competitive market structure) while undeniably a necessary measure, is not in itself sufficient to enable the country to diversify her economy and to develop the necessary economies of scale. It other words, one must realize Lebanon's meager prospects (in view of the smallness of its domestic market) for promoting increases in output that are 'diversified in accordance with domestic income elasticities of demand.' Such a diversification will not be sufficient to instigate output expansion. What in the final analysis Lebanon should do is to attempt an output expansion for export, which is 'diversified in accordance with regional comparative advantage.' The country, that is, should increase her dependence on export markets in order to utilize large scale production and thus compensate for her smallness.[1] If foreign trade is to compensate for the

---

[1] May be it should be mentioned again that it was this high dependence on export markets which enabled Switzerland to develop economies of scale in her major industries. For comparison, Switzerland's average export ratio (Exports as percent of national income) amounts to around 25 percent, whereas Lebanon's export ratio is only 10 percent (and is declining). The heavy export orientation of the Swiss economy is best illustrated by the fact that four important branches of industry (watches, dyes, pharmaceutical preparations, and embroideries) export 95 percent of their output. See W. A. Jöhr and F. Kneschaurek, op. cit., Table IV, p. 63. The export orientation should also demonstrate that a country's small size by no means implies that its market must be small.

smallness of Lebanon, exports must play a substantially larger part in the economy. The small domestic market, as already indicated, allows little room for output expansion. Only through increasing exports, therefore, can Lebanon get rid of the obstacles arising from market limitations and diseconomies of scale. This would mean, among other things, an increase in the already high dependence on foreign trade. But this may be the only effective way whereby the desired output expansion can be obtained.

CHAPTER SEVEN

DIVERSITY OF THE LEBANESE ECONOMY

Discussion here will be concerned with finding out the extent to which the generalization that the economic structure of small nations is less diversified than that of large nations, applies to the case of Lebanon. Diversity, as defined here, will encompass diversity of production, and also diversity of exports, and degree of dispersion (or concentration) of foreign markets. This broad concept of diversity is adopted because the assumption of the limited diversity of the economic structure of small nations is often coupled with the assumption that small nations concentrate on a few export industries, and that, more than larger nations, they rely on a few export markets, particularly those of their immediate neighbours. It is assumed for example that the structure of the export industries of small nations would have to follow their production structure. Since it is believed that small countries generally exhibit a limited degree of diversity in their overall economic structure,[1] the degree of diversity of their exports is expected to be limited too, and, as a result, they may find it easier to rely on a few export markets.

There are, therefore, three aspects of diversity that will be considered: diversity of production, diversity of exports (and also imports since there are some interesting relationships between the two), and degree of dispersion (or concentration) of foreign markets. Diversity of production will be measured in terms of the diversity of the occupational structure, namely, in terms of the labor force employed by the various sectors of economic activity, and in terms of the income arising in each sector. Diversity of exports (and imports) will be measured in terms of the percentage of total exports (and imports) contributed by the various groups of export (and import) products. Specifically, the degree of concentration of Lebanese exports and imports will be measured by the *Hirschman* coefficient of commodity concentration—

---

[1] For a discussion of the reasons making for the greater concentration of economic structure of small nations, see S. Kuznets, "Economic Growth of Small Nations," *op. cit.*, pp. 15-18.

$$\sqrt{\sum_{1}^{n} \left(\frac{\chi_i}{X}\right)^2}$$

where χ_i is the annual value of any good i exported or imported, and X is $\Sigma\chi_i$.[1] Degree of dispersion of foreign markets can also be measured by this coefficient for both exports and imports, and because of particular relevance to the case of Lebanon, by the percentage of total exports absorbed by the immediate neighbouring countries.

1. Diversity of Production

A general view of the diversity of the economic structure of Lebanon has already been partly conveyed by the analysis of national income estimates which indicated a unique structure characterized by a disproportionately heavy dependence on the services producing sectors. This dependence has reflected itself in the fact that around 70 percent of the country's national product is generated by the services-producing sectors and only the remaining 30 percent by the commodity-producing sectors. It was also indicated that there is a heavy concentration on trade activity which alone usually accounts for at least 30 percent of national product. In terms of the labor force employed, it has been roughly estimated that the agricultural sector alone employs 50 percent, industry 11 percent, and services combined employ around 40 percent of the total labor force.

A more detailed breakdown is, however, required if the degree of diversity of the country's economic structure is to be adequately conveyed. This is attempted in Table 59, where Lebanon's occupational structure (in terms of the labor force employed) is compared with similar data for Switzerland, United States and West Germany. The

---

[1] This coefficient, more commonly referred to in the literature as the *Gini* coefficient, was first used by Albert O. Hirschman to measure geographic concentration of trade in his *National Power and the Structure of Foreign Trade*, Berkeley, University of California Press, 1945. Recently, the coefficient has become suddenly popular. It was used by Michael Michaely, "Concentration of Exports and Imports: An Interpretational Comparison," *Economic Journal*, 1958, pp. 722-736; by Jan Tinbergen. *Shaping the World Economy*, New York, the Twentieth Century Fund, 1962, p. 268; by Joseph D. Coppock, *International Economic Instability*, New York, McGraw-Hill, 1962; and by B. F. Massel, "Export Concentration and Fluctuations in Export Earnings: A Cross-Section Analysis," *American Economic Review*, March 1964, pp. 47-63. Hirschman now claims that he is, and not Gini, the originator of the coefficient. In a recent note, he stands up to defent his case as the rightful father. See A. O. Hirschman, "The Paternity of an Index," *American Economic Review*, September 1964, p. 761.

Table 59

Occupational Structure in Lebanon, Switzerland, the United States, and Western Germany[1]*, Labor Force (%)*

	Lebanon	Switzerland	U.S.	W. Germany
Agriculture	50.0	16.5	11.7	6.7
Mining & Quarrying	0.3	0.3	1.6	5.7
Construction	8.0	8.1	6.0	8.0
Industry	10.7	37.1	26.9	41.2
of which:				
Food	2.9	4.0	2.8	4.2
Textiles	2.0	3.7	2.2	4.6
Clothing	1.2	5.2	2.1	3.8
Timber & Cork	0.3	2.9	2.1	3.6
Paper	0.1	0.9	0.8	0.9
Printing	0.5	1.5	1.4	1.0
Chemicals	0.2	1.6	1.6	2.3
Leather	0.3	0.5	0.7	0.6
Rubber	0.2	0.4	0.4	0.5
Non-metallic				
minerals	1.4	1.0	0.9	1.1
Basic Metals	—	4.5	4.0	6.4
Metal Products &				
Machinery	1.0	11.7	7.0	12.0
Miscellaneous	0.3	0.1	0.9	0.2
Commerce & Finance	14.0	11.7	22.5	10.0
Transport	5.0	4.5	6.1	7.4
Government	4.0	4.0	11.1	9.1
Other Services	8.0	17.2	14.1	11.9
TOTAL	100.0	100.0	100.0	100.0

Source: Figures for Switzerland, U.S., and Western Germany are based on
W. A. Jöhr and F. Kneschaurek, "Study of the Efficiency of a Small
Nation: Switzerland," in E. A. G. Robinson (ed.), *Economic Conse-
quences of the Size of Nations*, London: Macmillan & Co., p. 73; Figures
for Lebanon are based on Benjamin Higgins,*Financing Lebanese Development—
A Report on Fiscal Policy* (mimeographed), Beirut, 1960, p. 2, and on
Republic of Lebanon, Ministry of National Economy, *Industrial Census*,
1955, Beirut, 1957, p. 8, Table 2.

labor force absorbed by the agricultural sector in Lebanon (estimated
at 50 percent of total labor force) is considerably higher than the percentage of the labor force absorbed by the corresponding sector in
each of Switzerland, the United States, and West Germany where the
percentage shares are at 16.5 percent, 11.7 percent, and 6.7 percent

[1] Switzerland's, United States', and West Germany's figures are for 1950;
Lebanon's are for 1955.

respectively. The labor force absorbed by the industrial sector is also contrastingly different in Lebanon from the other three countries. Lebanon's 10.7 percent is considerably lower than Switzerland's 37.7 percent, United States' 26.9 percent, or Germany's 41.2 percent. The breakdown of the occupational structure within the industrial sector reveals that the degree of concentration (in terms of the labor force absorbed by main industries) is comparatively higher in Lebanon than that of the other three countries. For example, the four largest labor-employing industries in Lebanon absorb around 70 percent of total industrial labor force, while both in Switzerland and Germany they absorb 65 percent, and in the United States 59 percent of the industrial labor force. It can, therefore, be seen from this Table that Lebanon has had to concentrate on a few branches of industrial production, and that the Lebanese economy as a whole is less diversified than that of the United States, Germany and Switzerland. This is in line with the Kuznets generalization that a small country must by necessity be less varied than other larger countries. It is most interesting to observe, however, the remarkable similarity between the Swiss and German patterns and diversities of industrial production, and that contrary to the Kuznets assumption, the Swiss economy is hardly less diversified than that of the United States and Germany.

The extent of the limited diversity of industrial production[1] in Lebanon can also be seen in the relative amounts of 'value-added' by each of the main industries. The food industry alone generates 19.3 percent of total 'value-added' of industrial sector (and employs 18.3 percent of industrial labor force). Diversity of production is so limited that the value added by the four largest industries (the food, non-metallic minerals, tobacco, and textiles) amounts to around 60 percent of total value added by all industries. This is also almost true of the percentage of the labor force employed by these industries which amounts to around 55 percent of industrial labor force. Table 60 on the diversity of industrial production summarizes the breakdown of the labor employed and value added by main industrial categories.

2. Commodity Concentration of Trade

Since it is contended that the lack of diversity of economic structure

---

[1] No detailed data on patterns of production in other sectors of the economy are available. Data on industrial production are based on the second Census of industry undertaken during 1965.

Table 60

Diversity of Industrial Production in Lebanon, 1964

	Labor Employed 1964	Value Added 1964
	(as Per Cent of All Industries)	
Food & Beverages	18.3	19.3
Tobacco	4.5	13.0
Textiles	11.7	7.7
Clothing	10.1	7.1
Timber & Cork	4.4	2.5
Furniture	8.7	5.6
Paper	1.4	1.7
Printing	8.4	8.1
Chemicals	3.2	3.2
Leather	2.5	2.5
Rubber	0.6	0.4
Non-metallic minerals	14.4	19.1
Basic Metals	2.0	1.3
Metal products	7.0	6.1
Machinery	1.5	1.4
Miscellaneous	1.3	1.0
TOTAL	100.0	100.0

Source: Based on La Direction Centrale De La Statistique Au Ministère Au Plan, *Recensement De L'industrie Au Liban, Résultats Pour 1964.*

often results in a generally undiversified exports, it becomes of interest to measure the commodity concentration of Lebanese exports, and to compare this measure with the commodity concentration of exports of other countries. A measure of the geographic concentration of exports will also be attempted, since countries with a relatively few export commodities are expected (and may find it more convenient) to depend on a smaller number of export markets.

As stated earlier, the degree of concentration of Lebanon's exports was measured by the Hirschman coefficient of concentration. To render Lebanon's coefficients comparable with similar coefficients prepared for other countries (particularly those prepared by Michaely and Massell), Lebanese exports were classified on the basis of the Standard International Trade Classification (SITC) 150 *groups* (three-digit code).[1]

---

[1] In the SITC, commodities are classified into 10 *sections* (one-digit code), 52 *divisions* (two-digit code), 150 *groups* (three-digit code), and 570 *items* (five-digit code). The three-digit classification scheme was selected for practical considerations. Any other scheme, in the case of Lebanon, would have been either inconvenient or incomparable with schemes already employed in similar studies.

It is important that the same classification scheme be used since it has been pointed out that the value of the concentration coefficients depends on the level of commodity aggregation used. In fact it was demonstrated that the concentration index will be larger, the larger is the level of commodity aggregation.[1] Lebanon's coefficient of commodity concentration of exports, thus computed, amounted to 36.3 (which is multiplied by 100 for convenience). Michaely's coefficients for his sample of 44 countries ranged from 98.8 to 16.9 (the maximum possible range being from 100 to 8.2).[2] If these countries were arranged in decreasing order of coefficients of concentration and Lebanon's coefficient is included among them, Lebanon will be the 24th country on such a list. It must be noted also that Massell's similar coefficients for 36 countries ranged from 99.1 to 16.0. If these coefficients were also arrayed in decreasing order (Lebanon inserted among them), Lebanon will occupy the 23rd place. In both cases, Lebanon's coefficient (36.3) of commodity concentration of exports turns out to be lower than the means of the coefficients computed by Michaely and Massell. The arithmetical (unweighted) means of the coefficients of the forty-four countries of the Michaely sample, and of the thirty-six countries of the Massell sample amounted to 44.8 and 45.1 respectively. This should demonstrate that Lebanon's commodity exports are not conspicuously less diversified than the commodity exports of the average country included in the Michaely and Massell studies.

The Hirschman coefficient was also employed to measure the commodity concentration of Lebanese imports. The same SITC (three-digit) classification scheme was used, and the import coefficient thus

---

[1] B. F. Massell, *op. cit.*, computed the Hirschman coefficient for a sample of 35 countries on the basis of two classification schemes, differing in the level of commodity aggregation involved—the SITC one-digit and three-digit codes—and found out that the coefficients based on the scheme involving higher levels of aggregation (one-digit code) were appreciably larger than those based on the scheme involving lower levels of commodity aggregation (three-digit code). It should be also mentioned in this regard that M. Michaely, *op. cit.*, using a similar classification scheme, computed coefficients which corresponded fairly closely to Massell's coefficients; and that J. D. Coppock, *op. cit.*, who based his Hirschman co-efficients on a higher commodity aggregation scheme, computed indices which were considerably higher than those of Michaely and Massell.

[2] The coefficient of 100 would be for the case where a country's exports consist of one commodity only. The lowest possible coefficient of 8.2 would represent the case where a country's exports are distributed equally among all commodities. Since in the three-digit classification scheme used here the number of commodities is 150, the lowest possible coefficient would then be $\frac{100}{\sqrt{150}}$ or about 8.2.

measured amounted to 20.6. Only Michaely calculated similar import coefficients, and Lebanon's coefficient will therefore be briefly compared with Michaely's. The import coefficients he computed for the forty-four countries ranged, with one exception, from 30.5 to 15.6 (the maximum possible range, as with exports, is from 100 to 8.6 since the same classification scheme is used). If these coefficients are arranged by descending order and Lebanon's coefficient ranked among them, Lebanon would fall exactly half way down the list and occupy 23rd place. The arithmetical (unweighted) mean of Michaely's forty-four import coefficients amounts to 22.7. Lebanon's coefficient of 20.6 is lower than this average. So with respect to imports also, Lebanon seems to have a lower degree of concentration in its imports than the average of the forty-four countries included in the Michaely study. Michaely also computed the ratio between the coefficients of concentration of exports and of imports. The arithmetical average of this ratio is approximately 2 (ranging from 4.54 to 0.82). Lebanon's ratio between the export and import coefficients amounts to 1.76.

The fact that Lebanon's commodity exports are more concentrated than its commodity imports, while generally expected in a country like Lebanon, calls for some comment. Some of the factors that are likely to have influenced (either increased or decreased) the commodity concentration of Lebanese exports and imports, and that can partly justify their present degree of concentration and disparity, will therefore be briefly suggested. It must be mentioned for a start that such a disparity between the degree of commodity concentration of Lebanese exports and imports is in line with the classical assumption set forth by Mill, Marshall, and Taussig, that countries tend to specialize more in what they export than in what they import;[1] and in line with the Joan Robinson presumption that "In general, each country is more specialized in respect to the goods which it produces than in respect to the goods which it consumes,..."[2] and with Michaely's verification of this presumption. Michaely demonstrated that in the case of thirty-nine out of the forty-four countries investigated, exports were more concentrated than imports, and that on the average commodity exports were approximately twice as concentrated as commodity imports.[3]

---

[1] Charles P. Kindleberger, *Foreign Trade and the National Economy*, New Haven, Yale University Press, 1962, p. 145.

[2] Joan Robinson, "Beggar-My-Neighbour Remedies for Unemployment," A. E. A., *Readings in the Theory of International Trade*, London, Allen & Unwin, 1949, p. 400.

[3] Reference should also be made here to a study by Kuznets which also de-

One important factor which seems to influence the degree of concentration of exports and imports is the level of economic development. Since it is generally expected that a high level of economic development invariably means a more diversified production structure, it must then follow that the more developed countries would have less concentrated exports. This contention finds support in Michaely's study. Classifying countries into 'developed' and 'underdeveloped', he found out that the 'developed' countries have, on the average, significantly less concentrated exports than the 'underdeveloped' countries. The average export concentration coefficient of the former group amounted to 31.2, while the average coefficient of the latter amounted to 53.7.[1] A high level of economic development also means a high level of *per capita* consumption and a more diversified consumption pattern. This would suggest too that the more developed the country, the more diversified are its imports.[2] Lebanon's level of economic development is one of the highest in the region, but is still materially lower than development levels elsewhere in the world, and is not, which is more significant, equally distributed among the different sectors of the economy. While the 'services' sectors are highly developed, the 'goods' sectors still lag behind. Among other things, this has meant that a sizeable part of Lebanese exports are in the form of services.[3] Export statistics readily available and used in computing concentration coefficients include only exports of goods, and not those of services. If services exports were included, particularly in the case of a services-exporting economy like Lebanon, the degree of concentration of Le-

monstrates that the commodity concentration of exports is higher than that of imports. Using the two-digit SITC classification, it was found out that for a sample of 76 countries the single largest import group averages somewhat less than 20 percent of total imports; whereas the single largest export group averages 50 percent of total exports. Similarly, the average share of the three largest commodity groups is about 40 percent of total imports, whereas it is more than 75 percent of total exports. See Simon Kuznets, "Quantitative Aspects of the Economic Growth of Nations: Level and Structure of Foreign Trade: Comparisons for Recent Years," *Economic Development and Cultural Change*, Vol. XIII, No. 1, Part II, October 1964, Table 15, pp. 52-53.

[1] Michaely, *op. cit.*, *Economic Journal*, p. 729, Table II. 'Developed' Country was defined as a country whose *per capita* income exceeds U.S. $ 300.

[2] The magnitude of the association between concentration of exports and imports and economic development was analyzed in more detail in Chapter III.

[3] Receipts from the export of services, as will be indicated in the next Chapter, ranged from 51 to 53 percent of total foreign exchange receipts over the 1951-1961 decade, while receipts from merchandise exports declined from 26 to 18 percent over the same period. Exports of services, in other words, are more than twice the value of merchandise exports.

banese exports would have been substantially lower. A relatively advanced services sector has also contributed to increasing the diversity
of Lebanese imports, and can therefore partly account for the discrepancy between the concentration of commodity exports and imports.
The expanding touristic industry in Lebanon, for example, has generated a demand for a wide range of imported products. By and large, a
significant portion of these imports goes to satisfy tourists' demands
directly or indirectly.[1] The notable expansion in the construction industry, and the ensuing increase in the demand for a large variety of
imported durable consumers goods and capital equipment, is also a
factor making for more diversified imports. The 'demonstration effect'
has also had its influence on increasing the diversity of Lebanese imports. Such an effect should be given due importance since it has been,
in large measure, responsible for changing consumption habits (almost
radically) and creating new demands for imported goods which cannot
be produced domestically. All this plus the fact that import duties are
generally low and foreign exchange is freely available, both accommodate and generate an expanding capacity to import a large variety of
products which surpasses the diversity afforded by the limited structure of Lebanese domestic product.

Another factor which may have reduced the degree of concentration
of Lebanese exports and imports, is the geographical location of the
country, a factor partly responsible also for making trade the traditional and main vocation of the Lebanese. The central geographic location of Lebanon and its proximity to international trade centers must
mean reduced transportation costs. Other things equal, the smaller the
transportation costs, the larger is the number of products which a
country can trade in. This should be equally true of both exports and
imports. The convenient location of Lebanon has been instrumental in
developing its harbour and airport facilities, and in expanding the traf-
fic handled by them into their present impressive dimensions. Such a
development has greatly improved the means of transportation and
reduced their costs. This, to say the least, must have provided an added
impetus for the expansion and diversification of trade activity. Another element making for reduced transportation costs is the small
size of the country, and the resulting shorter lines of internal trans-

---

[1] It may not be possible to estimate the expenditure of tourists on imported
products. The magnitude of such an expenditure can be deduced however from
the fact that receipts from foreign travel in 1961 amounted to 21 percent of total
foreign exchange receipts.

portation. One should also consider the prevalence and convenience (other than means of transportation) of auxiliary activities to trade which can facilitate the free movement of goods. Entrepôt, transit and commercial activities have been generally enhanced by the existence of a free-zone area, a free foreign exchange market, and by a thriving and fairly developed banking system. The influence of such facilities (along with the relative absence of man-made obstacles to trade) on promoting the mobility of goods and the diversity of exports and imports, should not be underestimated.

There are, however, factors that have adversely affected the diversity of Lebanese exports and imports. One such factor is the degree of industrialization. It has been observed for example that the more industrialized the country, the wider is the range of its exports and imports. Manufactured production is generally more diversified than primary production, and therefore countries whose exports are composed largely of manufactured goods must, with exceptions of course, have more diversified exports than countries whose exports consist mainly of primary and agricultural products. Since industrial development, more often than not, entails the importation of a wide variety of capital products, this should mean also that the more industrially developed the country, the more diversified are its imports. Lebanon's industrial sector is still comparatively small and shows no signs of expansion (the relative share of industrial product, in fact, declined slightly from 13.6 percent to 13.2 percent of net national product between 1950 and 1966). Lebanon's exports, as a result, are still predominantly agricultural, i.e., crude foodstuffs in the form of fresh fruits and vegetables. Manufactured foodstuffs may have shown a slight tendency to increase, but they still constitute an insignificant portion (around 3 percent) of total exports, while it is estimated for example that fresh fruits and vegetables alone comprise around 51 percent of total Lebanese exports. And since it is also estimated that other consumers' goods make up 7 percent, intermediate goods 21 percent, raw materials 12 percent, and capital goods 9 percent of total merchandise exports,[1] it can then be roughly assumed that 'finished manufactures' at best can comprise a maximum of 25 percent of total exports. A similar breakdown of Lebanese imports indicates a significant difference. Manufactured products make up a larger portion (more than 50 percent) of total merchandise imports. If one is to accept the presumption that

---

[1] See Khalil Salem, *op. cit.*, p. 14.

manufactured production is generally more diversified than primary production, then this difference in itself can partly account for the fact that the Hirschman coefficient of commodity concentration of Lebanese imports is lower than that of commodity exports. So long, therefore, as Lebanon's industrial sector remains limited in scope, and so long as finished manufactures figure more in imports than they do in exports, Lebanese commodity exports will always tend to be less diversified than commodity imports.

A final factor which can adversely affect the diversity of trade (exports in particular) is the *size* of the economy. It is generally contended that small countries, because of relatively limited domestic markets and factor endowments, are likely to afford a relatively narrow variety in their production structure and, consequently, a limited diversity in their commodity exports. The extent and direction of the relationship between size of countries and degree of concentration of commodity trade were analyzed in some detail in Chapter Three above. It will only be mentioned here that findings of a relevant investigation which classified commodity concentration of exports by *size* of country and by degree of development,[1] suggest that *size* does not have as clear and strong an influence on the diversity of exports as does the degree of economic development. It was found out, for example, that only among the 'developed' countries did the so called 'small' countries have on the average higher export concentration coefficients than the 'large' countries. While among the 'underdeveloped' countries the contrary was true; the 'small' are reported to have on the average lower coefficients of commodity concentration of exports than the 'large' countries. The implication of this is that the effect of *size* on the diversity of exports may be important among the more advanced countries, but it is relatively unimportant among the underdeveloped countries. One, therefore, cannot say that a small country, by virtue of its smallness, must necessarily have more concentrated exports than a large country. The country's level of economic development should be taken into account. It is quite possible for a small and developed country to have more diversified exports than a larger but a less developed country. This is clearly borne out by Michaely's study and is *partly* supported by the Kuznets proposition "that the difference between small and large nations in range of diversity of the typical economic structure would be clear only in comparisons of nations at about the

---

[1] See M. Michaely, *op. cit.*, Table II, p. 729. A 'small' country was arbitrarily defined as one whose population was less than 10 million.

same level of devlopment... Even if we compared two nations, both underdeveloped, but one small and the other large, we would expect the range of economic activities to be wider in the latter than in the former... But the contrast in diversification would be particularly conspicuous for the two economically advanced countries."[1] It is only partly supported, for while it is true that the contrast in the diversity is more pronounced in the case of more developed countries, this is not true among the underdeveloped countries where the diversity is not necessarily wider as is contended by Kuznets.

This is not to argue that the 'smallness' of Lebanon need not be accounted for when analyzing the diversity of exports and imports. It is only to suggest that *size* by itself may not be an important cause of concentration in production and in exports. That Lebanon is small should not necessarily mean that its exports are concentrated and should not, therefore, preclude the possibility of diversified exports. If Lebanon's level of economic development permits, then there is no reason why the diversity of Lebanese exports cannot exceed that of larger countries whose level of development does not compare with Lebanon's. As a matter of fact, the Hirschman coefficient of Lebanese commodity exports (36.3), is significantly lower than Michaely's arithmetical mean of similar coefficients for 'large-underdeveloped' countries (57.8); and is also lower than the mean coefficient of the 'small-underdeveloped' countries (46.2), and that of the 'small-developed' countries (39.1). Only the mean coefficient of 'large-developed' countries (21.4) is lower than Lebanon's coefficient.

What about the size of Lebanon and the commodity concentration of its imports? Is 'size' in any way responsible for the wider diversity of imports? Is there, in other words, any relationship between the concentration of Lebanese exports and imports which can be attributable to the 'smallness' of Lebanon? One is strongly tempted to argue, in view of the country's narrow range of production and its relatively advanced level of development, that there is a negative correlation between concentration of exports and concentration of imports, namely, that the more concentrated Lebanese exports are, the more diversified will imports tend to be. This need not be the case in Lebanon. The small size of the economy must have handicapped the diversity of production and therefore of exports. The small size, along with the relatively decent level of economic performance, must have also meant

---

[1] S. Kuznets, "Economic Growth of Small Nations," *op. cit.*, p. 16.

a level and diversity of expenditure on consumption which exceed the level and diversity afforded by the domestic production structure. This is why expenditure on, and diversity of, imports are relatively high in Lebanon. Such an expenditure and diversity will also tend to increase with economic development. Diversity of exports is likely to increase too with economic development. But the increase in the diversity of imports, owing to the 'smallness' of Lebanon, will be wider than that of exports. What seems to be then more likely in Lebanon is for both diversities of exports and imports to move in the same direction. Both of them are, to a large measure, a function of the level of economic development, and both of them will, therefore, increase with development. But since the *size* of the economy, in itself, can obstruct the diversity of exports, and at the same time increase (if the level of development allows) the diversity of imports, then the expected increase in the diversity of the latter will exceed that of the former. The present discrepancy therefore between the degree of concentration of Lebanese commodity exports and imports (36.3 for exports vs 20.6 for imports) is likely to become wider in the future.

3. Geographic Concentration of Trade

We finally come to the third and last aspect of diversity discussed in this Chapter, namely, the geographic diversity of Lebanon's foreign trade. It is often asserted that small countries, more than larger countries, tend to have a higher degree of geographic concentration of foreign trade. This assertion has been clearly stated by Kuznets: "Accompanying the heavier reliance of small countries on foreign trade is a greater tendency on their part to rely on imports from and exports to but a few countries—with such concentration particularly noticeable in exports."[1] To what extent is this true of Lebanon? How does Lebanon's geographic concentration of exports and imports compare with other countries? Are Lebanese exports more geographically concentrated than imports? As an attempted answer to these questions, Lebanon's exports to and imports from the largest twelve markets will be taken as a measure of the degree of dipersion (or concentration)

---

[1] *Ibid.*, p. 21. The inverse relationship between size of a country and geographic concentration of both exports and imports, but particularly of exports, has been more recently confirmed by Kuznets. See his "Quantitative Aspects of the Economic Growth of Nations: Level and Structure of Foreign Trade: Comparisons for Recent Years," *op. cit.*, Table 10, p. 37.

of foreign markets. Lebanon's trade with its neighbouring countries will also be analyzed in order to determine the extent of the country's dependence on regional trade, and particularly on trade with its immediate Arab neighbours.

The sixteen-year (1951-1966) average of the share of Lebanon's merchandise exports taken up by the largest twelve import markets is given in Table 61 below. This share, to repeat, is used here as a measure of

Table 61

Lebanese Exports to the Twelve largest Markets (1951-1966)

Importing Country	Per Cent of Total Exports
Saudi Arabia	14.9
Syria	12.0
Jordan	8.6
Kuwait	6.8
Iraq	6.0
United States	5.9
United Kingdom	4.5
France	3.7
Italy	3.7
Egypt	2.9
U.S.S.R.	2.7
W. Germany	2.4
TOTAL	74.0

Source: Based on figures extracted from République Libanaise, Conseil Supérieur des Douanes, *Statistiques du Commerce Extérieur*, 1951-1966, Beirut.

geographic concentration of Lebanese exports. On the average, the twelve largest importing countries take up 74 percent of Lebanon's total merchandise exports.[1] Saudi Arabia alone receives around 15 percent, Syria comes second with 12 percent, and Jordan third with 8.6 percent. Six of these twelve importing countries are Arab countries that take up 51 percent of total exports. The remaining six (United States, France, United Kingdom, Italy, U.S.S.R., and Germany) re-

---

[1] It should be noted that the sixteen-year average does not hide any significant trend. Three-year moving averages of these percentages showed a slight tendency to increase during the fifties and to decrease during the sixties. They were 76 percent in 1960 and 72 percent in 1966.

ceive together 23 percent of total exports. That the five largest importing countries are Arab and that six Arab countries alone receive more than half of Lebanon's exports is indicative of the importance of the Arab countries as export markets, and of the relatively high regional concentration of Lebanese exports. Such a regional concentration, it must be added, has not shown any tendency to decrease. Exports to these six Arab countries, for example, amounted to 49 percent of total merchandise exports in 1951; by 1966 their share had increased to 53 percent of total exports.

Lebanon's geographic concentration of exports is noticeably higher than the geographic concentration of other countries, as it indicated by Table 62 below. With 74 percent of its exports taken up by the

Table 62

Regional Concentration of the Exports of Selected Countries 1954

Exporting Country	*Exports to Largest Twelve Markets as Percent of Total Exports*
Canada	90.1
Denmark	83.6
Sweden	77.0
Belgium-Luxemburg	73.7
Netherlands	69.0
Switzerland	66.9
Western Germany	64.2
France	59.9
Italy	58.2
United States	53.4
United Kingdom	50.1

Source: Jöhr & Kneschaurek, *op. cit.*, p. 76.

largest twelve importing countries, Lebanon's index exceeds that of Belgium-Luxemburg, Netherlands, and Switzerland, all of which belong to the category of small nations. One should also bear in mind the the fact that the index has not shown a tendency to decrease. This tendency may not be statistically significant; it is at least sufficient to demonstrate that the degree of geographic concentration of Lebanese merchandise exports does not show any significant declining trend.

Following Kuznets' assumption, one would expect the geographic concentration of Lebanese imports to be obviously lower than that of exports. This does not turn out to be the case. The sixteen-year (1951-

Table 63

Lebanese Imports from the Twelve largest Markets (1951-1966)

Exporting Country	Per Cent of Total Imports
Great Britain	18.6
United States	13.2
France	9.2
Syria	9.0
West Germany	7.5
Italy	5.8
Iraq	2.7
Switzerland	2.7
Belgium	2.6
Holland	2.5
Egypt	1.3
Jordan	1.0
TOTAL	76.1

Source: Based on figures extracted from République Libanaise, *Recueil de Statistique Libanaises, Année 1963,* for the years 1951-1963; and *Statistiques du Commerce Extérieur du Liban, 1961-1966,* for the years 1963-1966.

1966) average of the share of merchandise imports provided by the largest twelve markets amounts to 76.1 percent of total Lebanese imports. See Table 63 above. This is higher than the 74 percent of total exports that go to the twelve largest export markets. It must be mentioned, also that the import average (more than that of exports) has had a tendency to remain relatively stable. Three year moving average of the import percentage was around 77 percent in 1951 and 75 percent in 1966. Another difference is the relative unimportance of the Arab countries as major sources of merchandise imports. Five of the largest six sources of imports are not Arab countries. Syria, the largest Arab source, is in fourth place. Only four of the twelve markets are Arab (Syria, Iraq, Egypt, Jordan), and they provide together not more than 14 percent of total imports. The remaining eight, with Great Britain, the United States, France, Germany, and Italy heading the list, provide on the average more than 62 percent of Lebanese imports. This is not the case with the dispersion of exports. Arab countries are more significant as export markets.

Of special relevance to Lebanon, therefore, also as a measure of re-

Table 64

Lebanese Merchandise Trade with Immediate Neighbouring Countries[1]
1951-1966

	Exports LL mill.	Imports LL mill.	Exports As Per Cent of Total; (three-year moving averages)	Imports
1951	37.7	75.9		
1952	29.2	73.7	37.9	27.3
1953	30.2	102.5	36.2	30.0
1954	33.4	126.9	34.7	29.2
1955	32.5	103.3	32.2	27.0
1956	34.3	131.9	30.1	22.9
1957	39.0	117.8	20.3	20.9
1958	32.0	76.6	32.7	17.2
1959	43.8	84.0	36.4	13.8
1960	53.2	73.2	37.0	11.3
1961	52.4	69.9	34.1	8.3
1962	58.0	141.3	29.8	9.0
1963	50.1	145.7	27.8	10.6
1964	59.8	161.5	25.6	10.9
1965	76.3	189.8	24.9	10.5
1966	86.4	194.4		

Source: Years 1951-1960 are based on data extracted from M. A. Diab, *Inter-Arab Economic Cooperation 1951-1960*, Economic Research Institute, American University of Beirut, Beirut, 1964, Tables D-69 to D-73 and D-75 to D-80. Years 1961-1966 are from *Statistique de Commerce Extérieur du Liban, Années 1961-1966*.

gional concentration of trade, is the proportion of exports that go to, and imports that come from, the immediate neighbouring countries (Syria, Iraq, Jordan, and Egypt). This limited measure of regional concentration is justifiable since the general presumption is that small countries not only have a limited dispersion of foreign markets, but that they depend more heavily on their immediate neighbours for their exports and imports. Lebanon's trade with its four neighbouring countries is summarized in Table 64 above. The difference in the degree of regional concentration of exports and imports becomes quite noticeable. Lebanon's dependence on its immediate neighbours for exports is appreciably higher than its dependence on them for imports. The sixteen-year average of the share of exports (as percent of total exports) that go to immediate Arab neighbours amounts to 32 percent; the sixteen-year average of the share of imports is around 18 percent.

[1] Comprising Syria, Iraq, Jordan, and Egypt.

Three-year moving averages of merchandise exports to immediate neighbours (as percent of total exports) declined from around 38 percent in 1951 to around 25 percent in 1966, with a particularly strong and steady decline in the sixties.

The declining trend in imports from immediate neighbouring countries is perhaps more steady. With one exception, three-year moving averages of such imports (as percent of total imports) have declined from 27 percent to 10 percent between 1951 and 1966. This is a sizeable drop which already indicates that Lebanon's immediate neighbours tend to provide a decreasing share of its total imports. It is understandable why the country has had to rely more and more on non-Arab countries to meet the notable increase in demand for (and diversity of) imported products. The rapid expansion in some sectors of economic activity, particularly the real-estate and tourism industries, has generated a demand for capital and consumption (of the luxury variety) goods that cannot be imported from immediate neighbours.

The regional concentration of Lebanese exports, therefore, as measured by the proportion of total exports that goes to the country's immediate neighbours, is noticeably higher than the regional concentration of imports. It can be validly asserted, then, that Lebanon's tendency for relying on the immediate neighbouring markets for trade is particularly heavier in the case of exports. This supports the presumption, already referred to, that the geographic concentration of trade is more noticeable in exports. When, however, the geographic concentration was measured in terms of ratio of trade with the twelve largest markets, such a difference was not apparent. Exports, to repeat, showed a smaller (not a larger) degree of geographic concentration than imports.

CHAPTER EIGHT

LEBANON'S DEPENDENCE ON FOREIGN TRADE

A main consequence of the 'small' size of countries, generally referred to in the literature, is the high dependence on foreign trade.
It seems that small countries have to depend more heavily on trade, as
a means of expanding their limited domestic markets, if they are to
achieve the desired economies of scale in their main industries. Without such a dependence it may be difficult to account for the relatively
high level of economic performance which some of the 'small' countries have been able to enjoy. It is not a surprise, therefore, that foreign
trade is expected to be more important for smaller than for larger
countries. The nature of the association between size of country and
dependence of foreign trade was analyzed in some detail in Chapter
four. The present Chapter aims to assess the magnitude and economic
implications of Lebanon's dependence on foreign trade.

One of the most talked about features of the Lebanese economy is
the preponderance of the trade sector over all other sectors of the economy. National income estimates show that the trade sector alone
generates around 30 percent of national income. This exceeds the share
of any other sector. And if the financial sector is compounded to it,
as it should, since 'most banking, insurance and exchange transactions
are conducted in connection with trade activity,'[1] this would mean
that trade activity in Lebanon generates more than one third of total
national income. Hence the common description of Lebanon as mainly
a mercantile country. The relative shares of the trade and finance sectors in national income since 1950, given in Table 65, reached their
highest at around 38 percent in 1960. Since then they have stabilized
at around 34 percent. There is no evidence, therefore, of any substantial decline in the relative importance of trade activity. In fact, the
prevalent expansion in the auxiliary activities to trade, engendered by
the growth in the trade sector itself, speaks of further expansion in
the future which will further increase the relative magnitude of trade
and its auxiliary activities in the Lebanese economy.

For a thorough appraisal of the magnitude and consequences of

---

[1] Albert Y. Badre, "The National Income of Lebanon," *Middle East Economic
Papers*, 1956, Economic Research Institute, American University of Beirut, p. 20.

Table 65

Trade and Finance Sectors as % of Net National Product 1950-1966
(in Percentages)

	1950	1951	1952	1954	1955	1957	1958	1959	1960	1961	1962	1964	1965	1966
Trade	28.8	31.0	29.8	29.3	29.6	31.2	27.5	31.8	32.0	32.0	31.4	32.1	30.8	30.6
Finance	3.8	4.2	4.5	4.5	5.1	6.0	7.0	6.3	6.3	6.4	6.5	3.4	3.4	3.6
TOTAL	32.6	35.2	34.3	33.8	34.7	37.2	34.5	38.1	38.3	38.4	37.9	35.5	34.2	34.2

Source: Table 2 on Net National Product by sector, 1950-1966, in Statistical Appendix.

Lebanon's dependence on foreign trade, one has to turn to an analysis of the balance of payments. Such an analysis will highlight the peculiarities of the Lebanese balance of payments and, in so doing, bring out the salient features and economic implications of Lebanon's foreign sector. A summary of the balance of payments transactions for the years 1951-1966 (in the standard and abridged forms) is given in Tables 4 and 6 in Statistical Appendix.

1. LARGE MERCHANDISE TRADE DEFICIT

The first feature of the Lebanese balance of payments that presents itself is the large discrepancy between commodity imports and exports and the resulting deficit in the balance of trade. This sizeable and expanding deficit, as trends in trade data indicate, is likely to become a permanent feature of the Lebanese economy. The trade deficit (see Table 66) has more than quadrupled between 1951 and 1966. It increased from LL 260 million in 1951 to LL 1,138 million in 1966, at an average simple rate of 22 percent per annum. This increase in the trade deficit has come about because both exports and imports have been increasing at comparable rates of 24 and 23 percent per annum respectively. It should be noted, however, that during the fifties imports were increasing at a comparably faster rate than exports, but that during the sixties the growth rates were reversed with exports increasing faster than imports.[1] This difference in the rates of growth of merchandise imports and exports can also be seen in the change that has taken place in the ratio of imports to exports. The three-year mov-

---

[1] Compounded annual rates of growth for 1951-60 were 11.7 percent for imports and 5.9 percent for exports; for the whole period, 1951-66, the rate for exports is 13.5 percent, and for imports 11.4 percent.

Table 66

Ratio of Merchandise Imports (M) to Exports (X), and Merchandise
Trade Deficit (M-X), 1951-1966 (LL million)

	IMPORTS (M)	EXPORTS (X)	M/X	(M-X)
1951	385.3	124.9	3.1	260.4
1952	454.2	122.1	3.7	332.1
1953	373.7	134.4	2.8	239.3
1954	522.2	172.1	3.0	350.1
1955	693.5	196.5	3.5	497.0
1956	740.2	247.6	3.0	492.6
1957	759.8	210.5	3.6	549.3
1958	673.0	117.0	5.7	556.0
1959	762.0	152.0	5.0	610.0
1960	930.4	162.0	5.7	768.0
1961	1043.8	230.9	4.5	812.9
1962	1058.5	320.6	3.3	737.9
1963	1179.3	323.4	3.6	855.9
1964	1323.7	424.0	3.1	899.7
1965	1511.8	447.3	3.4	1064.5
1966	1722.4	584.1	3.0	1138.3

Source: Extracted from Appendix Table 5 on Balance of Payments of Lebanon,
1951-1966.

Table 67

Growth in Merchandise Imports, 1953-1961

	Per Cent Per Annum Compounded
Lebanon	11.7[1]
Kuwait	11.1
Jordan	11.0
Iraq	9.7
Industrial Areas of World	7.2
Syria	6.6
Egypt	6.4
Non-industrial Areas of World	5.0

Source: Frederic C. Shorter, "The Remarkable Upsurge in Arab
Trade." Paper delivered at the Fifty-Sixth Meeting
of the Princeton University Conference on *Arab Development in the Emerging International Economy*, April
25 and 26, 1963, Haskins Press, Princeton, New
Jersey, 1963, p. 6.

[1] Lebanon's rate for the period 1951-1966 is 11.4.

ing averages of this ratio increased from 3.2 to 5.1 between 1951 and 1961 and then decreased again to 3.2 in 1966. The merchandise imports are now three times the value of merchandise exports, the same ratio at which they were in 1951.

The uniqueness is not only in the large and expanding merchandise trade deficit, it is also in the high growth rates of both merchandise imports and exports. The growth in merchandise imports, for example, is higher than growth rates elsewhere in the world. It exceeds that of the industrialized areas of the world; it even exceeds, to a lesser extent, Kuwait's, a country well-known for its large financial capacity to import. See Table 67 above.

The expansion in merchandise imports and exports, and the disparity between the rates of growth of exports and imports, during the fifties and sixties reflect themselves in the behavior of the propensities to export and import and in the foreign trade ratio between 1951 and 1966. The export, import and foreign trade ratios (given in Table 68 below), other than providing evidence of the increasing importance of trade, demonstrate another unique feature of the Lebanese foreign trade sector.

Table 68

Ratios of Merchandise Exports (X), Imports (M), and Trade (X + M) to Net National Products, 1951-1966
(Percentages)

	X/NNP	M/NNP	(X+M)/NNP
1951	11.5	35.4	46.9
1952	10.9	40.7	51.6
1953	11.5	32.0	43.5
1954	13.7	41.6	55.3
1955	14.3	50.5	64.8
1956	17.5	52.2	69.7
1957	14.0	50.6	64.6
1958	8.8	50.8	59.6
1959	9.7	48.5	58.2
1960	9.7	55.7	65.4
1961	13.5	61.2	74.7
1962	17.9	59.2	77.1
1964	14.8	46.3	61.1
1965	14.2	47.9	62.1
1966	16.9	49.8	66.7

Source: Based on trade and national income figures given in Table 2 and 5 in Statistical Appendix.

2. HIGH PROPENSITY TO IMPORT

This feature is the high average propensity to import. On the average it amounts to around 48 percent for the period 1951-1966. This means that Lebanon spends around half its national income each year on merchandise imports. This is undeniably a high rate, which may exceed import propensities elsewhere in the world. The import ratio has also shown with the exception of the last three years, perhaps, a rising trend. The three-year moving averages of this ratio increased from 36 percent to 58.7 percent between 1951 and 1961. Since then the ratio dropped to 48 percent. Export ratios have behaved rather differently. On the average they amount to around 13 percent for the period 1951-1966. Three-year moving averages do not observe one directional trend during the fifties. The ratio in 1960 went back to its 1951 level of around 11 percent. In the sixties, however, export ratios increased to around 15 percent. Foreign trade ratios, exports as percent of net national product, have consequently shown an increasing trend, with the exception of the last three years. Three-year moving averages increased from 47.3 percent to 71 percent between 1951 and 1962 and then declined to 64 percent in 1966.

A high propensity to import, in itself, need not be cause for alarm. In a country like Lebanon, it is understandable why merchandise imports are relatively large. A small country, whose limited resources and domestic market do not permit the local production of certain goods, but whose level of economic performance permits the expenditure on them, will have to rely heavily on imports. Lebanon is a perfect example of a country where the level of economic performance warrants a diversity of expenditure on final goods which exceeds the diversity afforded by its structure of domestic product. Imports are therefore relatively large in Lebanon because the disparity between structure of final demand and that of the domestic product is large.

But when a high import ratio, such as Lebanon's, is coupled with a low export ratio, it becomes then a cause for some concern. There are many reasons why the ratio of merchandise imports to national income is expected to sustain its present high level. Economic growth itself may give rise to new needs and demands for products which cannot be supplied domestically. The current expansion in the construction industry in Lebanon and the resulting increase in the demand for imported raw materials and capital equipment are a case in point. Rising incomes and 'demonstration effect' are another reason for the high import ratio. Both (and particularly the latter) have partially transformed consumption habits and created new appetites for products which cannot be produced locally. The 'demonstration effect' can be quite strong in a small touristic country like Lebanon, where import duties are relatively low, import restrictions are non-existent, foreign exchange is freely and readily available, and where as a result a wide assorted variety of imported products flood the market; and where a constant and unrestricted flow of foreign capital resources generates a new capacity to import. These factors must have been instrumental in accommodating, if not partly accounting for, the already reputable capacity of the Lebanese to emulate the foreigner; a capacity which has expressed itself in the ostentatious and expensive habits that have already taken root among some Lebanese circles.

Imports are likely to continue to grow so long as the growth in income generates new needs and demands which cannot be statisfied domestically. There are certain forces, however, which beyond a certain point are expected to slow down the expansion in imports until the increase in imports becomes slower than the increase in incomes.[1] Such forces are not likely to manifest themselves in the behavior pattern of Lebanese imports. Imports in general, and Lebanese imports in particular, are rarely if ever 'inferior goods' whose consumption decreases absolutely with increases in income. Lebanese imports are not even of the variety whose consumption is expected to decline relatively as income increases.[2] They do not mainly consist of foodstuffs and simple materials. Around 52 percent of Lebanese imports are capital and intermediate goods, and 48 percent are consumption goods. It is also estimated that at least some 40 percent of the imported consumption goods are luxury items and durable consumers goods.[3] The income elasticity of demand for such products is not likely to change from greater than one to less than one, and imports, unless there is a drastic change in their composition which is not yet foreseeable, may not show therefore strong signs of decline in relative importance.

Another factor which can slow down the expansion in imports, since it constitutes a diversion of expenditure from imports to domes-

---

[1] In other words, until the income elasticity of demand for imports changes from greater than one to less than one.

[2] Reference here is made to Engel's Law where a country's imports, if mainly consisting of necessities, foodstuffs and simple materials, would beyond a certain point increase at a slower rate than national income.

[3] See Khalil Salem, *Balance of Payments of Lebanon*, 1961, Economic Research Institute, American University of Beirut, Lebanon, 1964, p. 14.

tic markets, is the growth of the services sector in national income. It is argued that while some services (insurance, tourism, ocean-shipping) are supplied internationally, a large part of these service is often supplied domestically. Kindleberger reports, for example, that in developing countries, labor employed in services rises from something like 24 percent of the total supply to 45 percent, as income per capita rises from $ 100 to $ 1,700, and this implies a proportionate diversion of expenditure from imports to domestic markets.[1] This diverting effect may not have exerted its influence on Lebanese expenditure on imported services, since these expenditures do not show a tendency to decline in relative importance between 1951 and 1966. Three-year moving averages of the expenditure on imported services (as a percent of total foreign exchange expenditures) did decline from 11.5 percent to 7.2 percent between 1951 and 1960, but then they steadily increased to 17 percent in 1966. However, imported services comprise only a minor portion of total foreign exchange expenditure, and therefore any change in their relative importance will not have a significant effect on the expansion in imports. What is more important in the case of Lebanon is the expenditure on merchandise imports which on the average make up around 87 percent of total foreign exchange expenditure. Three-year moving averages of merchandise imports (as a percent of total foreign exchange expenditure) increased from 87.8 percent to 92.2 percent between 1951 and 1960 and then decreased to 82 percent in 1966. See Table 69 below for exchange expenditure by source. So the diversion of expenditure from imports to domestic products suggested by Kindleberger to attend the growth of the services sector, cannot have the desired effect of reducing the growth rate of imports in view of the existing pattern of foreign exchange expenditure.

A final factor which may reduce the expansion in imports, and which is often talked about in developing countries, is the process of import substitution. Lebanon's capacity to develop such a process, while limited, is not without promise. There are obstacles, no doubt. Some are insuperable, but some are not. And these will partly disappear in the course of economic development. It is not within the proper scope of this section to look into the various prospects and to suggest what should Lebanon do. It will suffice to suggest that Lebanon should not resort to import restrictions in order to start off (or speed up) the process of import substitution. It must be remembered that import sub-

---

[2] Charles P. Kindleberger, *Foreign Trade and the National Economy*, New Haven: Yale University Press, 1962, p. 185.

Table 69

Foreign exchange Expenditure, by Source, 1951-1966

	Total Expenditure[1] (LL million)	Merchandise Imports	Services	Donations
		Percentage of Total Expenditure; three-year moving averages		
1951	434.8			
1952	504.3	87.8	11.5	0.7
1953	441.4	87.7	11.7	0.6
1954	591.4	88.0	11.5	0.5
1955	762.8	90.6	9.0	0.3
1956	798.5	91.7	8.0	0.4
1957	831.0	92.4	7.2	0.3
1958	722.0	92.5	7.1	0.4
1959	820.0	93.6	6.2	0.3
1960	983.0	92.2	7.2	0.6
1961	1,161.8	90.3	9.1	0.6
1962	1,213.6	88.2	11.0	0.8
1963	1,346.5	85.7	13.4	0.9
1964	1,607.9	83.8	15.0	1.2
1965	1,848.1	81.5	17.0	1.5
1966	2,138.4			

Source: Table 5 in Statistical Appendix.

[1] Excluding expenditure on imports of non-monetary gold. Data on capital movements are reported as 'net'. No separate figures on capital outflow are therefore available, except for 1961 and they have already been subtracted from the reported total for consistency.

stitution is a natural process in the course of economic development, and that it can take place without import restrictions.

3. HIGH DEPENDENCE ON SERVICES AND FOREIGN CAPITAL

In attempting to evaluate the magnitude and economic implications of Lebanon's dependence on foreign trade, two features of the Lebanese balance of payments have so far been discussed: The large disparity between merchandise imports and exports, and the high average propensity to import. A third feature which may also be peculiar to Lebanon is the relatively high dependence on services and capital movements. The magnitude of this dependence will become apparent once the services and capital transactions and, particularly, financing the trade deficit, are analyzed. Table 70 below, which summarizes total

Table 70

Foreign Exchange Receipts, by Sector, 1951-1966

	Total[1] Receipts (LL million)	Merchandise Exports	Services[2]	Donations[3]	Capital Movements (net)
			Percentage of Total Receipts; three-year moving averages		
1951	452.8				
1952	542.1	25.5	50.9	16.7	6.9
1953	510.5	24.8	48.7	17.5	9.0
1954	668.7	25.5	47.3	17.6	9.6
1955	798.8	26.8	45.6	17.0	10.7
1956	824.5	26.0	46.3	17.1	10.6
1957	902.2	23.0	44.1	19.1	13.8
1958	743.0	18.9	47.6	17.8	15.7
1959	853.0	16.6	48.3	15.4	19.7
1960	1,002.0	17.7	52.5	11.3	18.8
1961	1,255.9	19.5	54.7	9.6	16.2
1962	1,329.1	21.8	56.5	9.0	12.7
1963	1,400.5	23.9	55.7	8.0	12.4
1964	1,735.4	23.7	55.2	7.5	13.6
1965	1,883.5	24.7	53.5	6.4	15.4
1966	2,245.6				

Source: See Table 5 in Statistical Appendix.

[1] Excluding receipts from exports of non-monetary gold.

[2] Comprising foreign travel, transportation and insurance, investment income, government not included elsewhere, and miscellaneous services including transit.

[3] Comprising emigrants' remittances and transfers, foreign aid, and private donations to charitable and cultural institutions.

foreign exchange receipts by source, will help demonstrate the relative importance of services, donations and capital movements in the Lebanese balance of payments. Between them, they have on the average been responsible for not less than 78 percent of total foreign exchange receipts during the 1951-1966 period. The export of services alone accounts for more than 50 percent of total exchange receipts, and donations and capital account for the remaining 28 percent. This means that services alone generate as much foreign exchange as do merchandise exports, donations and foreign capital combined. And receipts from services have not shown any tendency to decline in relative importance. Three-year moving averages of the share of services (as percent of total foreign exchange receipts) have increased from around 51 percent to 54 percent between 1951 and 1966. They first declined in relative importance during the decade of the fifties, and then the trend was reversed during the last six years. It should be mentioned here that merchandise exports have to some extent followed a similar pattern. Three-year moving averages of merchandise exports (as percent of total foreign exchange receipts) dropped from around 26 percent to 18 percent between 1951 and 1961, and then increased to around 25 percent in 1966. Their relative importance, however, unlike services exports, had declined since 1951. This change in the structure of foreign exchange receipts is evidence of the increasing dependence on the services sector in the Lebanese economy. It should be noted also that the growth in services exports is appreciably higher than the growth in merchandise exports. While merchandise exports increased at a single annual rate of 24 percent between 1951 and 1966, exports of services increased at 28 percent annually. As the following data indicate, exports of services are, on the average, more than twice the value of merchandise exports. In 1951 exported services amounted to little less than twice the value of merchandise exports, in 1961 they amounted to three times the value of merchandise exports, and in 1966 they went back almost to their original 1951 level.

That merchandise exports have declined slightly in relative importance, that the exports of services have been growing at a faster rate than merchandise exports, are symptoms of Lebanon's increasing dependence on services in the foreign sector, symptoms that are an inevitable outcome of Lebanon's small domestic market, factor endowments, and the resulting composition of its services and merchandise exports. Merchandise exports consist mainly of basic consumers' goods, fruits and vegetables. Combined, these categories comprise around 80 percent of total exports.[1] Exported services are mostly composed of tourism, travel, transportation, trade and financial activities. Mention is here made of the composition of merchandise and 'services' exports because the difference in their composition and therefore the expected difference in their respective demand conditions, may account for the impressive expansion in 'services' and the resulting disparity between the rates of growth of 'services' and merchandise exports. Since merchandise exports consist of 'basic' commodities and services of 'higher' commodities, the income elasticity of demand for 'services' is expected to be higher than the income elasticity of demand

---

[1] It has been estimated that consumers goods amounts to 57 percent of total merchandise exports, and that the value of fruits and vegetables alone constitute 51 percent of the remaining 43 percent. See Khalil Salem, *op. cit.*, p. 14.

Table 71

Exports of Goods and Services, 1951-1966
(LL million)

	Merchandise Exports	Services[a] Exports	Ratio of Services to Merchandise Exports
1951	124.9	244.1	1.9
1952	122.1	288.6	2.3
1953	134.4	233.0	1.7
1954	172.1	314.7	1.8
1955	196.5	391.2	2.0
1956	247.6	335.4	1.4
1957	210.5	445.0	2.1
1958	117.0	315.0	2.7
1959	152.0	435.0	2.9
1960	162.0	517.0	3.2
1961	230.9	701.3	3.0
1962	320.6	758.2	2.4
1963	323.4	798.9	2.5
1964	424.0	922.5	2.2
1965	447.3	1,039.7	2.3
1966	584.1	1,164.8	2.0

Source: From Table 5 on Balance of Payments of Lebanon, 1951-1966, in Statistical Appendix.

[a] Comprising foreign travel, transportation and insurance, investment income, government not included elsewhere, and miscellaneous services including transit.

for merchandise exports. And this difference in the income elasticities of demand, in view of the growth in the incomes of the oil producing neightbouring countries and the ensuing increase in demand for services rendered by the Lebanese service-oriented economy, is in large part responsible for the discrepancy between the expansion rates of 'services' and merchandise exports. Concomitant with the increase in income and the resulting shift in the foreign demand for Lebanese services, a change in tastes in favour of services may have also taken place. This change in tastes is becoming more and more apparent, and should be considered as one of the forces, along with the increase in incomes, which has caused an upward shift in the foreign demand for services, and which therefore can partly account for the disparity between the growth of 'sevices' and the growth of merchandise exports. It may not be possible to indicate how much of the upward shift in demand has been the result of an income change and how much the result of a change in tastes. Neither change alone can provide adequate justification for the notable growth in the 'services' exports. Taken together, however, they may.[1]

We must, if briefly, analyze now the magnitude of Lebanon's dependence on donations and foreign capital, since such an analysis is part of the third feature of the Lebanese balance of payments currently under discussion. It has already been stated (and as shown in Table 70 on foreign exchange receipts by source) that donations and capital movements together make up on the average 28 percent of Lebanon's total foreign exchange receipts. This exceeds Lebanon's earnings from merchandise exports which amount to 22 percent of total foreign exchange receipts. Three-year moving averages of the combined share of donations and capital (as percent of total foreign exchange receipts) rose steadily from 23.6 percent to 35.1 percent during the fifties and then almost as steadily fell to 21.8 percent during the sixties. In other words, their combined share in 1966 is slightly less than their share in 1951. The pattern of foreign exchange receipts from donations and capital movements, therefore, is very similar to that of merchandise exports. The relative importance of these two components of foreign exchange receipts remains very comparable, at the beginning and at the end of the period under consideration.

When the shares of donations and foreign capital are separately analyzed, an observable change in the pattern of dependence on these two items is revealed. Donations at the beginning of the 1951-1966 period were more significant souces of foreign exchange than foreign capital. Three-year moving averages of the relative share of donations (as percent of total foreign exchange receipts) declined from 16.7 percent in 1951 to 6.4 percent in 1966. The relative importance of foreign capital has, on the other hand, increased. Three-year moving averages of the share of capital (as percent of total foreign exchange receipts) increased from 6.9 percent in 1951 to 15.4 percent in 1966. So by the end of the 1951-1966 period, foreign capital was a more important source of foreign exchange than donations.

There is, therefore, a noticeable tendency to rely less on donations and more on foreign capital. This increase in the relative importance of capital movements, and the change in the pattern of dependence on

---

[1] Another factor, worth noting here, which may have also contributed to the disparity, is the expenditure of tourists on Lebanese domestic products which would have otherwise been exported. Instead of exporting apples, for example, to Iraq and Egypt, the Iraqis and Egyptians as tourists consume Lebanese apples locally. Both transactions are a source of foreign exchange, one is treated as a merchandise export and the other an export of a 'service'.

Table 72

Financing the Merchandise Trade Deficit, 1951-1966

	Trade Deficit[1] (LL million)	Services[2] (net earnings)	Donations[3] (net earnings)	Capital Movements (net)
		Percentage of Trade Deficit: Three-year Moving Averages		
1951	260.4			
1952	332.1	73.1	29.5	13.0
1953	139.3	71.3	32.2	17.2
1954	350.1	68.9	32.3	18.1
1955	497.0	64.3	28.8	19.1
1956	492.6	63.6	27.3	17.5
1957	549.3	57.8	28.7	20.7
1958	556.0	59.7	25.4	22.3
1959	610.0	57.0	20.3	26.5
1960	768.0	64.7	15.4	26.4
1961	812.9	71.8	13.9	24.2
1962	737.9	76.6	13.6	21.0
1963	855.9	77.0	12.7	22.3
1964	899.7	71.8	11.6	24.5
1965	1,064.5	70.3	9.4	29.2
1966	1,138.3			

Source: Table 5 in Statistical Appendix.

[1] Excluding non–monetary gold.
[2] Comprising foreign travel, transportation and insurance, investment income, government not included elsewhere, and miscellaneous services including transit.
[3] Comprising emigrants' remittances and transfers, foreign aid and private donations to charitable and cultural institutions.

services, donations, and foreign capital, will become even more obvious when financing the trade deficit is analyzed.

One feature already emphasized about the Lebanese foreign sector is the chronic and expanding trade deficit. Despite this sizeable deficit, Lebanon has been able to accumulate a surplus (another peculiarity of the foreign sector) on its overall balance of payments. How this surplus has come about, and the respective shares of services, donations, and capital movements in accomodating the trade deficit, can be deduced from Table 72. Services, as is evident, defray the largest part of the trade deficit. Alone, net earnings from services have on the average paid for 68 percent of this deficit. Net earnings from donations have roughly been responsible for defraying 21 percent, and net capital movements approximately 22 percent of the deficit. (These percentages are more than a hundred because net earnings from services, donations, and capital movements combined exceed the trade deficit.) Such overall averages, however, conceal an important changing trend, and distort the true relative shares of these separate accounts in financing the trade deficit. Three-year moving averages of the relative share of net earnings from services (as percent of the trade deficit) maintain almost the same level at the beginning and end of the 1951-1966 period. Net earnings from donations have, however, declined noticeably in relative importance. Three-year moving averages of the share of donations (as percent of trade deficit) decreased from around 30 percent to 9 percent between 1951 and 1966. Only net earnings from capital movements have increased in relative importance. Three-year moving averages of capital movements (as percent of trade deficit) were quite low at the beginning of the 1951-1966 period. At 13 percent, they were less than half the relative share of donations. By the end of the period they had risen to 29.2 percent which is significantly higher than the share of donations.

It should be clear from the above that Lebanon still depends in the main on earnings from 'invisibles' to pav for a chronic, sizeable, and expanding merchandise trade deficit. This dependence may have declined, however, in relative importance or at least maintained the same magnitude (since earnings from the export of services as a ratio of total foreign exchange receipts have slightly decreased). Subsequently, Lebanon has had to rely more heavily on capital inflows in order to accommodate the growing trade deficit.

In describing the magnitude and consequences of Lebanon's dependence on foreign trade, this Chapter has singled out three features peculiar to the country's foreign trade sector, and, to some measure, an outcome of the 'small' size of the economy. They are: (1) A sizeable and expanding merchandise trade deficit (2) a high propensity to import caused by the relatively large disparity between the structure of final demand and that of the domestic product; and (3) an increasing dependence on services and, particularly, foreign capital to finance the expanding trade deficit. The implications of these features on the stability of the Lebanese economy are, in part, the subject matter of the next Chapter.

CHAPTER NINE

SIZE AND STABILITY OF THE LEBANESE ECONOMY

The previous chapters attempted to analyze the implications of the small size of the Lebanese economy on its structure and economic performance. The impact of size on the diversity of the Lebanese economy (particularly the diversity of trade), on its rate of economic growth, and on the degree of its dependence on foreign trade was investigated. An attempt was made to find out the extent to which the 'smallness' of the Lebanese economy has implied a limited diversity in economic structure (and hence a high concentration in trade), a slow rate of economic growth, or high dependence on foreign trade. It is equally important to find out whether 'smallness' has necessarily implied an irregular rate of economic growth. This is the main task of this Chapter. Despite its size, Lebanon has been able to enjoy a relatively moderate standard of living and has witnessed, over the last decade, an impressive pace of economic progress. Has Lebanon had to achieve this progress at the price of fluctuations in economic activity? Is Lebanon, on account of its 'smallness', more vulnerable to these fluctuations? It has been indicated for example that Lebanon has had to depend quite heavily on foreign trade as a means of escape from the limitations of the domestic market. Is this a precarious means of escape from 'smallness'? Lebanon has had also to rely increasingly on services and foreign capital to finance an expanding trade deficit, and to rely more heavily on its immediate neighbours as markets for its exports of goods and services. Such developments, it can be argued, can possibly impede the country's capacity to isolate itself from outside destabilizing influences, and can also subject Lebanon's foreign sector to control and manipulation by policy measures of neighbouring countries. The extent to which Lebanon can retaliate against such policy measures should also be taken into account since the power of retaliation can influence the country's ability to guard itself against outside developments threatening its economic stability. It should also be noted that just as Lebanon's high dependence on foreign trade may render the country more vulnerable to outside destabilizing developments, the same dependence on trade can possibly be a source of stability instead. Lebanon's high propensity to import may enable the economy to 'leak out' a sizeable part of the consequences of destabilising developments that originate inside the country.

In short, this Chapter will analyze some of the features (highlighted by the previous chapters) that are capable of impairing or facilitating the stability of the Lebanese economy, with emphasis placed on those factors that are related to, or are possibly an outcome of, the small size of the Lebanese economy.

1. Dependence on Trade and Stability

Lebanon's economic stability, since the country is heavily dependent on foreign trade, is to considerable measure dependent on the stability of the foreign sector. Three of the features of the foreign trade sector described by the previous Chapter—the increasing importance of foreign trade, i.e., a noticeable rise in the foreign trade proportions, the high propensity to import, and the increasing dependence on services and foreign capital to finance an expanding merchandise trade deficit—will be examined for possible impact on the stability of the Lebanese economy.

A. *Importance of Trade and Stability*

The incrasing importance of foreign trade is indicated by the steady rise in the foreign trade proportions (merchandise exports plus imports as percent of national income). The three-year moving averages of these proportions, to repeat, increased from 47 percent to 63 percent between 1951 and 1966. This increase was due to an increase in both the import proportions, and the export proportions. The three-year moving averages, referred to in the previous Chapter, of the import ratios increased from 36 percent to 48 percent, and those of the export ratios increased from 11.3 percent to 15.3 percent between 1951 and 1966. A high ratio of exports to national product which generally characterizes a small country is not apparently the case in Lebanon. It is usually this high export ratio which is often cited as a potential source of instability for a small country. A high export ratio renders a small country unusually sensitive to fluctuations in its exports. Any change in demand for a small country's exports will imply, because of the high ratio of exports to national product, a relatively large proportionate change in the demand for the country's total product. Likewise, any balance of payments disequilibria, which may result from a change in demand for a small country's exports, will imply a relatively large dis-equilibria in relation to the country's total product. The larger the export ratio, therefore, the more vulnerable the country becomes to fluctuations in its exports.

Not only is the magnitude of the export ratio in Lebanon low, and, hence, changes in the demand for Lebanese exports do not mean re-latively large changes in the total product, but the composition of Lebanese exports is such that they are not very sensitive to changes in demand conditions. Lebanese merchandise exports consist mainly of basic consumers' goods, fruits and vegetables. It has been estimated that these categories comprise around 80 percent of total merchandise exports. The elasticity of demand for these 'basic' commodities is not expected to be high. Consequently, the degree of responsiveness of merchandise exports to changes in demand conditions will not be re-latively high. Both the composition as well as the magnitude of mer-chandise exports, therefore, do not suggest that exports are a likely source of instability in the Lebanese economy. It should be noted however that any assessment of Lebanese exports as a potential source of instability is far from complete if exports of services are not con-sidered. The magnitude and composition of 'services' exports suggest a different conclusion. The nature, diversity and, hence, demand con-ditions for these exports are quite different from those of merchandise exports; and the relative importance of services has been increasing faster than merchandise exports. Exports of services comprise, on the average, more than 50 percent of total foreign exchange receipts, and the rate of increase in these services has been fairly impressive; they now amount to at least twice the value of merchandise exports. The stability implications of the dependence on services are analyzed under a different heading.

B. *Propensity to Import and Stability*

Another feature of Lebanon's dependence on trade whose stability implications ought to be considered is the high propensity to import. It has been observed, in the previous Chapter, that merchandise im-ports amount on the average to more than 48 percent of national product. The three-year moving averages, for example, of the import ratio in-creased from 36 percent to 48 percent between 1951 and 1966. Some of the factors accounting for this high ratio of merchandise imports to national income have already been discussed. It will be argued here that such a high propensity to import is capable of providing a stabilizing outlet for the Lebanese economy. A propensity to import of more than 48 percent constitutes a substantial 'leakage' in income and can therefore export some of the destabilizing forces initiated within the country. This leakage may have influenced the behavior of money and prices in Lebanon.

The magnitude of the import ratio in Lebanon becomes readily apparent when the ratio of imports to income and the ratio of money supply to imports are compared with similar ratios for other countries. This comparison is provided by Table 73. The ratios of money to

Table 73

Medians of Ratios of Money to Income (MO/Y) Imports to Income (M/Y), of Lebanon and Polaks' Groups of Countries

	MO/Y	*M/Y*	*MO/M*
High Income Countries (23)	.34	.28	1.3
Low Income Countries (21)	.19	.17	1.0
All Countries (44)	.26	.22	1.2
Lebanon	.49	.52	1.0

[1] J. J. Polak, "Monetary Analysis of Income Formation and Payments Problems," International Monetary Fund, *Staff Papers*, Vol. VI, No. 1, (Nov. 1957), p. 46.

Polak's Medians are for 1950-1954; Lebanon's for 1952-1966.

income, imports to income, and money to imports are compared with Polak's sample of forty-four countries. Lebanon's median ratio of money to income (0.49) is significantly higher than Polak's median for the high income countries (0.34), or the low income countries (0.19), or for the forty-four countries combined (0.26). Lebanon's median ratio of imports to income (0.52) is also significantly higher than Polak's median for the high income countries (0.28), the low income countries (0.17), and for all countries combined (0.22). As a result, Lebanon's median ratio of money to imports (1.0) is lower than the median ratio of the high income countries (1.3), and of the forty-four countries together (1.2). It is thus obvious that not only is Lebanon's ratio of imports to income quite high, but that imports are still equal to the money supply despite the notable expansion in the latter.

These median ratios hide certain trends, particularly in the ratios of money to income and imports to income. These trends are shown in Table 74. Lebanon's ratio of money to income, for example, was 0.38

Table 74

Lebanon's Ratios of Money to Income (MO/Y), Import to Income (M/Y), and Money to Imports (MO/M) (1952-1955)

	(MO/Y)	(M/Y)	(MO/M)
1952	.38	.39	.96
1953	.36	.36	.98
1954	.38	.44	.85
1955	.41	.52	.78
1956	.45	.54	.82
1957	.52	.53	.99
1958	.62	.51	1.22
1959	.64	.58	1.22
1960	.67	.65	1.06
1961	.71	.59	1.13
1962	.78	.59	1.33
1963	.66	.60	1.59
1964	.49	.46	1.05
1965	.48	.48	1.00
1966	.45	.50	.89
Median	.49	.52	1.00

in 1952, increased to 0.78 in 1962, and then dropped to 0.45 in 1966. Since this ratio is the inverse of the income velocity of circulation, this means that Lebanon's velocity of circulation has on the average tended to decrease during the period 1952-66. It is important to bear in mind such a drop in the income velocity of circulation when accounting for the behavior of money and prices in Lebanon. The ratio of imports to income also reveals an increasing pattern. In 1952 this ratio was less than 40 percent, in 1966 it had increased to 50 percent. The ratio of money to imports does not indicate any strong pattern. These two features, a declining income velocity of circulation, and a rising propensity to import may have contributed significantly to the relative stability of prices in Lebanon.

Despite a substantial increase in money supply and quasi-money, the level of prices, as reflected by the wholesale-price and cost-of-living indices, has failed to register any notable increase. Both the money supply and quasi-money, for example, have increased faster than net national product, (money supply was 38 percent of national income in 1952 and become 45 percent of national product in 1966; and quasi-money increased from 6.4 percent to 55 percent of national product between 1954 and 1966). Thus quasi-money and money supply

Table 75

Lebanon's Net National Product, Money Supply, and Quasi-Money, 1955-1966

	Net National Product	Currency in Circulation	Demand Deposits	Money Supply	Quasi-Money	Quasi-Money & Money Supply	Money Supply	Quasi-Money	Quasi-Money & Money Supply
			(in L. L. Millions)					(as Per Cent of NNP)	
1950	1,042								
1951	1,086								
1952	1,115			424			38.0		
1953	1,168	195	219	414			35.4		
1954	1,256	232	246	478	81	559	38.1	6.4	44.5
1955	1,374	255	299	555	111	666	40.4	8.1	48.5
1956	1,417	320	307	627	124	751	44.2	8.7	53.0
1957	1,503	343	447	790	165	955	52.5	11.0	63.5
1958	1,325	384	443	827	190	1,017	62.4	14.3	76.7
1959	1,570	378	621	999	243	1,242	63.6	15.5	79.1
1960	1,671	399	716	1,115	482	1,597	66.7	28.8	95.5
1961	1,707	403	796	1,199	590	1,789	70.2	34.6	104.8
1962	1,788	432	972	1,404	633	2,037	78.5	35.4	113.9
1963	1,951	466	1,419	1,885	695	2,580	96.6	35.6	132.2
1964	2,861	500	890	1,390	1,272	2,662	48.6	44.4	93.0
1965	3,154	548	962	1,510	1,706	3,216	47.9	54.1	102.0
1966	3,460	647	894	1,541	1,892	3,433	44.5	54.7	99.2

Source: Net National Product figures are those of Appendix Table 2; money and quasi-money are those reported by the International Monetary Fund, *International Financial Statistics.*

which together amounted to less that 45 percent of national product
in 1954, increased by such a magnitude that they amounted to around
100 percent of national product in 1966. Table 75 compares the increase in the money supply and quasi-money with the increase in net
national product. Money supply comprises currency in circulation and
demand deposits of the private sector as reported by banks, and quasi-
money comprises time deposits and foreign currency deposits.

The cost-of-living index shows an increase of around 16 percent between 1952 and 1962,[1] and the wholesale-price index shows hardly any
rise at all, while the money supply has more than tripled during the
same period. Prices, in other words, have not been very responsive to
changes in the money supply. This lack of responsiveness or relative
stability of prices can be accounted for for by several factors, one of
which must have been the high propensity to import. It must be mentioned that the wholesale-price index which includes commodities at
all stages of manufacture, exports, imports and goods domestically
produced for domestic use, is still based on 1950 weights. The cost-of-
living is still weighted by the 1943 expenditure for goods and services
of a salaried employee's family in Beirut. These weights, to say the
least, are no longer applicable to present-day living standards. Thus,
one reason why prices may have remained fairly stable despite a notable expansion in the money supply, is the inappropriateness of the
price indices, themselves. Another reason, also statistical, relates to
data on money supply. A good part of the money supply is in the form
of inter-bank deposits, and therefore, is not in actual circulation and is
not part of the money supply proper. Banks are also generally believed
to have improved, in recent years, their reporting procedures, and,
therefore, the real increase in the money supply is not as substantial
as figures indicate. Both of these facts may in part explain the reported
decline in the income velocity of circulation.

The real increase in national product and the relatively heavy spe-
culation on the stock and real estate markets must have absorbed a
part of the large increase in the money supply, and, hence, can provide
additional forces that account for the behavior of money and prices in
Lebanon. Data on the magnitude of speculative investments in stocks
and real estate are not available. The organized and expanded activity
on the stock market, and the lucrative and now-almost-fashionable investments in real estate, however, have become salient and predomi-

---

[1] A new set of price indices are presently under construction; more recent
estimates are not yet available.

nant features of the economic scene. That such activity must have left an impact on the price level cannot be denied.

The final factor which may have also contributed to the relative stability of the price level, despite the sizeable expansion in the money supply and quasi-money, is the high propensity to import itself. The magnitude and nature of merchandise imports, analyzed elsewhere, strongly suggest that expenditure on imports must have provided an outlet for the inflationary pressures that the increase in the money supply might have otherwise created. It is expected that the income e-lasticity of demand for imports is high (i.e., greater than one). Since the average propensity to import is rising, the marginal propensity to import must be greater than the average propensity, and the income elasticity of demand for imports must, consequently, be greater than one. Thus, any proportionate change in income is expected to lead to a larger proportionate change in imports. Any destabilizing development, in other words, that originates within the Lebanese economy is likely to be 'exported' in relatively large proportions through changing imports. The notable growth of Lebanese imports (at a compounded annual rate of 11.4 percent) attending the less impressive growth of the economy is a reflection of this phenomenon. The stabilizing impact of this import 'leakage' cannot be ignored.

C. *Services, Foreign Capital, and Stability*

The third feature of the foreign trade sector whose stability implications are now considered is the increasing dependence on services and foreign capital. In order to finance an expanding deficit in the balance of trade, Lebanon has had to depend more heavily on services and foreign capital. The magnitude and trend of such dependence were described in the previous Chapter. The relative share of services and capital movements in the balance of payments, and, particularly, the degree of control which Lebanon has over them, can be a considerable source of instability. The extent of dependence on services and foreign capital, in and of itself, need not be a source of instability. The determining factor is again the nature of these services and capital movements, the extent to which they are subject to sudden interruption or manipulation by foreign countries, and, hence, the degree of control which Lebanon has over them.

The magnitude of Lebanon's dependence on 'services' exports is much more pronounced than its dependence on merchandise exports.

The relative importance of merchandise exports, as indicated earlier, has remained constant and even declined, while the relative importance of 'services' has increased. Receipts from services amount, on the average, to 50 percent of total foreign exchange receipts, and are on the average two times the receipts from merchandise exports. Any change in the demand for these 'services', therefore, will imply a relatively large change in the demand for the country's total product; and any balance of payments disquilibria precipitated by a change in the demand for Lebanon's services, will also imply a relatively large disequilibria in relation to the country's total product. Thus, the dependence on services renders Lebanon vulnerable to fluctuations in its receipts from services. The degree of fluctuations in these receipts depends on the character of Lebanon's services, namely, on their degree of responsiveness to changes in demand, and also on their sensitivity to policy moves by other (and particularly neighbouring) countries. The nature of these exports suggests that their income elasticity of demand is quite high. Had this not been the case, the services sector may not have enjoyed its current prosperity. The rising incomes of the oil-producing Arab countries have increased the demand for Lebanese services, and have undoubtedly contributed to the consistent growth of the services exports. If Lebanese 'services' were not income elastic such a growth may not have been possible. This, however, does not mean that 'services' are not a possible source of instability. These 'services' still remain quite sensitive to policy moves by neighbouring countries. Lebanese services can be readily discriminated against for economic reasons, i.e., by countries with balance of payments difficulties seeking to cut down on their foreign exchange expenditure, or for purely non-economic reasons. Some of the restrictions frequently imposed by the neighbouring countries against Lebanese exports exemplify both cases. In so far as this is true about Lebanese services, namely, that they are income elastic and that they are vulnerable to outside developments and policy decisions, they will remain a potential source of instability in the economy. There is little that Lebanon can do on either score, save perhaps of attempting to diversify its services so as to accommodate possible shifts in demand resulting from change in income or sudden policy developments, or of developing the ability to employ effective retaliatory measures against outside developments impairing its stability. Lebanon is in no position to use the threat of retaliation, and, as such, does not possess the capacity to isolate itself from outside destabilizing forces.

Lebanon's increasing dependence on foreign capital is also a possible source of instability. Here again it is not only the magnitude of the dependence on foreign capital which is the deciding factor. It is more the nature of this capital and the degree to which it is subject to sudden interrruption. The relative share of capital movements in the Lebanese balance of payments has been increasing steadily. Lebanon provides almost a perfect demonstration that a small country can be a recipient of a large and steady inflow of foreign capital. How precarious this dependence on capital is, depends on how steady its flow is. And how steady the flow is, does not depend so much on, nor need it be impaired by, the small size of the Lebanese economy. It depends more on the factors that gave rise to this capital inflow. A good part of this inflow is in the form of emigrant remittances. This has been and is likely to remain a steady and reliable source of foreign exchange. For nostalgic or other reasons, emigrants, and they are plentiful (it is said that for every two Lebanese there is one emigrant abroad), seem to maintain strong ties with the old country. Their remittances have steadily increased over the years. From LL 58.4 million in 1951 they became LL 112 million in 1966.[1] In recent years, the earnings of young Lebanese seeking employment in the neighbouring countries (i.e., earnings of migrant workers), must have also contributed significantly to this increase.

The other part of the inflow of capital is mainly investment capital from the Arab countries. Some of this capital, it is argued, is 'flight' capital seeking refuge from political and economic instability in the surrounding countries. Hence, there is little control that Lebanon can command over such capital. This capital inflow could be suddenly interrupted if and when the factors that prompted its inflow no longer exist. No doubt, not all the foreign capital is being 'pushed' into Lebanon. The banking secrecy practice, the developed money market, and the general freedom that characterizes the Lebanese economy must have attracted a part of this capital. Admittedly, the bulk of it is in the form of short-term bank liabilities, which, if not ultimately invested in the country, is always subject to sudden withdrawal. The only form of attractive long-term investment which Lebanon has to offer this capital is real-estate. Hardly any of this capital goes into industry or agriculture. The building boom, which does not seem to

---

[1] See Edward Fei and Paul J. Klat, *The Balance of Payments of Lebanon* 1951 *and* 1952, American University of Beirut, 1954, pp. 5; and Elias Saba, *The Balance of Payments of Lebanon* 1966, American University of Beirut, p. 21.

end in Lebanon, has been largely made possible by this inflow of foreign capital. Other forms of investments are not as lucrative, and since these investments have not been able to induce the flow of domestic savings, they are not likely to attract foreign capital investments. The investment opportunities available for foreign long-term capital are still rather limited, and hence, Lebanon's possibilities to attract foreign capital and its ability to control the flow of this capital remain limited too. As such, the country's dependence of foreign capital could be a possible source of precariousness in the future.

2. Diversity of the Economy and Stability

The second feature which must be analyzed for possible impact on economic stability is the diversity of production and the degree of concentration in trade and particularly exports. It is generally assumed, for example, that the degree of economic instability is likely to be higher in a small country than in a large one, since a small country's economic structure is often characterized by a more limited diversity. This limited diversity also leads to a high commodity and geographic concentration in exports, and such concentration, in turn, may increase the instability of export proceeds. The unavailability of abundant and diversified resources in Lebanon, and the peculiarities and limited extent of its small domestic market, may have undoubtedly obstructed the country's capacity to accommodate sudden changes in demand for its major products. For the less diversified an economy is, the less capable it is in generating forces (or 'spontaneous or induced redress') to offset developments that are possible sources of fluctuations in economic activity. A small country has been aptly defined, for this purpose, as "one which is unable to resist outside influences and which must accept the worst of them together with the best", and a large country as "one which has enough autonomy and enough flexibility in its economic policy to provide a response to challenges from anywhere, so as to assure maximum stability and steadiness when decisive progress has to be imported from abroad."[1] Lebanon's ability to isolate itself from outside influences is to a large measure, therefore, dependent on the diversity of its production and exports. If Lebanon, in other wouds, is to protect itself against outside destabilizing forces, the elasticity of demand for its exports must be quite low. The elastici-

---

[1] See G. Leduc and J. Weiller, "The Size of the Economy and its Relation to Stability and Steady Progress: II," in E. A. G. Robinson (ed.), *op. cit.*, p. 218.

ty of demand for exports and diversity of exports are often related. One may venture to say, that the more diversified a country's exports are, the lower is their elasticity of demand likely to be, and the greater is the country's capacity to absorb changes in demand for its exports. Lebanon's merchandise exports, as we have seen, are not diversified, but they consist mainly of 'basic' commodities, and the elasticity of demand for basic commodities is not likely to be high. For this reason, merchandise exports are not a major source of instability. The exports of 'services', however, are more income elastic and, as such, are more vulnerable to outside influences. 'Services' exports (which, to repeat, are significantly larger than merchandise exports) are therefore a more likely source of instability.

While Lebanese merchandise exports, on account of the limited diversity of the economic structure, consist of a relatively few items, merchandise imports, as a result of a relatively diversified structure of final demand, comprise a wider variety of products. This difference in the degree of diversity of exports and imports suggests different elasticities of demand for exports and imports. Since imports are more diversified than exports, the income elasticity of demand for imports is expected to be lower than that for exports. These diversity and elasticity considerations of exports and imports may provide a clue as to the magnitude and frequency of balance of payments difficulties that a country is likely to encounter. Needless to mention, further complications, and consequently new factors which endanger a country's stability, will arise when the country's balance of payments difficulties (along with the balance of payments positions and policy measures of the neighbouring countries) are taken into account. It is suggested, for example, that if the income elasticity of demand for imports is low, and that for the exports is high, a country (irrespective of its size) would be more likely to experience balance tf payments disequilibria, i.e., either sizeable deficits or sizeable surpluses. There is no evidence which indicates that the income elasticity of demand for a small country's imports is necessarily lower, and that for its exports is necessarily higher, than those of a larger country. Thus, there is no reason to suppose that the smaller of two countries is more likely to encounter balance of payments difficulties. But there is reason to believe that the difference in the diversity of exports and imports (and hence in their elasticities of demand) is generally more pronounced in the case of small countries. This may mean that the income elasticity of demand for a small country's exports is high (because of their limited diversity), and that for imports is low (because of their relatively wide diversity). If it is true that such elasicity differences are more apparent in a small country, a small country would be more likely subjected to disequilibrating developments in its balance of payments. This situation has been summarized by Tarshis: "If the country's exports are highly income elastic, and its imports are not, the risk of serious difficulties, or for that matter of comfortable surpluses in its balance of payments, is high. In so far as a small country's exports are likely to consist of a relatively few products, and its imports of a wide range of items this situation is likely to exist, though there are certainly instances in which the reverse is true."[1]

Lebanese merchandise exports are not diversified, but since they are mainly 'basic' commodities their income elasticity of demand is not expected to be high. Services exports which are significantly larger than merchandise exports are, however, more income elastic. One is thus inclined to suppose that Lebanese exports in general tend to have a high (not a low) income elasticity of demand. Lebanese imports are observably more diversified than exports, but their nature (40 percent of the imported consumption goods, which comprise around half of total imports, are luxury and durable goods) suggests also a high income elasticity of demand. Thus, the situation referred to above, namely, where exports are highly income elastic and imports are not, and where, as a result, the chances of encountering balance of payments disequilibria are high, does not seem to apply to Lebanon. Both exports and imports appear to be income elastic, despite the difference in their degree of diversity. Lebanese exports, particularly services, have expanded steadily with the expansion in income in the neighbouring countries; and imports have also increased with the increase in demand for a wide variety of goods generated by a rise in the level of economic performance and made necessary by the limited diversity of the local market. The expansion in expenditure on imports (mainly merchandise) has outpaced the expansion in receipts from exports (mainly services), and Lebanon has had a consistent deficit on its current account since 1951.[2]

Another aspect of diversity which is an important source of in-

---

[1] L. Tarshis, "The Size of the Economy and its Relation to Stability and Steady Progress: I," in E. A. G. Robinson (ed.), *op. cit.*, p. 197.

[2] The net earnings on the capital account, it must be remembered, exceed the deficit on the current account, and Lebanon has had a consistent surplus on its overall balance of payments since 1951.

stability in Lebanon is the degree of geographic or regional concentration in trade, Lebanon's ability to isolate itself from (or resist) outside influences, the sensitivity of its exports to policy decisions by other (and mainly neighbouring) countries, and the degree of control which Lebanon commands over trade and capital movements, do not only depend on the nature of capital movements and on elasticity and diversity considerations of exports. An equally deciding factor is the extent to which Lebanon has to depend on its immediate neighbours as markets for its exports and as sources for capital. Such a dependence can endanger the stability of exports and capital inflow since they become ready targets for these countries, if and when these countries desire to cut down on their foreign exchange expenditure because of balance of payments difficulties.

The geographic or regional concentration in Lebanon's trade was described in a previous chapter. The association between size of country and commodity and geographic concentration in trade was also analyzed in some detail in Chapter Three. It should be recalled that Lebanon's geographic concentration of exports (measured by the percentage of exports taken up by the largest twelve markets) was found to be noticeably higher than the geographic concentration of other countries, and that six of these largest twelve markets are Arab countries that take up around half of Lebanon's total merchandise exports.[1] This should demonstrate the importance of Arab countries as export markets and the strong regional concentration of merchandise exports. It was also observed that such concentration has shown a tendency to increase. Figures then used did not include exports of 'services', the bulk of which, it is estimated is destined to the Arab countries. Their inclusion would have increased Lebanon's export regional concentration even further. Breakdown of capital movements by source is not available, but it is also estimated that the bulk of foreign capital is from Arab sources too. The flirtation with socialism in some of the neighbouring countries and the attempts at nationalization, are said to have increased Lebanon's share of Arab capital. Such capital may not have normally sought the Lebanese market.

Lebanon's dependence on its neighbours for imports is not as pronounced as its dependence on them for exports. The four immediate neighbours (Syria, Iraq, Jordan and Egypt) provide on the average 18 percent of total merchandise imports, and take up 32 percent of total

---

[1] See Tables 61 and 62.

merchandise exports. There is also a clear tendency for the relative share of imports from these countries to decline. Their share was around 27 percent in 1951 and steadily declined to 10.5 percent in 1966.[1] The expansion in economic activity which the country witnessed during the last decade has generated a demand for a variety of products that cannot be imported from the neighbouring countries. As a result, Lebanon has had to rely increasingly on non-Arab countries to accommodate the rising imports.

The stability implications of the regional concentration of Lebanon's trade may not be readily apparent. This concentration, admittedly, has made possible to a large measure the current pace of the country's economic development. Had it not been for the increase in demand for Lebanese services, prompted by the expanding incomes of the oil producing countries, and had it not been for the Arab capital which has almost constantly sought the Lebanese market, such a pace may not have been achieved. Admittedly too, Lebanon has in the process acquired comparative regional advantages in the production of some services which cannot be easily rivaled by the other countries of the region. These would remain a reliable source of income. Others, however, which the neighbouring countries has had to rely on Lebanon for, may in time be developed by these countries, and Lebanon's income from these services will be reduced. Investment opportunities in these countries are also likely to improve in the future, and Lebanon's share of the foreign capital will decrease as some of this capital seeks domestic outlets instead. Some of the factors which instigated the flight of capital into Lebanon may also disappear, and Lebanon will have little control over the sudden interruption of this capital. Balance of payments difficulties will prompt these countries to impose a variety of restrictions, and Lebanon may not be in a position to resist their influences, let alone to retaliate against them. It is in such considerations that the precariousness of the regional concentration lies.

To conclude, this Chapter has attempted to assess the stability implications on the Lebanese economy of some of the factors that are possibly an outcome of the 'smallness' of the country. Two such factors were chosen—the country's dependence on trade, and the diversity of its production and (mainly) trade—and were examined for their impact on the stability of the Lebanese economy. The increasing dependence on merchandise trade was not found to be a likely source of

---

[1] See Table 64.

instability. The magnitude of the export ratio and the composition of merchandise exports are such that they are not very sensitive to changes in demand conditions, and that any change in the demand for exports will not imply a relatively large change in the total product. The uniquely high import ratio and the nature of merchandise imports may have had a stabilizing effect on the economy. The propensity to import is one important factor contributing to the relative stability of prices despite a notable expansion in the money supply. The increasing dependence on 'services' and capital movements, and the extent to which they are subject to interruption or manipulation, suggested that both items could be possible sources of instability. And finally, concentration in trade, and particularly regional concentration, was found to reduce Lebanon's capacity to isolate itself from outside influences, and as such to be a possible source of precariousness. Past trends do not reveal this precariousness, but the possibility is there. The economic flexibility, the ability to accommodate sudden shifts in demand, and to 'provide a response to challenges from anywhere so as to assure maximum stability and steadiness', are still limited in Lebanon. A good example of a small country, Lebanon has not been able to resist influences and has had to 'accept the worst of them together with the best'. So far, however, these influences have not been of the 'worst' variety and Lebanon has stood to gain from them.

CHAPTER TEN

CONCLUSION

The study in its two parts has been an attempt to evaluate the implications of the size of nations on their (1) economic stability, (2) diversity of production and trade, (3) degree of dependence on foreign trade, and (4) economic growth and development. The first part (Chapters two through five) was in the main an interpretation of the nature and magnitude of the association between size of country and the four mentioned aspects, and also an analysis of some of the factors that can plausibly influence this association. For this purpose, two-variable analysis and multi-variant analysis with two independent variables were utilized. The second part (Chapters six through nine) comprised an assessment of the impact of the small size of the Lebanese economy on each of these four aspects. Some of the salient features that characterize the Lebanese economy and that are possibly an outcome of 'smallness', were analyzed for their implications on the diversity, stability, and pace of growth of the economy. This final Chapter will highlight the main conclusions suggested by the foregoing investigation.

Analysis of the relationship between size and the different aspects of economic instability considered here, does not provide any support for the claim that small countries, by virtue of their 'smallness', are generally expected to be more vulnerable than large countries to fluctuations in their economic activity. The two-variable analysis, rankings and simple correlations, indicated the following results—there is no significant association between size and instability of national income; there is a significant positive association between population size and export instability; there is no association between size and import instability; there is also no association between size and instability of capital movements; and finally there is no association between size and either of the fluctuations of foreign exchange reserves or of the terms of trade. 'Smallness', therefore, is not an important source of instability.

Multi-variant analysis (cross-classifications and multi-correlations) supports the same conclusion and suggests the following results—that it is not likely either for the level of economic development or for the rate of economic growth to influence the association between size and income instability; that dependence-on-trade is not a likely source of extra income instability; and that commodity export concentration and geographic export concentration are both also not likely sources of extra income instability. Multi-variant analysis provides similar results with respect to export instability—namely—that there is no significant association between export instability and size; that neither economic development nor economic growth are likely to change the association between export instability and size; and that commodity and geographic export concentration both are not important sources of extra export instability. Finally, analysis of import instability suggests also similar results—that there is no significant association between import instability and size; that there is no evidence that this association is likely to change due to economic development or due to economic growth; and that there is also no evidence of an association between dependence on trade and import instability.

Some of the results suggested above by the analysis of the relationship between size and economic instability have important implications for the economies of small nations. Not only do these results suggest that size is not a significant source of instability, but they also suggest that dependence on trade, commodity export concentration, and geographic export concentration are not sources of extra instability in income, exports, and imports. Even if small countries turn out to have relatively higher degree of dependence on trade and higher export concentration, small countries are not, as a result of these features, likely to experience extra instability in their incomes, exports, or imports. These results are contrary to plausible a priori reasoning, and they suggest that small countries need not be very apologetic about their dependence on trade and their export concentration. Nor should they expect, however, that policies designed to reduce their dependence on trade and their export concentration, to be very effective in reducing the instability of their income and export proceeds.

In analyzing the relationship between size and concentration in trade, three different aspects of concentration were considered—commodity concentration of exports, commodity concentration of imports, and geographic concentration of exports. Two-variable analysis, rankings and simple correlations, do provide some support, but not unqualified support, for the claim that commodity and geographic concentration of exports are generally more conspicuous in the case of small countries. An inverse association between size and commodity export concentration, no significant association between size and commodity import concentration, and a weak inverse association between size and geographic export concentration were all observed. Some of the correlation coefficients of these relationships were statistically significant and could be taken with some confidence, and the rankings of the median concentration, more often than not, revealed a declining pattern.

The three-variable analysis which examines the impact of economic development and dependence on trade on the association between size and export concentration, also reveals a mild inverse association between size and export concentration, and suggests that neither economic development nor dependence on trade are likely to have a significant influence on export concentration. An inverse pattern was observed between economic development and export concentration, but this pattern is not statistically significant and is not, therefore, expected to change the association between size and export concentration. No apparent relationship was observed between dependence on trade and export concentration and, hence, dependence on trade also is not expected to change the association between size and export concentration. Regardless of the country's level of economic development and degree of dependence on foreign trade, the same association between size and export concentration is likely to prevail. This is contrary to conclusions of a similar investigation which suggested that the level of economic development can alter the association between size and commodity export concentration.

The interpretation of the association between size and degree of dependence on trade was based on three different aspects of involvement in foreign trade: Foreign trade proportions, export proportions, and foreign capital and donations proportions. The two-variable analysis, rankings and simple correlations, suggested the following results—First, the association between foreign trade proportions and size is not as strong as is often claimed. An inverse relationship was observed, the correlation coefficients, however, were not all statistically significant, and in one case a positive pattern was even indicated. Second, a significant inverse association between dependence on exports and size was observed. The correlation coefficients were significant and the rankings also observed declining patterns. Third, a tendency for small countries to depend more heavily than large countries on foreign capital was also observed, but this tendency is not as significant and as pronounced as their tendency to depend on exports. The association between dependence on foreign capital and donations and size is relatively weaker and remains fairly ambiguous. Therefore, only with respect to dependence on exports is a clear inverse association established. As for dependence on foreign trade (both exports and imports) and dependence on foreign capital and donations, an inverse pattern is observed but it is not as significant as the inverse association between dependence on exports and size.

The three-variable analysis, multiple-correlations and cross-classifications, examined the impact of economic development and economic growth on the association between size and degree of dependence on foreign trade. Results revealed by such analysis suggested that neither economic development nor economic growth are likely to influence the association between dependence on foreign trade and size. This is, again, contrary to qualifications suggesting that economic development could offset the relationship between dependence on trade and size.

Finally, part I of this investigation treated the relationship between size and economic development and growth, and suggested the following results—First, that there is no significant association between size and rates of growth of GNP, nor between size and increases in per capita GNP, and that the association between size and growth of exports, also, cannot be taken with much confidence. Second, that there is no significant association between population size and per capita GNP; large countries, in terms of population, do not have higher per capita GNP. The two-variable analysis, therefore, indicated that size is not a significant factor in economic growth and economic development and, as such, size cannot be assumed to be an obstacle to either growth or development. The three-variable analysis, which examined the impact of dependence-on-trade and export concentration on the association between size and economic growth and development, suggested these additional results: First, that dependence on trade does not seem to have any influence on the association between size and economic development, and that export concentration (both commodity and geographic) is also not likely to have a strong influence on the association between size and economic development. In other words, both dependence on trade and export concentration are not significant obstacles to economic development. Second, that dependence on trade does not have any strong influence on the association between size and economic growth, and that export concentration (commodity and geographic) also does not have any influence on the association between size and economic growth. Neither dependence on trade nor export concentration, therefore, are significant factors in economic growth. The relevance of these results to the economies of small nations should be obvious. They demonstrate that 'smallness' in itself is not necessarily an obstacle to economic growth and economic development, and that dependence on trade and export concentration, both of which are to some measure attributes of smallness, are not also important obstacles to economic growth and development.

To summarize, the implications of the size of nations on economic stability, concentration in trade, dependence on trade, and economic growth and economic development suggested by this investigation should be hopefully apparent. Size does not have any clear impact on economic stability nor on economic growth and development. 'Smallness' is not a source of extra instability, nor is smallness necessarily an obstacle to economic growth and development. The impact of size on dependence on trade and concentration in trade is relatively less ambiguous. In some instances significant inverse relationships were observed between size and degree of dependence on trade, and between size and concentration in trade. These relationships, however, were not as significant as is often claimed or suggested by plausible a priori reasoning. But regardless of the strength of these relationships, both dependence on trade and concentration in trade turned out to be neither sources of extra instability nor important obstacles to economic growth and economic development.

Part II treated the Lebanese economy as an example of a small nation and analyzed some of the features that are possibly attributes of the size of the economy. One distinguishing feature of the Lebanese economy which is largely a consequence of the size of the country and which must have influenced the stability and performance of the economy is the unsymmetrical distribution of the national product. With the indispensable requisites for the development of an efficient and well-balanced industry and agriculture almost completely lacking, Lebanon has had to rely heavily on, and acquire a notable advantage in, the production of services. Admittedly, this reliance on services has contributed significantly to the relatively decent standard of living of the country. But it has also generated an economic structure which could be a major source of precariousness and instability. An extension of the small domestic market through output expansion for exports, and a possible achievement of the necessary economies of scale in the country's goods producing sectors, could be instrumental in correcting this economic structure. The limited domestic market allows little room for output expansion. The country, therefore, should try to increase her dependence on export markets in order to get rid of the obstacles emanating from market limitations and diseconomies of scale and thus compensate for her smallness.

Another feature which is often attributed to the small size of an economy is a lack of diversity in production and a relatively strong concentration in trade. Lebanon's diversity of production, as measured in terms of the diversity of the occupational structure and of the income arising in the various sectors of economic activity, was found to be rather limited. The commodity concentration of Lebanese exports, however, measured by the Hirschman coefficient of concentration based on the SITC three-digit code classification, did not turn out to be higher than the means of the coefficients similarly computed (by Michaely and Massell) for two different samples of forty-four and thirty-six countries. The commodity concentration of Lebanese imports, also measured by the Hirschman coefficient and based on the same SITC classification, was significantly lower than the concentration of exports, and also lower than the mean of the import concentration coefficients similarly computed (by Michaely) for a sample of forty-four countries. Some of the factors that may have affected the diversity of Lebanese exports and imports and that may, therefore, account for the relatively low commodity concentration of exports and imports despite the limited diversity of production were suggested. The geographic concentration of Lebanese exports and imports were also measured. Lebanon's exports to and imports from the largest twelve markets, and her trade with immediate neighbours were analyzed as a measure of the degree of dispersion or concentration of foreign markets. Lebanon's geographic concentration of exports was noticeably higher than the geographic concentration of other countries (such as Belgium-Luxemburg, Netherlands, Switzerland) which belong to the category of small nations. Lebanon's geographic concentration of imports was not lower, as suggested by Kuznets, than that of exports. It was observed, however, that Lebanon's dependence on her immediate neighbours for exports is higher than her dependence on them for imports.

A third feature which is generally characteristic of small nations and which is strikingly obvious in the case of Lebanon is the strong dependence on foreign trade. In analyzing the magnitude and implications of this dependence, three distinguishing qualities of Lebanon's foreign sector were emphasized—A large and expanding merchandise trade deficit caused by impressive rates of growth of both merchandise exports and imports; a uniquely high propensity to import caused by the large discrepancy between the structure of final demand (warranted by the country's level of economic performance) and that of the domestic product (afforded by the limited local market); and, an increasing dependence on services and, particularly, foreign capital to finance the expanding trade deficit.

Finally, the stability implications of some of the features that characterize the Lebanese economy and that are to some measure a consequence of its size were examined. Two such features—the country's strong dependence on foreign trade, and the concentration in production and trade—were chosen and analyzed for their impact on the stability of the economy. The dependence on merchandise trade was not found to be a likely source of instability. The magnitude of the export ratio and the composition of merchandise exports both suggest that exports are not very sensitive to changes in demand and that a change in demand for exports will not imply (because of the low export ratio) a relatively large change in the total product. On the other hand, the high import ratio and the nature of merchandise imports may have had a stabilizing effect on the economy. The propensity to import, among other factors, can account for the relative stability in prices despite a substantial increase in the money supply. The increasing dependence on services and capital movements, however, and the extent to which they are subject to manipulation by foreign (and particularly neighbouring) countries, suggest that both items could be possible sources of instability. The second feature, i.e., concentration in trade, and mainly regional concentration, was found to reduce Lebanon's ability to isolate itself from outside influences and to render the trade sector more vulnerable to policy measures of neighbouring countries, and as such to be a possible source of precariousness and instability.

APPENDIX A

STATISTICAL TABLES

Table 2

Net National Product, by Sector, 1950-1966 (at Current Factor Cost)
(in LL million)

Sector	1950	1951	1952	1953	1954	1955	1956	1957	1958	1959	1960	1961	1962	1964[a]	1965[a]	1966[a]
Agriculture	206	211	216	221	226	223	231	238	219	229	235	241	254	381	409	442
Industry	141	147	155	161	166	175	183	189	181	192	203	206	210	411	462	512
Construction	43	35	48	47	60	60	50	41	38	52	59	59	60	178	200	231
Transportation	44	46	45	50	60	75	78	80	57	62	66	68	84	258	291	306
Trade	300	337	333	344	368	407	410	469	365	499	535	546	562	1,028	1,085	1,183
Finance & Insurance	40	46	50	51	57	70	80	91	93	99	105	109	116	108	124	141
Real Estate	96	97	98	101	112	116	130	139	155	172	184	189	194	250	269	284
Government	72	64	64	71	73	83	95	108	113	125	131	132	146	245	284	319
Services	100	103	106	122	134	165	160	148	104	140	153	157	162	341	398	445
TOTAL	1,042	1,086	1,115	1,168	1,256	1,374	1,417	1,503	1,325	1,570	1,671	1,707	1,788	3,200	3,523	3,867

Source: For the years 1950-1958, A. Y. Badre, as published in the United Nations, Economic Development of the Middle East 1956-1957, and later revised and published in the FAO Mediterranean Development Project, Lebanon: Country Report, Rome 1959; figures for the years 1959-1962 were privately obtained from the American Embassy in Beirut; years 1964-1966 are gross domestic product figures as published in Republique Libanaise, Direction Centrale de la Statistique, Les Comptes Economiques De L'année 1966, table 4, p. 12.
(a) Gross Domestic Product at current factor cost.

Table 3

Annual Variations in Net National Product, by Sector, 1950-1966
(at Current Factor Cost)
(in Percentages)

Sector	1951	1952	1953	1954	1955	1956	1957	1958	1959	1960	1961	1962	1965	1966
Agriculture	+ 2.4	+ 2.4	+ 2.3	+ 2.3	− 1.3	+ 3.6	+ 3.0	− 8.0	+ 4.6	+ 2.6	+ 2.5	+ 5.4	+ 7.4	+ 7.9
Industry	+ 4.3	+ 5.4	+ 3.9	+ 3.1	+ 5.4	+ 4.6	+ 3.3	− 4.2	+ 6.1	+ 5.7	+ 1.5	+ 1.9	+12.6	+10.7
Construction	−18.6	+37.1	− 2.1	+27.7	+ 0.0	−16.7	−18.0	− 7.3	+36.8	+13.5	—	+ 1.7	+12.4	+15.4
Transportation	+ 4.6	− 2.2	+11.1	+20.0	+25.0	+ 4.0	+ 2.6	−28.8	+ 8.8	+ 6.4	+ 3.0	+23.5	+12.6	+ 6.4
Trade	+12.3	− 1.2	+ 3.3	+ 7.0	+10.6	+ 0.7	+14.4	−22.2	+36.7	+ 7.2	+ 2.1	+ 2.9	+ 5.5	+ 9.0
Finance & Insurance	+15.0	+ 8.7	+ 2.0	+11.8	+22.8	+14.3	+13.8	+ 2.2	+ 6.4	+ 6.1	+ 3.8	+ 6.4	+15.3	+13.2
Real Estate	+ 1.0	+ 1.0	+ 3.1	+10.9	+ 3.6	+12.1	+ 6.9	+11.5	+11.0	+ 7.0	+ 2.7	+ 2.6	+ 7.6	+ 5.5
Government	−11.1	+ 0.0	+10.9	+ 2.8	+13.7	+14.5	+13.7	+ 4.6	+10.6	+ 4.8	+ 0.8	+10.6	+15.9	+12.5
Services	+ 3.0	+ 2.9	+15.1	+ 9.8	+23.1	− 3.0	− 7.5	−29.7	+34.7	+ 9.3	+ 2.6	+ 3.2	+16.7	+11.7
TOTAL	+ 4.2	+ 2.7	+ 4.7	+ 7.5	+ 9.4	+ 3.1	+ 6.1	−11.9	+18.5	+ 6.4	+ 2.2	+ 4.7	+10.1	+ 9.7

Source: Based on Table 2. Rates for 1965 and 1966 are based on Gross Domestic Product estimates. Those for 1963 are not available.

Table 4

Capital Formation, 1948-1957
(LL million)

	1948	1949	1950	1951	1952	1953	1954	1955	1956	1957
PUBLIC	25	24	30	18	22	23	25	49	49	53
PRIVATE	97	91	130	113	128	132	140	157	176	150
Building	56	48	74	56	69	69	71	98	92	73
Industry	15	14	23	15	15	15	15	13	24	27
Agriculture	6	8	12	14	15	17	20	15	22	18
Services	13	13	13	14	14	15	16	14	19	17
Transportation	7	8	8	14	15	16	18	17	19	15
TOTAL	122	115	160	131	150	155	165	206	225	203
Net National Product	n.a.	n.a.	1,042	1,086	1,115	1,168	1,256	1,374	1,417	1,503
Capital Formation as % of NNP			15.4	12.1	13.5	13.3	13.1	15.0	15.9	13.5

Source: Prepared by A. Y. Badre as quoted by Food and Agricultural Organization of the United Nations, *Lebanon: Country Report,* FAO Mediterranean Development Project, Rome 1959, p. II 25.

APPENDIX B

DESCRIPTION OF THE INDICES USED IN ANALYZING THE IMPLICATIONS OF SIZE

1. INSTABILITY INDICES $(Y_1 - Y_8)$

Y_1: *Instability Index of National Income*

The instability index of national income (and also that of export proceeds and imports) is a close approximation of the average year-to-year percentage variation, adjusted for trend. In algebraic terms the formula is

$$V_{log} = \frac{\Sigma (\log \frac{X_t + 1}{\Delta t} - m)^2}{N}$$

The instability index = antilog $\sqrt{V_{log}}$, where X_t is the value of a country's national income in year t; N, the number of years minus 1; m, the arithmetic mean of the differences between the logs of X_t and X_{t+1}, X_{t+1} and X_{t+2}, etc.; and V_{log}, the logarithmic variance of the series. This measure of instability was developed by J. D. Coppock,[1] and computed for a sample of sixty countries. Values of the index range from 1.6 (Costa Rica) to 66.8 (Philippines).

Y_2: *Instability of Export Proceeds (Coppock)*

This is the same as the index used for measuring instability of national income, computed by Coppock for a sample of eighty-three countries. Values of the index range from 6.2 (Switzerland) to 73.8 (Iran).[2]

Y_3: *Instability Index of Exports (Massell)*

This is one of two instability indices, both trend-corrected, developed by B. F. Massell. This measure which he terms the "normalized standard error", is the standard error of estimate (square root of the unexplained variance), divided by the mean of the observations. It is,

---

[1] See J. D. Coppock, *op. cit.*, Ch. 2, particularly pp. 23-26 for an explanation of the index; values of the index are given in Column X_2 of Appendix Table A-2.

[2] *Ibid.*, Column Y of Appendix Table A-2.

in other words, a pure number and is thus independent of the over-all level, or the rate of growth, of a country's exports. Values of this index, computed for a sample of 36 countries, range uniformly from .057 (Canada) to .184 (Columbia), with the exception of .284 (Malaya).[1]

Y_4: *Instability Index of Imports*

Same as the index used for measuring instability of national income, also computed by Coppock for a sample of eighty-three countries. Values range from 9.6 (Jordan) to 50.7 (Lebanon).[2]

Y_5: *Instability Index of Capital Movements (Correlation Coefficients, r)*

This index consists of applying the standard linear correlation technique, with time on the X-axis and the net capital movements on the Y-axis. Low r-values represent high instability. The logarithmic variance method used in measuring the instability of national income, exports and imports was not applicable here because of the presence of both negative and positive values in this time series. The index was computed by Coppock for a sample of sixty-seven countries for the period 1947 to 1958. Values range from —.879 (Morocco) to —.003 (Finland).[3]

Y_6: *Instability Index of Capital Movements (U. N. Method)*

This method (used by the United Nations Secretariat in its 1952 study, *Instability in Export Markets of Underdeveloped Countries*), consists of obtaining the absolute difference in values from year to year, expressing this difference as a percentage of the *larger* of the two annual values, and then averaging these percentages. Unlike the 'log variance' method developed by Coppock, the U. N. method does not make any adjustments for trend. Figures used here are computed by Coppock for sixty-seven countries. Values of the index range from 15 (Jordan) to 26 (Finland)[4].

Y_7: *Index of Fluctuations of Foreign Exchange Reserves*

This index constructed by M. Michaely for a sample of thirty-two countries (for the period 1948-1958), is essentially the same as the U. N.

---

[1] See B. F. Massell, *op. cit.*, Table 2, p. 51. Formula of index in algebraic terms is on p. 49.

[2] J. D. Coppock, *op. cit.*, Column X_3 of Appendix Table A-2.

[3] *Ibid.*, Column X_{28} of Appendix Table A-2.

[4] *Ibid.*, Column X_{30} of Appendix Table A-2.

method. For each year, the percentage change of foreign exchange reserves from the previous year is computed, using the earlier year as a base (the U. N. index uses the *larger* of the two annual values as a base); and then the mean (arithmetic average) of the *absolute* changes in each of the years is computed. Values of this index range from 3.7 (Portugal) to 38.3 (France).[1]

Y_8: *Index of Fluctuations of the Terms of Trade*
This index also computed by Michaely for a sample of thirty-six countries, stands for the range between the highest and lowest positions of the country's terms of trade for the period 1948-1958, expressed as a ratio of the average level of the terms of trade during that period. Values of the index range from 11.4 (Norway) to 87.9 (Brazil and Egypt), with the exception of 94.8 (Malaya).[2]

2. CONCENTRATION INDICES ($Y_9 - Y_{15}$)

Y_9: *Commodity-Group Export Concentration Index*
This is the 'Hirschman index' applied to the exports of each of seventy-eight countries (for 1957) grouped according to the Standard International Trade Classification (SITC) 10 *sections* (one-digit code). Values of the index computed by Coppock range from 41.6 (U.S.S.R.) to 96.4 (Costa Rica).[3]

Y_{10}: *Country-Export Concentration Index*
The 'Hirschman index' also applied by Coppock to the exports of each of eighty countries to all other countries. Values of the index range from 19.9 (United Kingdom) to 96.9 (Panama).[4]

Y_{11}: *Regional Export Concentration Index*
This is also the 'Hirschman index' applied to the International Monetary Fund regional classification, and calculated by Coppock for the exports of each of eighty-three countries. The values of the index range from 45.5 (United States) to 94.1 (Puerto Rico).[5]

---

[1] See M. Michaely, *Concentration in International Trade*, Amsterdam: North-Holland Publishing Co., 1962, Table 20, p. 121. An explanation of the index and its formula in algebraic terms are found on pp. 68-69.
[2] *Ibid.*, Table 21, pp. 124–125.
[2] See Coppock, *op. cit.*, Column X_{26} of Appendix Table A-2.
[4] *Ibid.*, Column X_{38} of Appendix Table A-2.
[5] *Ibid.*, Column X_{27} of Appendix Table A-2.

Y_{12}: *Percent of Exports to Region Receiving Most of Country's Exports*

The regions and the percentages are those used by the International Monetary Fund: United States and Canada, Latin America, Continental European Fund, Sterling Area, and the Rest of the World. The percentages for eighty-three countries computed by Coppock for 1957 range from 21 (Egypt) to 94 (Puerto Rico).[1]

Y_{13}: *Coefficients of Commodity Concentration of Exports*

This is the 'Hirschman index' applied by M. Michaely to the 1954 exports of a sample of forty-four countries classified according to the SITC 150 *groups* (three-digit code). Values of the coefficients range from 16.9 (Netherlands) to 98.8 (Mauritius).[2]

Y_{14}: *Coefficients of Commodity Concentration of Imports*

This is also the 'Hirschman index' applied by Michaely to the 1954 imports of a sample of forty-four countries classified according to the SITC 150 *groups* (three-digit code). With the exception of one country, values of the index range from 15.5 (Belgium-Luxemburg) to 30.5 (Trinidad and Tobago).[3]

Y_{15}: *Ratio of Commodity Concentration of Exports to Imports*

This is the ratio of Michaely's coefficients of commodity concentration of exports (Y_{13}) to commodity concentration of imports (Y_{14}). Both coefficients are measured by the 'Hirschman index' of concentration. Values of this index range from 0.82 (Yugoslavia) to 4.54 (Egypt).[4]

3. Dependence on Trade Indices ($Y_{16} - Y_{20}$)

Y_{16}: *Foreign Trade as Per Cent of GNP*

Exports plus imports (both goods and services) expressed as a percentage of gross national product for a sample of eighty countries, prepared by Coppock, based on 1957 data. Values of the index range from 2 percent (U.S.S.R.) to 127.4 percent (Puerto Rico).[5]

---

[1] *Ibid.*, p. 95, and Column X_6 of Appendix Table A-2.

[2] See M. Michaely, "Concentration of Exports and Imports: An International Comparison," *Economic Journal*, 1958, Table I, p. 725.

[3] *Ibid.*, Table I, p. 725.

[4] *Ibid.*, Table I, p. 725.

[5] See Coppock, *op. cit.*, Column X_4 of Appendix Table A-2.

Y_{17}: *Foreign Trade Per Capita*

Exports and imports of goods and services per capita in U.S. $ per year, 1957. Values of the index, computed by Coppock for a sample of eighty-three countries, range from $ 7.0 (China) to $ 1029.1 (Norway).[1]

Y_{18}: *Exports of Goods and Services as Per Cent of GNP*

Ratios of exports of goods and services to gross national product (unweighted averages) for the years 1950-1956, or for any number of years within this period for which data were available. These ratios, computed by Michaely for a sample of thirty-two countries, range from 5.0 (United States) to 45.3 (Mauritius).[2]

Y_{19}: *Foreign Capital as Per Cent of GNP*

Ratios of foreign capital (private capital and official and banking long-term capital) to gross national product; unweighted averages for the years 1953-1958, or for any number of years within this period for which data were available. These ratios, computed for sixty-five countries, range from —3.25 (Switzerland) to 9.33 (Rhodesia-Nyasaland).[3]

Y_{20}: *Foreign Capital and Donations as Per Cent of GNP*

These are ratios of foreign capital (private and official and banking long-term capital) and donations (private and official) to gross national product; unweighted averages for the years 1953-1958, or for any number of years within this period for which data were available. Values of these ratios, computed for a sample of sixty-four countries, range from —4.33 (Malaya) to 25.32 (Greece).[4]

4. ECONOMIC GROWTH AND DEVELOPMENT (Y_{21} — Y_{25})

Y_{21}: *Percent Increase in GNP Per Year* (1951-1957)

These are average annual rates of growth of gross national product for the years 1951 to 1957, adjusted for price changes. The rates for thirty countries for which data are available range from —.5 (Australia) to 11.4 (Venezuela).[5]

---

[1] *Ibid.*, Column X_{31} of Appendix Table A-2.

[2] M. Michaely, *Concentration in International Trade*, *op. cit.*, Table 17, p. 110.

[3] Foreign capital data used in the preparation of these ratios are those of the International Monetary Fund, *Balance of Payments Yearbook*, Vol. II, 1957-1958, pp. 1-12.

[4] Source of data used in preparing this index is same as Y_{19}.

[5] See Coppock, *op. cit.*, Column X_{18} of Appendix Table A-2.

Y_{22}: *Increase in Per Capita GNP* (1951-1957)

Average increase in per capita gross national product per year for the years 1951 to 1957, in absolute terms (U.S.$), adjusted for price changes. Rates, for thirty-one countries for which data are available, range from —6.8 (Australia) to 99.1 (Canada).[1]

Y_{23}: *Per Capita GNP* (1951-1957)

This is the average per capita gross national product (in U.S.$) for the years 1951 to 1957, adjusted for price changes. Figures, for the thirty countries for which data are available, range from $ 47.0 (Burma) to $ 1713.0 (Canada).[2]

Y_{24}: *GNP Per Capita*, 1957

Per capita gross national product in 1957, in U.S. dollars. Figures, for the eighty countries reported by Coppock, range from $ 25 (Indonesia) to $ 2582 (United States).[3]

Y_{25}: *Growth of Exports (log.)*

These are logarithmic rates of growth of exports, i.e., slopes of least-squares lines through logarithms of annual export proceeds of each of eighty-three countries for the period 1946 to 1958, or for any number of years within this period for which data were available. Values of these rates, prepared by Coppock, range from —.0044 (Uruguay) to .1268 (Japan).[4]

---

[1] *Ibid.*, Column X_{20} of Appendix Table A-2.
[2] *Ibid.*, Column X_{16} of Appendix Table A-2.
[3] *Ibid.*, Column X_{22} of Appendix Table A-2.
[4] *Ibid.*, Column X_{25} of Appendix Table A-2.

APPENDIX C

SUMMARY OF REGRESSION LINES AND CORRE-
LATION COEFFICIENTS

I. SIMPLE REGRESSIONS AND CORRELATIONS

1. *Instability Regressions*

$Y_1 = 0.0192X_1 + 9.9007$
$\quad\quad (.14) \quad\quad (1.72)$ $\quad\quad\quad\quad r = .03$

$Y_1 = 0.0037X_2 + 10.0652$
$\quad\quad (.12) \quad\quad (2.02)$ $\quad\quad\quad\quad r = .01$

$Y_2 = 0.0868X_1 + 16.0237$
$\quad\quad (.08) \quad\quad (.98)$ $\quad\quad\quad\quad r = .20$

$Y_2 = 0.1609X_2 + 14.3122$
$\quad\quad (.06) \quad\quad (1.04)$ $\quad\quad\quad\quad r = .45$

$Y_3 = -0.0001X_1 + 0.1187$
$\quad\quad (.000) \quad\quad (.002)$ $\quad\quad\quad\quad r = .12$

$Y_3 = -0.0001X_2 + 0.1190$
$\quad\quad (.000) \quad\quad (.003)$ $\quad\quad\quad\quad r = .10$

$Y_4 = 0.0013X_1 + 22.1866$
$\quad\quad (.02) \quad\quad (.37)$ $\quad\quad\quad\quad r = .01$

$Y_4 = -0.0205X_2 + 22.7681$
$\quad\quad (.02) \quad\quad (.56)$ $\quad\quad\quad\quad r = .13$

$Y_5 = 0.0004X_1 - 0.0642$
$\quad\quad (.001) \quad\quad (.01)$ $\quad\quad\quad\quad r = .07$

$Y_5 = 0.0003X_2 - 0.0654$
$\quad\quad (.001) \quad\quad (.02)$ $\quad\quad\quad\quad r = .05$

$Y_6 = -0.0985X_1 + 147.6659$
$\quad\quad (.25) \quad\quad (3.54)$ $\quad\quad\quad\quad r = .05$

$Y_6 = -0.2638X_2 + 152.5028$
$\quad\quad (.26) \quad\quad (6.07)$ $\quad\quad\quad\quad r = .13$

$Y_7 = -0.0231X_1 + 17.9365$
$\quad\quad (.02) \quad\quad (.48)$ $\quad\quad\quad\quad r = .22$

$Y_7 = -0.0053X_2 + 17.4844$
$\quad\quad (.04) \quad\quad (1.05)$ $\quad\quad\quad\quad r = .02$

$Y_8 = -0.0321X_1 + 36.3363$
$\quad\quad (.05) \quad\quad (1.23)$ $\quad\quad\quad\quad r = .10$

$$Y_8 = -0.0235X_2 + 36.1668$$
$$(.12) \qquad\qquad (2.80) \qquad\qquad\qquad r = .03$$

2. Concentration Regressions

$$Y_9 = -0.0278X_1 + 67.0076$$
$$(.04) \qquad\qquad (.80) \qquad\qquad\qquad r = .08$$
$$Y_9 = -0.1407X_2 + 70.3183$$
$$(.04) \qquad\qquad (1.13) \qquad\qquad\qquad r = .41$$
$$Y_{10} = -0.0288X_1 + 42.6932$$
$$(.04) \qquad\qquad (.66) \qquad\qquad\qquad r = .11$$
$$Y_{10} = -0.0118X_2 + 42.4818$$
$$(.04) \qquad\qquad (1.02) \qquad\qquad\qquad r = .04$$
$$Y_{11} = -0.0282X_1 + 65.1359$$
$$(.02) \qquad\qquad (.33) \qquad\qquad\qquad r = .14$$
$$Y_{11} = 0.0128X_2 + 64.3268$$
$$(.01) \qquad\qquad (.46) \qquad\qquad\qquad r = .10$$
$$Y_{12} = -0.0230X_1 + 53.1800$$
$$(.03) \qquad\qquad (.46) \qquad\qquad\qquad r = .08$$
$$Y_{12} = 0.0252X_2 + 52.0508$$
$$(.02) \qquad\qquad (.64) \qquad\qquad\qquad r = .14$$
$$Y_{13} = -0.0871X_1 + 45.0035$$
$$(.05) \qquad\qquad (.97) \qquad\qquad\qquad r = .28$$
$$Y_{13} = -0.2420X_2 + 48.6691$$
$$(.10) \qquad\qquad (2.27) \qquad\qquad\qquad r = .38$$
$$Y_{14} = -0.0096X_1 + 20.6111$$
$$(.01) \qquad\qquad (.24) \qquad\qquad\qquad r = .13$$
$$Y_{14} = -0.0165X_2 + 20.7816$$
$$(.03) \qquad\qquad (.56) \qquad\qquad\qquad r = .10$$
$$Y_{15} = -0.0045X_1 + 2.1321$$
$$(.002) \qquad\qquad (.04) \qquad\qquad\qquad r = .29$$
$$Y_{15} = -0.0062X_2 + 2.2295$$
$$(.01) \qquad\qquad (.11) \qquad\qquad\qquad r = .43$$

3. Dependence-On-Trade Regressions

$$Y_{16} = -0.5203X_1 + 62.3085$$
$$(.29) \qquad\qquad (3.45) \qquad\qquad\qquad r = .34$$
$$Y_{16} = 0.0130X_2 + 55.8855$$
$$(.25) \qquad\qquad (4.29) \qquad\qquad\qquad r = .01$$

$$Y_{17} = \quad 0.1309X_1 + 236.5547$$
$$(.57) \qquad\quad (8.10) \qquad\qquad r = .03$$
$$Y_{17} = -0.1970X_2 + 244.6849$$
$$(.36) \qquad\quad (11.30) \qquad\qquad r = .06$$
$$Y_{18} = -0.0509X_1 + \quad 24.4440$$
$$(.02) \qquad\quad (.59) \qquad\qquad r = .36$$
$$Y_{18} = -0.1659X_2 + \quad 27.2091$$
$$(.05) \qquad\quad (1.14) \qquad\qquad r = .54$$
$$Y_{19} = -0.0072X_1 + \quad 1.7603$$
$$(.005) \qquad\quad (.06) \qquad\qquad r = .19$$
$$Y_{19} = -0.0075X_2 + \quad 1.8367$$
$$(.005) \qquad\quad (.11) \qquad\qquad r = .20$$
$$Y_{20} = \quad 0.0246X_1 + \quad 2.9442$$
$$(.01) \qquad\quad (.16) \qquad\qquad r = .27$$
$$Y_{20} = \quad 0.0015X_2 + \quad 3.2514$$
$$(.01) \qquad\quad (.29) \qquad\qquad r = .02$$

4. *Economic Growth and Development Regressions*

$$Y_{21} = \quad 0.0060X_1 + \quad 5.1989$$
$$(.03) \qquad\quad (.39) \qquad\qquad r = .04$$
$$Y_{21} = \quad 0.0231X_2 + \quad 4.8714$$
$$(.03) \qquad\quad (.45) \qquad\qquad r = .17$$
$$Y_{22} = \quad 0.1761X_1 + \quad 21.2894$$
$$(.28) \qquad\quad (3.18) \qquad\qquad r = .12$$
$$Y_{22} = -0.0826X_2 + \quad 24.8936$$
$$(.19) \qquad\quad (3.79) \qquad\qquad r = .08$$
$$Y_{23} = \quad 12.8839X_1 + 377.5040$$
$$(4.31) \qquad\quad (52.68) \qquad\qquad r = .51$$
$$Y_{23} = \quad 1.6569X_2 + 505.8917$$
$$(4.05) \qquad\quad (71.06) \qquad\qquad r = .08$$
$$Y_{24} = \quad 3.1919X_1 + 418.1200$$
$$(1.00) \qquad\quad (14.39) \qquad\qquad r = .34$$
$$Y_{24} = \quad 0.6938X_2 + 441.8055$$
$$(.67) \qquad\quad (21.22) \qquad\qquad r = .12$$
$$Y_{25} = -0.0004X_1 + \quad 0.0543$$
$$(.000) \qquad\quad (.001) \qquad\qquad r = .09$$
$$Y_{25} = \quad 0.0001X_2 + \quad 0.0425$$
$$(.000) \qquad\quad (.001) \qquad\qquad r = .22$$

II. Multiple Regressions and Correlations

1. *Income Instability Regressions*

$Y_1 = \quad 0.1265X_1 - \quad 0.0088Y_{23} + \quad 13.0910$
$\qquad\qquad (.157) \qquad\qquad (.006) \qquad\qquad (2.86) \qquad\quad R = .269$

$Y_1 = \quad 0.1642X_2 - \quad 0.0069Y_{23} + \quad 10.7946$
$\qquad\qquad (.107) \qquad\qquad (.005) \qquad\qquad (3.20) \qquad\quad R = .359$

$Y_1 = \quad 0.0128X_1 + \quad 1.0546Y_{21} + \quad 4.4177$
$\qquad\qquad (.143) \qquad\qquad (.868) \qquad\qquad (4.82) \qquad\quad R = .242$

$Y_1 = -0.0212X_2 + \quad 1.0852Y_{21} + \quad 4.7784$
$\qquad\qquad (.117) \qquad\qquad (.880) \qquad\qquad (4.73) \qquad\quad R = .244$

$Y_1 = -0.0284X_1 - \quad 0.0514Y_{16} + \quad 13.1388$
$\qquad\qquad (.023) \qquad\qquad (.049) \qquad\qquad (2.48) \qquad\quad R = .198$

$Y_1 = -0.0110X_2 - \quad 0.0505Y_{16} + \quad 12.8718$
$\qquad\qquad (.026) \qquad\qquad (.053) \qquad\qquad (2.90) \qquad\quad R = .126$

$Y_1 = -0.0241X_1 - \quad 0.0238Y_9 + \quad 12.3137$
$\qquad\qquad (.024) \qquad\qquad (.104) \qquad\qquad (7.24) \qquad\quad R = .136$

$Y_1 = -0.0243X_2 - \quad 0.0296Y_9 + \quad 12.9260$
$\qquad\qquad (.026) \qquad\qquad (.106) \qquad\qquad (7.50) \qquad\quad R = .128$

$Y_1 = -0.0208X_1 + \quad 0.0732Y_{10} + \quad 7.3235$
$\qquad\qquad (.023) \qquad\qquad (.088) \qquad\qquad (3.84) \qquad\quad R = .169$

$Y_1 = -0.0187X_2 + \quad 0.0692Y_{10} + \quad 7.6208$
$\qquad\qquad (.024) \qquad\qquad (.089) \qquad\qquad (3.98) \qquad\quad R = .157$

2. *Export Instability Regressions*

$Y_2 = \quad 0.1144X_1 - \quad 0.0021Y_{23} + \quad 16.8558$
$\qquad\qquad (.097) \qquad\qquad (.004) \qquad\qquad (1.77) \qquad\quad R = .226$

$Y_2 = \quad 0.1618X_2 - \quad 0.0005Y_{23} + \quad 14.5809$
$\qquad\qquad (.062) \qquad\qquad (.003) \qquad\qquad (1.86) \qquad\quad R = .455$

$Y_2 = \quad 0.0856X_1 + \quad 0.0245Y_{21} + \quad 16.2092$
$\qquad\qquad (.087) \qquad\qquad (.528) \qquad\qquad (2.94) \qquad\quad R = .197$

$Y_2 = \quad 0.0269X_2 + \quad 0.0083Y_{21} + \quad 16.8491$
$\qquad\qquad (.072) \qquad\qquad (.545) \qquad\qquad (2.93) \qquad\quad R = .077$

$Y_2 = \quad 0.0019X_1 + \quad 0.0021Y_9 + \quad 19.0402$
$\qquad\qquad (.019) \qquad\qquad (.082) \qquad\qquad (5.72) \qquad\quad R = .014$

$Y_2 = \quad 0.0227X_2 + \quad 0.2748Y_9 + \quad 16.6932$
$\qquad\qquad (.020) \qquad\qquad (.082) \qquad\qquad (5.85) \qquad\quad R = .154$

$Y_2 = -0.0009X_1 - \quad 0.0906Y_{10} + \quad 23.3374$
$\qquad\qquad (.018) \qquad\qquad (.070) \qquad\qquad (3.03) \qquad\quad R = .171$

$$Y_2 = \underset{(.019)}{0.0165X_2} - \underset{(.070)}{0.0812Y_{10}} + \underset{(3.12)}{22.4606} \qquad R = .205$$

3. Import Instability Regressions

$$Y_4 = \underset{(.122)}{-0.0357X_1} - \underset{(.005)}{0.0030Y_{23}} + \underset{(2.23)}{23.9369} \qquad R = .182$$

$$Y_4 = \underset{(.086)}{0.0325X_2} - \underset{(.004)}{0.0038Y_{23}} + \underset{(2.57)}{23.4077} \qquad R = .188$$

$$Y_4 = \underset{(.096)}{-0.0643X_1} - \underset{(.583)}{0.1830Y_{21}} + \underset{(3.24)}{22.3789} \qquad R = .151$$

$$Y_4 = \underset{(.079)}{-0.0558X_2} - \underset{(.590)}{0.1244Y_{21}} + \underset{(3.17)}{22.2700} \qquad R = .159$$

$$Y_4 = \underset{(.020)}{-0.0022X_1} - \underset{(.043)}{0.0492Y_{16}} + \underset{(2.17)}{24.646} \qquad R = .151$$

$$Y_4 = \underset{(.022)}{-0.0342X_2} - \underset{(.045)}{0.0749Y_{16}} + \underset{(2.46)}{26.7860} \qquad R = .252$$

4. Concentration Regressions

$$Y_9 = \underset{(.170)}{-0.2618X_1} - \underset{(.007)}{0.0074Y_{23}} + \underset{(3.09)}{76.3990} \qquad R = .474$$

$$Y_9 = \underset{(.117)}{-0.2251X_2} - \underset{(.006)}{0.0118Y_{23}} + \underset{(3.51)}{79.4651} \qquad R = .511$$

$$Y_{10} = \underset{(.220)}{-0.6231X_1} + \underset{(.009)}{0.0080Y_{23}} + \underset{(3.99)}{48.0728} \qquad R = .501$$

$$Y_{10} = \underset{(.149)}{-0.4824X_2} - \underset{(.007)}{0.0024Y_{23}} + \underset{(4.48)}{54.5418} \qquad R = .549$$

$$Y_9 = \underset{(.044)}{-0.0276X_1} + \underset{(.095)}{0.0023Y_{16}} + \underset{(4.82)}{66.8913} \qquad R = .084$$

$$Y_9 = \underset{(.045)}{-0.1615X_2} - \underset{(.092)}{0.1130Y_{16}} + \underset{(5.05)}{76.3831} \qquad R = .431$$

$$Y_{10} = \underset{(.036)}{-0.0226X_1} + \underset{(.078)}{0.0866Y_{16}} + \underset{(3.94)}{38.3608} \qquad R = .179$$

$$Y_{10} = \underset{(.041)}{0.0063X_2} + \underset{(.083)}{0.0990Y_{16}} + \underset{(4.57)}{37.1703} \qquad R = .161$$

5. Dependence-On-Trade Regressions

$$Y_{16} = \underset{(.328)}{-0.7555X_1} + \underset{(.013)}{0.0164Y_{23}} + \underset{(6.01)}{54.7130} \qquad R = .412$$

$$Y_{16} = -0.5216X_2 + \quad 0.0034Y_{23} + \quad 61.5769$$
$$\quad\quad (.232) \quad\quad\quad (.011) \quad\quad\quad\quad (6.94) \quad\quad R = .404$$
$$Y_{16} = -0.5173X_1 - \quad 0.4995Y_{21} + \quad 64.9055$$
$$\quad\quad (.296) \quad\quad\quad (1.79) \quad\quad\quad\quad (9.95) \quad\quad R = .342$$
$$Y_{16} = \quad 0.0280X_2 - \quad 0.6500Y_{21} + \quad 59.0519$$
$$\quad\quad (.257) \quad\quad\quad (1.93) \quad\quad\quad\quad (10.36) \quad\quad R = .069$$

6. *Economic Development and Growth Regressions*

$$Y_{23} = \quad 14.6623X_1 + \quad 3.5319Y_{16} + \quad 167.6832$$
$$\quad\quad (4.43) \quad\quad\quad (2.79) \quad\quad\quad\quad (177.17) \quad R = .545$$
$$Y_{23} = \quad 2.1978X_2 + \quad 1.0398Y_{16} + \quad 439.8338$$
$$\quad\quad (4.37) \quad\quad\quad (3.39) \quad\quad\quad\quad (225.32) \quad R = .101$$
$$Y_{23} = \quad 10.5891X_1 - \quad 6.4065Y_9 + \quad 848.8575$$
$$\quad\quad (4.75) \quad\quad\quad (5.71) \quad\quad\quad\quad (423.36) \quad R = .540$$
$$Y_{23} = -1.4396X_2 - \quad 12.6521Y_9 + \quad 1435.7097$$
$$\quad\quad (4.08) \quad\quad\quad (6.04) \quad\quad\quad\quad (448.70) \quad R = .394$$
$$Y_{23} = \quad 15.0639X_1 + \quad 4.2007Y_{10} + \quad 162.7421$$
$$\quad\quad (4.91) \quad\quad\quad (4.48) \quad\quad\quad\quad (235.10) \quad R = .530$$
$$Y_{23} = \quad 0.7540X_2 - \quad 1.8560Y_{10} + \quad 604.8509$$
$$\quad\quad (4.92) \quad\quad\quad (5.53) \quad\quad\quad\quad (303.36) \quad R = .104$$
$$Y_{21} = \quad 0.0026X_1 - \quad 0.0064Y_{16} + \quad 5.6019$$
$$\quad\quad (.036) \quad\quad\quad (.023) \quad\quad\quad\quad (1.50) \quad\quad R = .067$$
$$Y_{21} = \quad 0.0231X_2 - \quad 0.0072Y_{16} + \quad 5.2763$$
$$\quad\quad (.027) \quad\quad\quad (.022) \quad\quad\quad\quad (1.29) \quad\quad R = .186$$

III. COEFFICIENTS OF MULTIPLE CORRELATION (R)
HIGHEST R-VALUES

Variables		R
Dependent	Independent	
Y_{10}	$X_2 - Y_{23}$	.549
Y_{23}	$X_1 - Y_{16}$	.545
Y_{23}	$X_1 - Y_9$	.540
Y_{23}	$X_1 - Y_{10}$	.530
Y_9	$X_2 - Y_{23}$	.511
Y_{10}	$X_1 - Y_{23}$	.501
Y_9	$X_1 - Y_{23}$	.474
Y_2	$X_2 - Y_{23}$	455
Y_9	$X_2 - Y_{16}$	.431

Y_{16}	$X_1 - Y_{23}$	.412
Y_{16}	$X_2 - Y_{23}$	.404
Y_{23}	$X_2 - Y_9$	.394
Y_1	$X_2 - Y_{23}$	.359
Y_{16}	$X_1 - Y_{21}$	.342

BIBLIOGRAPHY

OFFICIAL PUBLICATIONS

Républic of Lebanon, Ministry of National Economy. *Bulletin Statistique Trimestriel.* Beirut.
——. *Industrial Census of Lebanon,* 1955, Beirut, 1957.
République Libanaise, Conseil Supérieur Des Douanes. *Statistiques Du Commerce Extérieur.* Beirut.

BOOKS

Benedict, Burton (ed.). *Problems of Smaller Territories,* University of London, The Athlone Press, 1967.
Churchill, Charles. *The City of Beirut.* Economic Research Institute, American University of Beirut, 1954.
Coppock, Joseph D. *International Economic Instability.* New York: McGraw-Hill Book Co., Inc., 1962.
Demas, William G., *The Economics of Development in Small Countries with Special Reference to the Carribbean.* Montreal: McGill University Press, 1965.
Diab, M. A. *Inter-Arab Economic Cooperation, 1951-1960.* Economic Research Institute, American University of Beirut, 1963.
Fei, Edward and Klat, Paul J. *The Balance of Payments of Lebanon, 1951 and 1952.* Economic Research Institute, American University of Beirut, Beirut, September 1954.
Food and Agriculture Organization of the United Nations. *FAO Mediterranean Development Project.* Italy, 1959.
——. *Lebanon: Country Report.* FAO Mediterranean Development Project, Rome, Italy, 1959.
Hirschman, Albert O. *National Power and the Structure of Foreign Trade.* Berkeley & Los Angeles: University of California Press, 1945.
Holtrop, Marius W. *Monetary Policy in an Open Economy: Its Objectives, Instruments, Limitations, and Dilemmas.* International Finance Section, Princeton University, Essays in International Finance, No. 43, September 1963.
Institut de Formation En Vue du Développement. *Le Liban, Face à son Développement.* (Présentation Condensée de la Première Etude IRFED 1960-1961) Beyrouth, 1963.
Kindleberger, Charles P. *Foreign Trade and the National Economy.* New Haven: Yale University Press, 1962.
Kuznets, Simon. *Six Lectures on Economic Growth.* Illinois: The Free Press of Glencoe, 1959.
Macbean, Alasdair I. *Export Instability and Economic Development.* London: George Allen and Unwin, 1967.
Michaely, Michael. *Concentration in International Trade.* Amsterdam: North-Holland Publishing Company, 1962.
Robinson, E. A. G. (ed.). *Economic Consequences of the Size of Nations.* London: Macmillan and Co., Ltd., 1960.
Salem, Khalil. *Balance of Payments of Lebanon 1961.* Economic Research Institute, American University of Beirut, 1964.

Sayigh, Yusif A. *Entrepreneurs of Lebanon: The Role of the Business Leader in a Developing Economy.* Cambridge: Harvard University Press, 1962.

Siksek, Simon G., Daouk, Bashir J., Baaklini, Sami E. *Preliminary Assessment of Manpower Resources and Requirements in Lebanon.* Economic Research Institute, American University of Beirut, Beirut, 1960.

Tinbergen, Jan. *Shaping the World Economy.* New York: The Twentieth Century Fund, 1962.

United Nations, Department of Economic Affairs. *Commodity Trade and Economic Development.* New York, 1954.

——, Department of Economic & Social Affairs. *Economic Developments in the Middle East, 1956-57.* Supplement to World Economic Survey, 1957, United Nations Publications, Sales No: 58.II.C.2.

——, United Nations Economic & Social Office in Beirut, *Studies on Selected Development Problems in Various Countries in the Middle East,* 1967, 1968, 1969.

Woytinsky, W. S., & E. S. *World Commerce and Governments.* Twentieth Century Fund, 1955.

ARTICLES AND PERIODICALS

Ali, Anwar. "Banking in the Middle East," International Monetary Fund, *Staff Papers,* Vol. VI, No. 1.

Asfour, Edmond Y. "Industrial Development in Lebanon," *Middle East Economic Papers, 1955,* Economic Research Institute, American University of Beirut, pp. 1-16.

Badre, Albert Y. "The National Income of Lebanon," *Middle East Economic Papers,* 1956, Economic Research Institute, American University of Beirut, pp. 1-37.

Belassa, Bela. "Country Size and Trade Patterns: Comment," *American Economic Review,* March 1969.

De La Vinelle, L. Duquense. "Study of the Efficiency of a Small Nation: Belgium," E. A. G. Robinson (ed.), *Economic Consequences of the Size of Nations,* London: Macmillan & Co., Ltd., 1960.

Diab, Muhammad. "Foreign Trade of Lebanon (1951-1960)," *Middle East Economic Papers, 1962,* Economic Research Institute, American University of Beirut, pp. 16-37.

Doblin, Ernest M. "The Ratio of Income to Money Supply: An International Survey," *Review of Economics and Statistics,* Vol. 33 (1951-52), pp. 201-213.

Fabricant, S. "Study of the Size and Efficiency of the American Economy," E. A. G. Robinson (ed.), *Economic Consequences of the Size of Nations,* London: Macmillan & Co., Ltd., 1960.

Hakim, George. "Land Tenure Reform," *Middle East Economic Papers, 1954,* Economic Research Institute, American University of Beirut, 1955.

Hannush, Basim A. "The Present Socio-Economic Conditions in Lebanon and the Prospects for Economic Development," *Middle East Economic Papers, 1962,* Economic Research Institute, American University of Beirut, pp. 40-52.

Hirschman, A. O. "The Paternity of an Index," *American Economic Review,* (September 1964).

Hoss, Salim. "Capital Movements and the Lebanese Balance of Payments," *The Arab Economic Report,* Confederation of the Chambers of Commerce, Industry and Agriculture of the Arab Countries, (December 1962).

Hoss, Salim A. "Economic Concentration in Lebanon," *Middle East Economic Papers, 1963,* Economic Research Institute, American University of Beirut, pp. 55-74.

Itō, Taikichi. "The High Growth of the Japanese Economy and the Problems of Small Enterprises," *The Developing Economies*, Vol. 1, Number 2, (July-December, 1963), pp. 137-168.

Jöhr, W. A. and Kneschaurek, F. "Study of the Efficiency of a Small Nation: Switzerland," E. A. G. Robinson (ed.), *Economic Consequences of the Size of Nations*, London: Macmillan & Co., Ltd., 1960.

Keesing, D. B. "Population and Industrial Development: Some Evidence from Trade Patterns," *American Economic Review*, June 1968.

Klat, Paul J. "The Future of Economic Development in the Arab World," *Middle East Economic Papers, 1956*, Economic Research Institute, American University of Beirut, 1957.

——. "Whither Land Tenure in the Arab World," *Middle East Economic Papers, 1955*, Economic Research Institute, American University of Beirut, 1956.

Kuznets, S. "Economic Growth of Small Nations," A. E. G. Robinson (ed.), *Economic Consequences of the Size of Nations*, London: Macmillan & Co., Ltd., 1960.

——. "Quantitative Aspects of the Economic Growth of Nations: IX Level and Structure of Foreign Trade: Comparisons for Recent Years," *Economic Development and Cultural Change*, Vol. XIII, Number 1, Part II, (October 1964).

——. "Toward a Theory of Economic Growth," in Robert Lekachman (ed.), *National Policy for Economic Welfare at Home and Abroad*, New York: Double-day & Co., 1955.

Leduc, G. and Weiller, J. "The Size of the Economy and its Relation to Stability and Steady Progress: II," E. A. G. Robinson (ed.), *Economic Consequences of the Size of Nations*, London: Macmillan & Co., Ltd., 1960.

Marsan, V. A. "The Experience of Italy," E. A. G. Robinson (ed.), *Economic Consequences of the Size of Nations*, London: Macmillan & Co., Ltd., 1960.

Massell, Benton F. "Export Concentration and Fluctuations in Export Earnings: A Cross-Section Analysis," *American Economic Review*, (March 1964), pp. 47-63.

Michaely, M. "Concentration of Exports and Imports: An International Comparison," *The Economic Journal* (December 1958), pp. 722-736.

Myint, H. "The Classical Theory of International Trade and the Underdeveloped Countries," *The Economic Journal* (June 1958), pp. 317-337.

Penrose, Edith. "Money, Prices, and Economic Expansion in the Middle East, 1952-1960," *Rivista Internazionale di Scienze Economiche e Commerciali*, Anno IX (1962), N. 5.

Perroux, François. "Matériaux pour une Analyse de la Croissance Economique," *Cahiers de l'I.S.E.A.*, Series D., No. 8.

Polak, J. J. "Monetary Analysis of Income Formation and Payments Problems," International Monetary Fund, *Staff Papers*, Vol. VI, No. 1, (November 1957).

Polak, J. J. & White, William H. "The Effect of Income Expansion on The Quantity of Money," International Monetary Fund, *Staff Papers*, Vol. IV (1964-1955).

Robinson, Joan. "Beggar-My-Neighbour Remedies for Unemployment," American Economic Association, *Readings in the Theory of International Trade*, London: Allen & Unwin, 1949.

Saba, Elias S. "The Implications of the Foreign Sector in the Lebanese Economy," *Middle East Economic Papers, 1962*, Economic Research Institute, American University of Beirut, pp. 140-154.

Seers, Dudley. "Big Companies and Small Countries: A Practical Proposal," *Kyklos*, Vol. XVI, (1963), Fasc. 4, pp. 599-607.

Sayigh, Yusif, A. "Lebanon: Special Economic Problems Arising from a Special

Structure," *Middle East Economic Papers, 1957*, Economic Research Institute, American University of Beirut, pp. 60-88.

Shorter, Frederic C. "The Remarkable Upsurge in Arab Trade," Paper delivered at the Fifty-Six Meeting of the Princeton University Conference on *Arab Development in the Emerging International Economy*, April 25 and 26, 1963, Haskins Press, Princeton, New Jersey, 1963.

Tarshis, L. "The Size of the Economy and its Relation to Stability and Steady Progress: I," E. A. G. Robinson (ed.), *Economic Consequences of the Size of Nations*, London: Macmillan & Co., Ltd., 1960.

Vakil, C. N. and Brahmananda, P.R. "The Problems of Developing Countries," E.A.G. Robinson (ed.), *Economic Consequences of the Size of Nations*, London: Macmillan & Co., Ltd., 1960.

UNPUBLISHED MATERIALS

Doxiadis team. *Economic Data for the Ekistic Programme for Lebanon*. Beirut, 1957. (Mimeographed.)

Higgings, Benjamin, *Financing Lebanese Development—A Report on Fiscal Policy*. Beirut, August 16, 1960. (Mimeographed.)

Institut International de Recherche et de Formation en Vue du Développement. Intégral et Harmonisé (Mission I.R.F.E.D.—Liban). *Etude Préliminaire sur les Besoins et les Possibilités de Développement au Liban*, 1959-1960. Beirut, Lebanon. (Mimeographed.)

Salem, Khalil. *Credit and Economic Growth in Lebanon*. Unpublished Ph. D. Thesis, Department of Economics and Business Administration of Vanderbilt University, Nashville, Tennessee, July 1964.

INDEX